ENDORSEMENTS

"I love Todd's passion for students and the world. He not only believes that students can change the world, he gives a clear and compelling path to getting there."

Brian Mosley
President, The RightNow Campaign

"Todd Ahrend is a leader, thinker, historian, networker, and mobilizer who knows students and missions. He speaks—and writes—with great vision and passion. I read every word of *In This Generation*. So should you!"

Steve Shadrach
Director of Mobilization, U.S. Center for World Mission

"The Student Volunteer Movement has gone down in history as one of the most strategic mobilization movements in the history of the Church. Over the years I have heard dozens of students ask if it could ever happen again. *In This Generation* by Todd Ahrend gives us the blueprint for how this generation of students can, once again, be mobilized around the world to extend the gospel of Christ to new frontiers. I know of few leaders who understand the mind and heartbeat of college students today like Todd Ahrend. This book shows how this vibrant movement in our past can be translated into an effective force of mobilization today. This is the book we have been waiting for. May it be the spark which lights a new flame of mobilization around the world."

Timothy C. Tennent
President, Asbury Theological Seminary

"*In This Generation* is so right on! Loaded with perspective and wisdom. Thoroughly biblical, historical, visionary, challenging, and practical. Todd really knows students, the present culture's influence on them, and the issues they wrestle with most concerning their role in God's purpose for all peoples. I will have every man I disciple read this book, discuss it with them and apply it!"

Roger Hershey, Campus Crusade for Christ

"The missions book that pastors have been waiting for! This book should be in the hands of every church leader. Todd has opened up missions' history by unveiling its key players and movements. God used normal people to do some extraordinary things and their successes and failures will equip and inspire you."

Donnie Smith
Lead Pastor, The Fellowship, Round Rock, Texas

"*In This Generation* is a powerful tool because in it Todd captures what I have watched in his life for the past 15 years, as his pastor and friend: how one person can be used of the Lord to touch thousands for eternity. He shows the guiding truths from those who mobilized an entire generation 100 years ago—and packages those truths into simple yet life-changing choices anyone can make to become part of the ancient, eternal mission Christ left us all to accomplish. Bravo, Todd! Thanks for hearing, following, and now pointing us to follow Jesus, going to every people."

John Barnett
Pastor, Calvary Bible Church, Kalamazoo, Michigan

"This story of God's Spirit igniting student movements for His glory among the nations will certainly ignite a like-minded passion in your heart. I have not only learned about challenging students into radical World Christian living; I have been freshly stirred to give up my small ambitions for God's glory among the nations."

Mark Bradley
Director of Mobilization, OMF International

"Todd Ahrend has provided us with one of the most comprehensive and compelling overviews of the Student Volunteer Movement, distilling practical lessons that missions activists can apply to be more effective today. *In This Generation* is an excellent resource that will inform and inspire you to do your part in the Great Commission."

Steve Moore
President & CEO, The Mission Exchange

"The Student Volunteer Movement mobilized more students to go and serve the nations in their first year than in the previous century! How in the world did they do it? Todd Ahrend answers that question in this engaging and practical book. Todd combines his personal wisdom gained over a decade of mobilizing students with a historical survey of the Student Volunteer Movement, which is perhaps the most underappreciated mobilizing work of God in the last two centuries. Reading this book gives you access to the mind and passion of a master mobilizer."

Joey Shaw,
Minister of International Mission
The Austin Stone Community Church, Texas

"This book is a must read for anyone working with college students. Through his extensive study of the Student Volunteer Movement, Todd pulls out practical, timeless principles that will help campus ministers mobilize students to change the world."

Mike Schatzman
WSN Director Red River Region, Campus Crusade for Christ

"One of the most remarkable and least recognized movements in history was the Student Volunteer Movement. Ultimately 20,000 of America's 'best and brightest' scattered across the globe in response to the compelling vision they'd discovered in the Scriptures. Todd Ahrend unveils the powerful secrets of the S.V.M., renews the call in today's generation, and points the way forward for God's world changers."

Steve Richardson
President, Pioneers – U.S.A.

"*In This Generation: Looking to the Past to Reach the Present* is a thoughtful yet extremely practical book on how to motivate this generation for missions. Todd Ahrend analyzes the questions, issues, and practices around the Student Volunteer Movement and compares them to today. This is a great history of the S.V.M. but it is much more than that. Todd shows that we can learn from the past as long as we don't live there. I highly recommend this for anyone interested in missions today."

Jim Tebbe
Urbana Director
Vice President for Missions, InterVarsity Christian Fellowship

"I've known of Todd's passion for mobilization for years. In this book he combines years of thinking and studying with practical experience and methods that will greatly aid anyone interested in reaching the nations."

Brian Phillips
Campus Outreach Director, Brisbane, Australia

"This book is more than a collection of biographical sketches. It is more than the account of an awe-inspiring God-centered movement of students. It is both a challenge and a practical guide to participation in the fulfillment of the Great Commission. I can't wait to get this resource in the hands of people in my ministry."

Brian Zunigha
Director of Campus Ministries, California Baptist University

IN THIS GENERATION

Looking to the Past to Reach the Present

For Jess.

*You believed in me before
I believed in myself.*

CONTENTS

FOREWORD

Where does the U.S.A. Church fit in the future of global missions? And—if the U.S.A. Church is destined to play a part—how can this Church be mobilized, especially the younger college-age members of this Church? These and many other related questions are the focus of Todd Ahrend in this significant work.

When I first met Todd Ahrend after he had given his testimony at the Urbana Student Missionary Conference, I recognized him as a gifted mobilizer—one of those unusual individuals called by God not to go and serve cross-culturally but rather to call others to go and serve.

Since the late 1990s, Todd has dedicated himself to the mobilization of students, so it's not surprising that his first major written work takes us back over a century to the Student Volunteer Movement. The Student Volunteer Movement (S.V.M.)—arguably the greatest movement of missions mobilization that Christian history has ever known—provides the foundation upon which Todd builds in this work. The intent is clear: to observe the S.V.M. methodology and connect it to the 21st century. What principles are relevant? Which are best left to history? These are the questions Todd invites us to consider.

I consider myself privileged to introduce this work for three reasons. First, I think we need to look back—as Todd does—to the Student Volunteer Movement to glean both ideas and inspiration for motivating and mobilizing students today. If the writer of Ecclesiastes is correct—that there is "nothing new under the sun," then "looking to the past to reach the present" is critically important.

Second, I see Todd as a person who has an "inside scoop" on students in the 21st century. His extensive exposure to students through The Traveling Team adds a credibility to his observations here from which I and every other "mobilizer" can learn.

Finally, I believe in the mission behind Todd's desire to write this book: students can be and must be mobilized to go into all the "nations" of the world to invite others to share in worshiping Jesus. If we are to welcome the day when every tribe, tongue, language, and people worship Jesus (Revelation 5:9; 7:9), the younger generation must be mobilized to prayer, witness, and cross-cultural ministry. And if the Student Volunteer Movement has something to teach us toward that end, then so be it!

Paul Borthwick, author of over a dozen books on missions and church leadership, including *How to Be a World-Class Christian*, **serves as consultant to InterVarsity Missions and the Urbana Student Mission Convention, teaches global Christianity courses at Gordon College, and trains international leaders through Development Associates International.**

ACKNOWLEDGMENTS

Someone once said, "Life is a journey and only you hold the map." We make decisions that dictate where we will end up tomorrow, in five years, and in fifty years. This would be a daunting thought if along the way there were no pointers! These are people who come along and help direct us to the way of God, encourage us to stay on it, and help us thrive to our fullest potential. I have had many pointers; influencers who have aided my journey and I cannot imagine trying to decipher my map without them. It is time to pause and say thanks for the directions along the way.

I think of the first pointer, Danny Ferguson. He influenced me to the cross. I think of Nick and Ted Shimer—brothers who sought me out, trained me in the spiritual disciplines, and poured their lives into me. These two men showed me how to spend time in the Word, pray, and share my faith. Invaluable tools needed along the way.

I think of Bill Stearns who was one of the first and best mobilizers I've ever known. He left such an impression on me that I wanted to be on the same journey he was on. I know I join with many in missing him dearly.

I would like to say thanks to Steve Shadrach who was the first to share the story of the Student Volunteer Movement with me. Shad influenced me to turn my map right-side up!

David Smithers taught me to actually compare my map with the maps of those who have gone before. More than any other man I know, Smithers is looking to the past to reach the present.

Paul Borthwick has mastered that which I aspire to: taking the map to others around the world and teaching them to read it. It's second nature to this man.

I think of Timothy Tennent. He took my missions understanding from knee deep in the streams and exposed me to oceans of thought.

I think of Claude Hickman. It seems our journeys are parallel. Same dorm in college, married two weeks apart, kids four months apart, same ministry for over a decade. He is the most talented person I know and truly mentors what it means to be a friend that sticks closer than a brother.

I think of my father and mother, who have consistently encouraged and guided me. They've always wanted the best for my journey. I am also grateful to my sisters, Theresa and Alicia, for making the journey a precious and unforgettable one.

I think of my wife, Jess. There's no one else I would rather journey with!

THE MOVERS
AND THE MOVEMENT

"There is one thing stronger than all the armies in the world; and that is an idea whose time has come."

-Victor Hugo

CHAPTER 1
THE STORY

I never imagined I'd be at this crossroads. I never pictured myself at the ripe age of nineteen already facing the biggest question of my life. I enrolled in college with one goal: to be a third-grade teacher. My plans were simple. Not only would I teach, but I would marry a teacher; we would never work a holiday, I would have my summers free to golf, and eventually we'd retire in a beautiful Winnebago. I had my life laid out and was excited about the path it was on. I was a believer, but for some reason I'd just left God out of the big decisions and relegated Him to the Sunday morning department. My assumption was that I would happily join the ranks of countless Christians who aspire to the American Dream, never questioning my course but seeking only for God to bless it. Then my freshman year in college something happened—I met a guy who had purpose. He used a completely different grid to make decisions. He invited me to be in a Bible study where we prayed for the world. This was weird. I'm thinking, "why not pray more about me?" We met internationals on campus, we shared our faith, and we invited others to join us. He showed me passages in the Bible that revealed God's desire to see the nations reached; they were everywhere! My world started to turn upside down.

I realized that although I had been a believer for nearly five years, no one had challenged me to take personal responsibility for evangelizing the world. I had not even heard about missions! Sitting on my bed in my dorm room at the end of the year, I had a choice to make; I was at a crossroads. Was I going to allow God to interrupt my life with His purpose and push mine aside? Or was I going to cling to the life I had always wanted? Until that point, I had never pursued seriously what the Bible had to say about missions. I had never wondered about the destiny of the lost or the exclusive claims of Jesus as they related to the world. I couldn't even recall any specific sermons about missions. Why was I at this crossroads after being a Christian for so long? What would my family think of my change of direction? Wasn't I supposed to hear God "call" me? In that moment a flood of questions and convictions seemed to apex into what many have called a crisis of belief.

The definition of a missionary is someone who allows God to interrupt their life.

Incredibly, these are the questions that Christian students have had to come face-to-face with for the past two hundred years. As you study history it becomes apparent— the definition of a missionary is *someone who allows God to interrupt their life*. I wasn't the first nor will I be the last. Come, join me on the journey of tracing interrupted lives throughout history and see if it is worth giving up your dreams, even your Winnebago!

THE STUDENT VOLUNTEER MOVEMENT

College-aged students, more than any other group, have yielded an incredible harvest of laborers for the mission movement. Though God can and does use people from all seasons of life, *most* missions momentum has always come from students, individuals in this unique four- to six-year time frame. If we charted the history of missions it would look like a mountain, the peak of which would represent approximately thirty years from 1886-1920 when an organization called the Student Volunteer Movement (S.V.M.) was thriving. Let me briefly tell you the story that will be further developed throughout this book.

I am not sure what you think of when you think of the Y.M.C.A. today. I know for me it was where I played eighth grade basketball and then went swimming. One hundred years ago it looked quite different. The Young Men's Christian Association (Y.M.C.A.) was founded by George Williams in London in 1844. By 1858, a mere fourteen years later, it had spread so rapidly that it had made its way throughout Europe and onto American college campuses.[1] The Y.M.C.A. was equipping students to lead Bible studies, do evangelism on campus, and pray. In 1885 a man named Luther Wishard was the collegiate minister for the entire Y.M.C.A. During his day, the Y.M.C.A. was considered the "spiritual nerve center" of

---

[1] Clarence P. Shedd, *Two Centuries of Student Christian Movements: Their Origin and Intercollegiate Life* (New York: Association Press, 1934), 92-94.

[2] Shedd, 272-275.

the American colleges and Wishard sought to use it as the vehicle to recruit students to missions.[2] His method? He decided to host a four-week summer training project in Mount Hermon, Massachusetts, not only to disciple students in the basics of the Christian walk, but also to mobilize students to go to the world.

In preparation for this project, which began in July of 1886, Wishard invited two students from every campus to come. The result was that 251 students from eighty-nine campuses actually attended. One of these students was a senior from Princeton University, Robert Wilder. When the project's keynote speaker, D. L. Moody, took the stage, Robert Wilder took to prayer. By the end of the summer they had successfully mobilized exactly one hundred students to be foreign missionaries. These came to be known as the Mount Hermon One Hundred. But the impact had only begun.

Mount Hermon One Hundred

Realizing the mass amount of Christian students not represented at the project, Wishard invited a few of the Mount Hermon One Hundred to travel from campus to campus and share God's purpose of reaching the nations. After one year, 162 campuses were visited and the result was that 2,106 students volunteered to be missionaries.

After that incredibly momentous first year it was decided to give this movement a name. They called it the Student Volunteer Movement because it seemed day after day students were laying down their plans, allowing God to interrupt their lives and, upon graduation, *volunteering* to board a boat and live in a distant land for the gospel. Over the entire course of its existence, this mobilization organization yielded approximately 20,000 missionaries who went forth to the field and 80,000 who stayed behind to support those who went.[3]

John Mott, who led the Student Volunteer Movement for over thirty years, gives a glimpse as to the missionary recruitment that was going on before the Movement began: "Before the Volunteer Movement was organized, comparatively little was being done to inform, still less to educate, students on the subject of foreign missions. In a few institutions missionary meetings were held from time to time. Now and then a missionary on furlough would visit a college or seminary."[4] Just to put it in perspective, the cumulative total of Protestant missionaries sent out from America by the year 1870 was two thousand.[5] In the first year of the Student Volunteer Movement's existence alone,

---

[3] Michael Parker, *The Kingdom of Character: The Student Volunteer Movement for Foreign Missions 1886-1926*, 2nd ed. (Pasadena, CA: William Carey Library, 2008), 56.

[4] The Students and the Modern Missionary Crusade, Addresses Delivered before the Fifth International Convention of the Student Volunteer Movement for Foreign Missions, Nashville, Tennessee, Feb. 28-March 4, 1906, 45.

it recruited more students to go as missionaries than had been sent from the United States in the preceding century.[6] Amazing! College presidents were even awed at the commitment of students. The president of Princeton University said, "Christians cannot but notice this event occurring before their eyes.... Has any such offering of living young men and women been presented in our age? In our country? In any age or in any country since the days of Pentecost?"[7]

By 1920, after thirty years of ministry, John Mott could look back in amazement and say, "The Volunteer Movement has furnished approximately 75% of the male missionaries of North America and 70% of the unmarried women missionaries."[8] It was a time when the right men joined with the right methods for the right moment in history that would later be recognized as the most potent missionary mobilization force the world has ever seen.[9]

---

[5] Parker, XI.

[6] Parker, XII.

[7] C. Howard Hopkins, *History of the YMCA in North America* (New York: Association Press, 1951), 299, 316.

[8] "North American Students and World Advance," Addresses Delivered at the Eighth International Convention of the Student Volunteer Movement for Foreign Missions, Des Moines, Iowa, Dec. 31, 1919 – Jan. 4, 1920, 62.

[9] The impact of these 20,000 missionaries was quite remarkable. Both men and women took their training from the university, committed long-term to the field, shared their faith, and did good works in the nation they went to. At one point in 1936 John Mott addressed an audience of students and shared over 35 stories of what had been accomplished by those who went out. The common theme was that they proclaimed their faith in Christ while at the same time serving those around them in a practical, humanitarian way. Mott states, "I myself, in my world travels, have met thousands of these former student volunteers, absorbed in their great unselfish cause of making Christ known and regnant in the life of the peoples with whom they have identified themselves." John R. Mott, *Addresses and Papers of John R. Mott Volume 1: The Student Volunteer Movement for Foreign Missions* (New York: Association Press, 1946), 249. See also Parker, *The Kingdom of Character*, 239.

THE LANDSCAPE

This movement proves that God delights to move in fresh ways that exceed our highest expectations; it breathes hope for what He might do in our own generation. While God's overall purpose in the world is changeless, His ways are unpredictable and unprecedented. Our every missional endeavor need not be characterized by the same steps of obedience that He asked of Abraham, Paul, the Student Volunteer Movement, or any other prior agent of His work. But what if we could better understand the inner workings of the Student Volunteer Movement, take a deeper look at their writings, speeches, and journals and gather common principles that are relevant no matter what the context? Think about the impact we could have by utilizing the best resources from this incredible movement!

David Smithers, an expert in revival history, says, "It's OK to look back at history as long as we don't stare." We reflect on history not as an end in itself, but to take what we learn from it and look forward. History is rich with life lessons that drive us on today.

The goal of this book is to understand *how to mobilize Christian students to be World Christians* and we will do that by taking a peek into the past. By way of introduction, my first desire is to set the stage with the movers of the Movement—those who were the key leaders of the S.V.M. As you will see there is much to be drawn from their lives. In the second section, we will look at the shifting of theology that occurred over the century that spans between our generations. We live in such a different world than in 1910 and this section will bring us into our cultural and theological context today. In the third section we will compare and contrast the primary methods employed in the past with those used today. From there, I hope to bring to light the issues that students have struggled with both today and in the S.V.M.'s era. Finally, we will conclude by unpacking some common principles from the Student Volunteer Movement that can be applied to today's missions mobilization.

This movement breathes hope for what He might do in our own generation.

I have spent the last decade circling the United States mobilizing on college campuses and one thing is sure—God is moving. He is bringing students to a crossroads and they are asking, *Am I going to allow God to interrupt my life*? Will they say yes to embracing God's heart for the world and whatever that means for them? Or will they allow obstacles and excuses to distract, hinder, and eventually keep them from the World Christian lifestyle? Let's learn from the past to reach the present!

John Mott

CHAPTER 2
JOHN R. MOTT

" Elijah was a man with a nature like ours..." (James 5:17, ESV). Sometimes it is just good to hear that.

There are no superheroes. We all have struggles and issues. The line in the sand between the masses and those who are remembered is a willingness to surrender ourselves to God for His purpose. Those who make history are those who submit to the One who orchestrates it. That's what is so apparent in the leaders of the Student Volunteer Movement; people who said yes to God. Real people just like you. They said yes to the hard things. And their impact will be felt for eternity.

As I introduce you to five of these extraordinary people, let me give you two reasons that you will want to know their stories. First, these movers of the Movement are, in many ways, the very foundation of this epic era in history. The lives of those who came after them and the very Movement itself truly took on the rich character qualities and spiritual depth that these people possessed. The second reason is that you will be personally challenged and encouraged by their hearts to see God move among the nations. These five individuals were men and women "with a nature like ours" and God used each one to greatly impact a generation.

Those who make history are those who submit to the One who orchestrates it.

The progress and impact of the Student Volunteer Movement owes no man more than John Mott (1865-1955). Not only was he the founder, but for thirty-two years he was the organization's chairman—its leader.[1] Through Mott, thousands of students found their way to the foreign field. Mott was born in Livingston Manor, New York, and was the only son among three daughters. Soon after his birth the family moved to Postville, Iowa, where his father owned a lumber company which he intended to leave to John when he retired. At age sixteen Mott attended Upper Iowa

---

[1] C. Howard Hopkins, *20th Century Ecumenical Statesman John R. Mott: 1865-1955* (New York: Eerdmans Publishing Company, 1979), 569.

University, a Methodist preparatory school. He soon realized that UIU was unable to provide the training he needed to enter his desired profession. Mott was also feeling pressure that the UIU was placing on all students to go into a religious field.[2] Mott appeared, at this time in his life, externally religious, but inside he still clung to his own desires and plans. Commenting on this period he later said:

> What hinders our placing our lives at the disposal of Christ, henceforth to do his will and not our own? With some of you it may be, as it once was with me, a selfish ambition. Let it be repeated, there are two views of one's life. One is that a man's life is his own, to do with as he pleases; the other is that it belongs to another, and in the case of the Christian, that the other to whom it belongs is Christ himself. At first, although I bore the name of Christian, I held the former or selfish view.[3]

This inner struggle along with the religious stress of UIU was enough to make Mott transfer. So at age twenty Mott enrolled at Cornell University and found himself in the company of Christian students there as well. Though Mott was still wrestling with giving his whole heart to Christ, his friends observed in him a potential gifting of spiritual leadership. After being at Cornell only four months, he gave in when the Y.M.C.A. elected him to be their vice president.

God was working deeply in Mott's life and, through his involvement in the Y.M.C.A., he experienced what he later called "the most decisive hour of his life." Late one night

---

[2] Basil Mathews, *John R. Mott: World Citizen* (New York: Harper and Brothers Publishers, 1934), 28.
[3] Clarence P. Shedd, *Two Centuries of Student Christian Movements: Their Origin and Intercollegiate Life* (New York: Association Press, 1934), 291.

while he and his roommate Arthur Grant were studying, they pushed their books aside to talk about what it meant to be "called into the ministry." During their discussion these two men knelt before God and it was placed on their hearts that they should be men who give their whole life to ministry. They both tried to confirm this conviction by opening up to random passages in hopes that they would land on something remotely relevant. Mott opened up to Daniel 12:3: "Those who are wise will shine like the brightness of the heavens, and those who lead many to righteousness, like the stars forever and ever."[4] Undeniable confirmation of this conviction came soon enough as Arthur "randomly" stumbled on to the Great Commission (Matt 28:18-20). That same week a guest speaker, the famous English athlete J. E. K. Studd, came to preach to Cornell's Christian students.[5] Here is an excerpt from Mott's journal about that meeting:

> I hesitated long as to whether to go to Studd's first meeting... I arrived after the meeting had begun. As I took my seat, I heard Studd give three sentences: "Seekest thou great things for thyself? Seek them not. Seek ye first the Kingdom of God" (Jer. 45:5; Matt. 6:33, KJV). These words went straight to the springs of my motive life.

Of the next day Mott continues:

---

[4] Hopkins, 19.

[5] J. E. K. Studd was one of the three famous Studd brothers along with George and Charles Thomas (C. T.). Luther Wishard invited J. E. K. Studd to travel to campuses in America telling the story of the Cambridge Seven—high-profile athletes who committed to missions after graduation. It was on the campus of Cornell that J. E. K. Studd met John Mott. For more information on the Studd brothers see Norman Grubb, *C. T. Studd: Famous Athlete and Pioneer* (Grand Rapids, MI: Zondervan, 1933).

At 2:30, I mustered courage to seek an interview with Studd, and found him in his sports clothes, bent over his Bible. In a most discerning way he made me see the reasonableness of consulting for myself the source book of Christianity, the New Testament, and the wisdom of using my will to follow the gleam of light leading Christ's way.[6]

Mott had looked forward to a legal and political career, but after Studd's visit to Cornell he knew the course of his life would be in Christian work—there was no looking back. That semester Mott wrote a six-page letter home to his father and mother, trying to bridge the gap between what God was doing in his heart and his parents' aspirations. Here is a portion:

Feb. 7th, 1886 (Ithaca, New York)

My own spirit says, "you are gifted for the legal profession—by work you can achieve eminence in that field..." Again the same spirit says, "go into business your father has built up"...This same spirit says, "you can do enough good for the world in either of these spheres..." This spirit stops not here, it taunts me still more saying, "just think what your friends and acquaintances will say; think how foolish they will call you for relinquishing such fine opportunities as you have in the political, commercial or farm life."

---

[6] Ruth Rouse, *The World's Student Christian Federation* (London: S.C.M. Press LTD., 1948), 48.

His hope was to explain that God had been leading in a direction that, in hindsight, had been slowly building to an ultimate surrender to full-time ministry. He continues:

> That spirit, ma, is the spirit of the flesh, of the world, and of the devil! …On the other hand there is a still small voice saying… "Go ye into all the world and preach the gospel to every creature—the harvest is great but the laborers are few—he who would save his life shall lose it, but he who would lose his life for my sake the same shall save it."[7]

Right about this time, an invitation to the Mount Hermon summer project was sent to him by Luther Wishard.[8] Mott saw the decision to go to this project as the first decision of any importance that he made without his parents' advice. As Mott boarded the train to Mount Hermon, Massachusetts, that July, he had no idea what was waiting for him and how the summer would shape his life.

During these four weeks at the Mount Hermon summer project the leading American evangelist D. L. Moody and a few other men taught on various topics. However, throughout the summer there was an undercurrent of recruitment to missions being stirred by a Princeton student, Robert Wilder. Mott met Wilder as they were walking to the river for a swim and the two began a conversation on German philosophy. Wilder wove in the subject of missions and, even though Mott tried to avoid it, Wilder was relentless. As the month progressed, so did Mott's desire to fully

---

[7] Matthews, 39-40.
[8] The official name was the "College Students' Summer School."

consecrate himself to the Lord for missions work. At the end of the four weeks, one hundred men signed a pledge dedicating themselves to be missionaries. Mott was number twenty-three, though he was still unsure as to when and where the Lord might lead.[9] In order to keep the fires going Luther Wishard elected four of the one hundred at the project to travel to various campuses and spread the vision of missions. Mott committed to be one of the four but because of his parents' disapproval he withdrew his commitment.

With all of his talent and ability, Mott could have done many things after graduation. He decided to devote one year to full-time ministry on staff with the Y.M.C.A., a position that earned him $1,500 per year. This one-year commitment gave Mott the foundation he needed and launched him naturally into a lifetime of mobilization as he remained the leader of the Student Volunteer Movement until 1920.

Mott went on to marry Leila White in 1891 and that same year took his first overseas trip. He and his wife traveled to Europe in order to measure the prospects for carrying on student work there.[10] This short trip cast vision for Mott to join together the Christian students of the world. Between the years of 1895-1897 he and Leila took a twenty-month tour of numerous countries in the quest of challenging Christian students with the values and tools the S.V.M. had developed. A short sampling of countries shows just how extensive their travels were for these twenty months: Britain, Germany, Sweden, Norway, Turkey, Syria, Israel, Egypt, India, Australia, New Zealand, China, and Japan. The result was the founding of the World Student Christian Federation in 1895.

[9] Hopkins, 27.
[10] Matthews, 98-99.

To see all that Mott accomplished in his generation is fascinating. He crossed the Atlantic over one hundred times averaging thirty-four days on the ocean per year for fifty years. He delivered thousands of speeches, pioneered many organizations, all of which have become the foundation-stones of other greater world organizations. He also raised over $300 million for

Very early in his career he began to earn the title, "that young man who thinks in continents."

religious initiatives. Very early in his career he began to earn the title, "that young man who thinks in continents."[11] In 1946, under the endorsement of President Harry Truman, John Mott was awarded the Nobel Peace Prize for his life's work. Mott not only created an organization in the S.V.M. that would impact the United States, but he also extended that organization's influence to the ends of the earth. John Raleigh Mott died at age eighty-nine and is buried in the Washington Cathedral. His life was centered on a single passion to see the evangelization of the world in his generation. This for Mott was not simply an ivory-tower notion, but an achievable task and vision. What began as a reluctant conversation with Robert Wilder turned into a life of fruitful service to Christ in pursuit of reaching the nations.

---

[11] Rouse, 49-51.

Robert Wilder

CHAPTER 3
ROBERT WILDER

I f any man could tap into a person's full potential, it was Robert Wilder. Robert was born on August 2, 1863 in Kolhapur, India, and was the fifth and final child of his missionary parents, Royal and Eliza Wilder.[1] Royal Wilder attended Andover Seminary and moved to India where he and his wife worked until forced to return home in 1875. The family decided to move to Princeton and Royal Wilder founded the monthly journal *The Missionary Review of the World*. The journal became the foremost magazine of its day featuring the needs and situation of missions of all denominations.

---

[1] Robert Wilder's father, Royal Wilder, attended Andover Theological College in the 1840s and heard the story of the Haystack Prayer Movement. He also met their successors and heard stories describing their work in India and Persia. He married Eliza and they set sail for India in September 1846. Elizabeth Goldsmith, *Roots and Wings: Five Generations and Their Influence* (Waynesboro, GA: Paternoster Publishing Publication, 1998), 5, 8. Also see James Patterson, "The Legacy of Robert P. Wilder," *International Bulletin of Missionary Research,* January 14, 1991, 1.

In 1881 Robert Wilder entered Princeton University where his primary scholastic interests included Greek, philosophy, and music.[2] In the autumn of 1883 Wilder, intending to enroll in seminary himself someday, attended a spiritual life conference for seminary students hosted by noted author and pastor A. J. Gordon. It was there that Wilder heard an address from Dr. Gordon challenging the students to yield to the inspiration and control of the Holy Spirit. After the conference, Wilder returned to Princeton in order to accomplish two things: first, to pray and work for a revival on his campus and second, to stir up missionary interest. The result of these two initiatives was the formation of the Princeton Foreign Missionary Society, a gathering of students desiring to go overseas.

Wilder and a handful of others met on Sunday afternoons in his father's home to pray and study missions. This tiny band of missions-minded students continued to flourish, but made no apparent efforts to spread the movement beyond the walls of Princeton and onto other college campuses.[3] However, intent upon pursuing missions as their life work, one went to Japan, two to China, two to India, one to Bulgaria, and two to Thailand.[4] Seeing the great interest that his peers had in missions service, Wilder decided to introduce a declaration of commitment for the members of their group to sign: "We are willing and desirous, God permitting, to become foreign missionaries." Two and a half years later (1886), this would become the Volunteer Declaration adopted by the one hundred volunteers at the

[2] Ruth Wilder Braisted, *In This Generation: The Story of Robert P. Wilder* (New York: Friendship Press, 1941), 14.

[3] Timothy C. Wallstrom, *The Creation of a Student Movement to Evangelize the World* (Pasadena, CA: William Carey International University Press, 1980), 11.

[4] Robert P. Wilder, *The Great Commission: The Missionary Response of the Student Volunteer Movement in North America and Europe; Some Personal Reminiscences* (London: Oliphants Publishers, 1936), 16.

D. L. Moody

famous Mount Hermon summer project.[5]

Robert Wilder received an invitation from Luther Wishard to attend this Mount Hermon project. At first he was hesitant in light of the fact that he was a senior at Princeton and would have been unable to return to college and apply what he had learned. He eventually accepted the invitation, but was totally unaware he was about to influence the spawning of arguably the greatest mobilization movement in history. Upon arrival at the four-week summer project Wilder realized he was not alone in his desire to spread the missions vision. Out of the 251 men present, already twenty-one were seriously considering overseas service. They all signed the declaration and committed to recruit more volunteers from among those present. The summer project speaker, D. L. Moody, did not intend for world evangelization to be taught from the platform, but Wilder convinced him of the urgent importance of this message. At Wilder's suggestion, Moody allowed ten students from different countries to have three minutes each to share.[6] This occurred halfway through the

---

[5] Wilder, 22.
[6] Goldsmith, 41.

summer project and was indeed the climax of the summer—the pinnacle of the Holy Spirit's work to penetrate the hearts of many men with a deep commitment to global Christian involvement. Throughout the course of the next two weeks men were burdened for the world's needs and responded in obedience. Looking back on the summer project, Wilder reflects on the fruit of the event, "Before the conference closed, while the

He was about to influence the spawning of arguably the greatest mobilization movement in history.

ninety-nine who had signed the declaration were meeting for prayer, another joined our ranks. So we closed the conference with exactly one hundred volunteers for foreign service."[7]

Wilder was one of the four men asked to travel from campus to campus extending the invitation to thousands of students to be involved in the urgent work of world evangelization. The others chosen were Mott from Cornell, Riley from DePauw, and Taylor from Yale. The concept was powerful—students recruiting students—what could have more impact? The plan was set, the campuses were lined out, and everyone involved anticipated what God was going to do

---

[7] Wilder, 22.

through this new initiative. Then this budding Movement was dealt a devastating blow. Wilder writes, "I confess I am surprised, disappointed, and pained at the action... I find it utterly impossible to comprehend and sympathize with the 'reason,' the 'obstacles,' the 'difficulties' which the fellows present."[8] What could have occurred to compromise the Movement so greatly and cause such distress to Wilder? What kind of obstacle could present such a threat? Riley got engaged. Taylor got scared. Mott's parents made him go back to finish college. Wilder alone was left to carry out this vision. And he faced his own internal obstacle. He had just received word from the doctors that his father would not live another six months. With the future of missions hanging in the balance, Robert struggled. He could not have known the weight of his decision and the subsequent revolution that was to occur in missions, but God knew.

Days before his projected solitary launch on the campus tour and still asking the question of whether or not he should go, Robert's father called him into his study. A man of God and missions zealot himself, he said, "Son, let the dead bury their dead. You go and preach the kingdom of God."[9] Relieved, Robert did just that. The students of the world were changed. History was written. Without this act of obedience it is easy to imagine that this Movement would never have existed.

While Wilder was working out his personal decision to obey despite his circumstances, God was making provision for him by stirring the heart of John Forman. After

---

[8] Wilder, 23.
[9] Wilder, 23.

Wilder committed himself to the work, Forman joined him and the two labored together that following year (1886-1887) on the campus tour. Beginning in Maine, Wilder and Forman traveled to over 162 colleges presenting the message of missions and successfully recruited 2,106 volunteers—550 of whom were women.[10] This is also the year that saw the enlistment of great future missionaries such as Samuel Zwemer and missions mobilizers such as Robert Speer.

With the future of missions hanging in the balance, Robert struggled... but God knew.

In light of Wilder's desire to serve in India, the next year he decided to enter Union Theological Seminary. He left, however, after one year to travel again to different campuses for the S.V.M. during the 1888-1889 school year. After this year of travel Wilder finished seminary and was appointed by the Presbyterian Board of Foreign Missions to India. On June 28, 1891, at age 27, he departed to India. Wilder was scheduled to travel through Europe in order to get there. The stop in Europe caused him to consider two alternatives to his initial plan, both involving his love of student mobilization. The first was to stay in England and recruit students to the missions movement. The second was to actually enroll as a student in one of the universities to

---

[10] Tissington Tatlow, *The Story of the Student Christian Movement of Great Britain and Ireland* (London: Student Christian Movement Press, 1933), 19.

give him first-hand exposure and influence with students. One month later he was granted thirteen minutes to speak at the annual Keswick convention, England's premier conference on spiritual life. During these thirteen minutes he not only captivated his audience, but he caught the ear of the entire nation.[11] As a result he was inundated with requests to stay in England and mobilize students on British campuses presenting the story of the Student Volunteer Movement. Wilder reported on this pivotal meeting:

> After that thirteen-minute address which I gave on Saturday morning, Fraser insisted on my coming to Glasgow University, and Professor Drummond's secretary invited me to Edinburgh, and Rennie MacInnes, who is now the Anglican Bishop in Jerusalem, invited me to Cambridge, where he was studying. So after a good deal of thought and prayer, I decided to delay going to India long enough to visit the leading British universities.[12]

By April 2, 1892 Robert Wilder was able to witness the birth of the Student Volunteer Missionary Union of Great Britain and Ireland. During this time in Great Britain a short visit to Norway allowed him to meet his wife, Helen Olsson.

---

[11] The Keswick conventions in England, the Cambridge Seven, and Henry Drummond's work in Edinburgh all contributed to the establishment of the British Student Volunteer Movement. John Mott attended the 1891 and 1894 Keswick Convention in Britain. He stated that one could, without much difficulty, imagine himself at the Mount Hermon summer project. However he desired to make it clear that the Student Volunteer Movement was not to be confused with the Keswick Convention. Hopkins writes, "This was, in a sense, a distinction without a difference, because both movements shared largely in the evangelical currents that had swirled back and forth across the Atlantic." C. Howard Hopkins, *20th Century Ecumenical Statesman John R. Mott*: 1865-1955 (New York: Eerdmans Publishing Company, 1979), 114. See also Ruth Rouse, *The World's Student Christian Federation* (London: S.C.M. Press LTD, 1948).

[12] Robert Wilder, "Early Days in the Movement," *SVM Bulletin* 7, no. 3 (Dec. 1926): 71.

Eight months later Robert and Helen Wilder set sail for India to work with students.

He worked in Pune, India, for almost a decade until he had to leave in order to recover from illness. He chose Vevey on Lake Geneva as his retreat location where he and his wife shared a home with 70-year-old Hudson Taylor, pioneer missionary and founder of the faith mission movement.[13] In 1904 he received an invitation from Rev. Tissington Tatlow to spend three months serving the Movement of Great Britain and Ireland. Because health issues were still hindering him from going back to India, he decided to accept the invitation. These three months turned into eleven years of work among British undergraduates. In 1916 John Mott, who was still presiding over the Student Volunteer Movement in America, invited Wilder to come back to the U.S. and work for him. The invitation was timely as World War I was underway and funds to support the British Movement were dwindling, so Wilder accepted. He held this strategic position until 1927 when, at the age of sixty-five, Wilder resigned.

His last full-time position was with the Near East Christian Council which took him to Cairo, Egypt. For six years he tried to unite the Church in an area where Islam was a dominant force.[14] He spent the last years of his life in Norway with his wife. He died in 1938 at age seventy-five and is buried in Oslo. James Patterson sums up the legacy of Robert Wilder well:

---

[13] Goldsmith, 66.
[14] Patterson, 4.

In the final analysis, Robert Wilder left his mark in ways that are difficult to measure by the standards normally applied to the missionary leaders of his generation. He was neither a brilliant mission theorist nor an innovative strategist. He is not remembered as an orator who overwhelmed audiences with his eloquence and his published writings are not voluminous or especially profound. Yet Wilder grasped better than most of his contemporaries the real essence of servanthood and discipleship. Through a life of humble and sacrificial service, he faithfully persevered, despite chronic physical problems, in his overarching commitment to world evangelization. Thus he modeled qualities that are vital and relevant in any missionary era.[15]

Yes, Luther Wishard knew just the kind of man he needed at the Mount Hermon summer project. He knew that others would follow a humble, persistent servant. He knew that a disciple-maker would leave a legacy. So he pursued Robert Wilder and, as it turns out, Wishard chose the right man.

---

[15] Patterson, 6.

Luther Wishard

CHAPTER 4
LUTHER WISHARD

I t is said of Luther Wishard that "his laugh would ring out above all others and people would laugh to hear him laugh, and you would hear people sitting near you say in an undertone 'That's Wishard.'"[1] Born in Danville, Indiana on April 6, 1854, Wishard grew to be a man of incredible influence. His father worked with disabled soldiers and his mother was a schoolteacher. His father also happened to be very inspired by the Y.M.C.A. and passed that enthusiasm on to Luther. At Princeton University where he enrolled in 1875, Wishard was one of the best known and most popular men.

---

[1] C. K. Ober, *Exploring a Continent* (New York: Association Press, 1929), 69.

LUTHER WISHARD

Wishard's commitment to the Y.M.C.A. extended to the degree that he actually initiated an entirely new division of it—one that was solely focused on college students (previously, the Y.M.C.A. had been open to a much broader definition of "young men").[2] This made Luther the first full-time college minister in America. The position offered a limited salary and came with a lengthy job description including traveling to various campuses and meeting with students. Somehow, Wishard still found time to pursue a seminary degree at Union Theological Seminary.

In class at seminary Wishard heard the story of Samuel Mills and the Haystack Prayer Meeting that took place among the students at Williams College eighty years earlier and launched America's first missionaries.[3] Wishard, realizing the connection between what Mills desired to do and what God had placed on his own heart said:

---

[2] The division was called the Intercollegiate Young Men's Christian Association Movement. Luther Wishard met with those in charge of the Y.M.C.A. to put forth a proposal of what the role of the collegiate division would be. The executives of the Y.M.C.A. agreed with the proposal under the condition that a full-time staff would be appointed to supervise and organize the work. It was understood that Wishard would accept this new role to ensure the success of the Y.M.C.A. on campuses. For more information on the I.Y.M.C.A.M. see Clarence P. Shedd, *Two Centuries of Student Christian Movements: Their Origin and Intercollegiate Life* (New York: Association Press, 1934), 145. Ober, 68.

[3] As an incoming freshman at Williams College, friends of Samuel Mills described him as a tall, quirky guy with a squeaky voice. But Samuel Mills had Asia on his mind. The problem was that up to this point America had not sent a single missionary. To make matters worse, had there been a willing candidate, there were still no existent missions agencies in America. In a field just off campus at Williams College, Massachusetts, in what seemed to be an ordinary Bible study, a storm approached and five students sought shelter next to a haystack. When the storm passed Samuel Mills challenged them with the words "We can do this if we will," referring to the spread of the gospel to Asia. From then on, these five students called themselves the "Society of the Brethren" in order to mobilize even more students. They would go on to see the first missionary launched in 1812 and to found the first six missions agencies in the United States. For more on the life of Samuel Mills see Thomas C. Richards, *Samuel J. Mills: Missionary, Pathfinder, Pioneer and Promoter* (Boston: The Pilgrim Press, 1906).

Let the students in these closing years of the century consummate what our fellow students in the early part of the century attempted. Let us engraft a missionary department upon this Intercollegiate Movement. We are their lineal spiritual descendants and successors; what they had begun it is ours to complete. They had willed, but our wills must now be brought into the plan to consummate their daring purpose.[4]

What they had begun it is ours to complete.

Learning of Samuel Mills and his goal of mobilizing students to reach the world, Wishard set out to leverage his influence and position within the Y.M.C.A. to carry on where Mills left off. So now, when he traveled campus to campus his emphasis was on publicizing the story of Samuel Mills and the Williams College Haystack Prayer Meeting. He also held regular missionary meetings, established a missionary library, and challenged students to either go as a missionary or to support the missionary cause from home. Wishard said that if all these things can be done, "it won't be long until a thousand educated men who remain in this country will send their prayers and their means into all the world that the gospel may be preached to every creature."[5]

Wishard's work was becoming increasingly demanding and, as more of his heart and time were being consumed, he had to come face-to-face with his own

---

[4] Luther Wishard, *The Beginning of the Students' Era in Christian History* (New York: YMCA Library, 1917), 97.
[5] Shedd, 158.

missionary burden. He would have to make a personal decision to either go to the field himself or stay behind and mobilize others. Wishard made his decision after receiving some wise counsel from a friend:

> I sympathize with your desire to go to the foreign missionary field and I would ordinarily be the last man to detain you. You seem, however to be providentially detained. You are doing a great work, which you may not be able to delegate. I have long been guided by a principle which has served me at some important crises of my life, namely, never to move forward until the door in front of me is open and the door behind me is closed. A door great and effectual is clearly opened to you. Is the door behind you closed?[6]

After attending a prayer meeting that confirmed this counsel, Wishard said, "I walked out of the room assured that I was destined for a period of years to remain in America for the sake of foreign missions and so my heart was fixed and my path was clear at last and from then until the fullness of time had come I never wavered."[7]

"I am willing to go anywhere, at any time, and do anything for Jesus."

Four years later, in 1883, Wishard was able to personally visit Williams College to see the monument that stood as a memorial to

---

[6] Wishard, 86.
[7] Shedd, 161.

the missionary vision of Samuel Mills. Wishard knelt in the snow and made an unreserved surrender, "I am willing to go anywhere, at any time, and do anything for Jesus."[8]

Eight years had passed since Wishard began his full-time student work and he felt a growing dissatisfaction with the spiritual growth opportunities offered by the Y.M.C.A. Even though Wishard observed the organization's incredible numerical growth across the country, still there was no national conference at which to gather college students and harness momentum. Wishard couldn't shake the feeling that there needed to be a student summer project "to gather up, consolidate, and perpetuate the missionary interest" among them.[9] Wishard took the matter up with D. L. Moody.

In April of 1886, Luther Wishard visited D. L. Moody in Atlanta and, over dinner, they contemplated and discussed opportunities for Christian students to gain greater preparation for service.[10] Together they realized one possibility was to offer an

Haystack Prayer Monument

---

[8] Shedd, 255-256.

[9] Shedd, 240.

[10] C. Howard Hopkins, *20th Century Ecumenical Statesman John R. Mott: 1865-1955* (New York: Eerdmans Publishing Company, 1979), 274.

entire summer for students to grow in their knowledge of and skills in studying the Bible. Both men liked the idea of a four-week summer project and Wishard asked if Moody would be the keynote speaker. Moody balked, thinking he could not interest or inspire college students. Realizing that time was short for Wishard and his assistant, Charles Ober, to recruit students to come, Moody hesitantly replied, "Well, I guess we'd better try it."[11]

Both Wishard and Ober immediately began recruiting. They divided the eastern and southern U.S. between them in order to most effectively enlist students to attend. Ober went to Cornell to invite John Mott while Wishard went back to his alma mater, Princeton, and urged Robert Wilder to join them.[12] As I mentioned earlier, Wilder initially refused, but Wishard was more resolute and insisted that Wilder come in order to mobilize others.

As students converged from all over the U.S., Wishard had an aggressive agenda to challenge the students with ministry skills and vision. During the summer, Wishard took charge of an hour every day to teach the students methods of ministering to others back on campus. He showed the students how to lead others to Christ; then he would ask students during that hour to give a testimony.[13] Wishard also aimed to raise an awareness of missions and see students sent out to the nations. One onlooker stated, "The missionary spirit is rampant among students now. The interest is strong, vigorous, and healthful... The leading of Mr. Wishard is nothing if not energetic, nothing if not

---

[11] Shedd, 243.

[12] Ober, 71.

[13] John R. Mott, *Addresses and Papers of John R. Mott Volume 1: The Student Volunteer Movement for Foreign Missions* (New York: Association Press, 1946), 276.

inspiring. The young men answer readily to his call. He is joyous."[14]

After the Lord swept through the Mount Hermon summer project and one hundred of the 251 students responded, Wishard knew that something needed to be done to keep the momentum going. He proposed that a group of students visit the colleges of North America as the Cambridge Seven had done in Britain.[15] Robert Wilder followed through with the idea and visited many campuses, reporting back to Wishard all along the way.

Wishard departed on a short five-month tour of Europe on April 2, 1888, to expand student ministries on campuses internationally. He then took a much longer tour from September 18, 1888 to April 20, 1892 to continue visiting colleges in foreign countries. On every college visit he would tell the story of the Mount Hermon summer project and the American missions movement. Luther Wishard had given his life to student work and he would challenge anyone who would listen to do the same, "You want a life work? This is the greatest field in the world."[16] It was through his mentorship that John Mott absorbed the concept of a worldwide fellowship of Christian students.

When Wishard returned to America he expected to assume his earlier role in the American student movement.

---

[14] D. L. Moody, "Study of the Bible at the Mt. Hermon School," *Springfield Magazine*, August 2, 1886, 5-3.

[15] C. T. Studd was the captain of the Cambridge cricket team and on track to go pro. As a premier athlete on campus something happened to him that would permanently alter his heart and plans—he was mobilized to missions by D. L. Moody. C. T. Studd was not content to go alone; he wanted to stir the campus and the nation. The result was that seven of the top athletes committed to work in China. They were known as the Cambridge Seven. Before they launched in February of 1885 these seven students traveled for eighteen months on college campuses all over England and, as a result, 165 other students committed to join them. For more information on the Cambridge Seven see Norman Grubb, *C. T. Studd: Famous Athlete and Pioneer* (Grand Rapids, MI: Zondervan, 1933).

[16] Shedd, 59.

However, under Mott's leadership, the work was prospering beyond Wishard's dreams. Therefore, Wishard accepted a new and strategic leadership position as the first Administrative Secretary of the Foreign Department of the Young Men's Christian Association.[17]

Three years after his return to the States, Wishard accompanied John Mott on Mott's first world tour. They went to Britain, Germany, and Scandinavia together, contributing to the formation of the World Student Christian Federation. When they eventually separated, Wishard went to Edinburgh and South Africa while Mott moved throughout East Asia.[18]

There is no doubt that Luther Wishard set the stage for John Mott to fulfill many of his dreams. Wishard's vision, more than anyone else's, was to reach students to reach the world. What a fantastic contribution he made to this end! After a life of fruitful service among students and among the nations, he died in 1925 at age seventy-one.

Wishard's role in this Movement was a unique one. He was driven by pouring vision into those who could run with it. He challenged and developed Wilder's gifts to their full extent. He made Mott's success possible in many ways. Behind the scenes, he mentored the Student Volunteer Movement in its most impressionable stages. This visionary role he shares with one other man who sought to give wisdom and guidance to the younger generation, A. T. Pierson.

---

[17] Shedd, 335.
[18] Hopkins, 131-132.

A. T. Pierson

CHAPTER 5
A. T. PIERSON

A. T. Pierson died in 1911 at the peak of mission mobilization in America. It's a shame, because he was a significant reason there was a peak at all. Yet few have heard his story.

Arthur Tappan Pierson was born in New York on March 6, 1837 as the ninth of ten children. Pierson grew up in a devout Presbyterian home and while attending a revival meeting at age thirteen, he accepted Christ. At age fifteen he graduated from high school but was too young to be accepted into college. He decided to join the newly begun Y.M.C.A. in New York City. He had no idea just how much that decision would impact his life and that his involvement with this organization would last more than fifty years. Looking back on his choice to get involved with the Y.M.C.A. Pierson says, "It helped me at a critical period of life; helped to keep me within moral and religious restraints; turned my attention anew toward the ministry; helped to train me in debate; it helped my heart, conscience, and will."[1] That following year Pierson entered Hamilton College and had an incredible ministry writing articles, giving sermons, and leading many peers to Christ. After college he attended Union Theological Seminary. In seminary he and his friends talked themselves out of becoming foreign missionaries by such arguments as "let the rude, rough, uncultured men bear the Gospel to the brutal pagans; we who have refinement, accomplishment, urban culture, will remain at home," for "the home field offers the amplest yield in honors, salaries, and temporal rewards."[2]

After graduating from seminary in 1860, his first pastoral role came in Binghamton, New York. Excited about his new role at age twenty-three, Pierson preached with such conviction, at times even to the displeasure of the church.[3] The Civil War broke out and the church entered into financial difficulty. As a married man with two young daughters, Pierson found himself unemployed. He soon was hired as the pastor of another church in Waterford, New

---

[1] Dana Robert, *Occupy Until I Come: A. T. Pierson and the Evangelization of the World* (Grand Rapids, MI: Eerdmans Publishing, 2003), 14.

[2] Robert, 129-130.

[3] Delavan Leonard Pierson, *Arthur T. Pierson: A Biography* (London: James Nisbet and Co, 1912), 86-87.

York, and upon his arrival he realized they had a vision for the world. A vision he did not share. He realized that if he was to lead this flock, he would need to grow in his knowledge of the world and what God was doing. It was in this pursuit that Pierson gained the world vision that he would spend the rest of his life living out. He explains:

He realized that if he was to lead this flock, he would need to grow in his knowledge of the world.

I found myself to be lacking in my knowledge of missionary history and biography and set myself to gather new facts through the study of missions, the trials and triumphs. Thus I began to see more clearly, on the one hand, the awful spiritual destitution of the world and on the other hand the perfect adoption of the Gospel to human need… As I studied the needs of the world and our Lord's commission I became conscious that I had never been true with God on the subject of consecration to missionary work. I wanted power in my ministry to convert souls at home, but I could get no peace with God until I reconsidered the entire question… I told Him that if He called me now to the foreign field I would leave my pastorate and, with my family, consecrate myself to this work.[4]

---

[4] Pierson, 94-96.

Pierson believed there was a direct connection between Christ's return and the cause of foreign missions. Pierson took a literal interpretation of Matthew 24:14 (ESV), "And this gospel of the kingdom will be proclaimed throughout the whole world as a testimony to all nations, and then the end will come." He believed that Christ would return when the gospel had been plainly preached to all nations though it was not necessary that the conversion of the world take place prior to His coming.

> Every saved soul is called to be a herald and a witness; and we are to aim at nothing less than this: to make every *nation*, and every *creature* in every nation, *acquainted* with God. This is the first and ever-present duty of the Church: it is the heart of the whole missionary plan… The first need of the world is to hear the Gospel, and the first duty of the Church is to go everywhere and tell every human being of Christ, the world's Savior. To stop, or linger anywhere, even to *repeat* the rejected message, so long as there are souls beyond that have never heard it, is at least unjust to those who are still in absolute darkness.[5]

As he continued to grow in his understanding of missions and to preach on the subject, his invitations to speak elsewhere also increased. The time came for him to move on from Waterford's pulpit to a larger audience. The opportunity came in the form of an invitation to pastor the congregation at Fort Street Presbyterian Church of Detroit, Michigan. He

---

[5] Arthur T. Pierson, *The Divine Enterprise of Missions*, 2nd ed. (London: Hodder and Stoughton, 1891), 99-100.

accepted. Pierson tripled the attendance of this already large church and began to be called "a prince among preachers." His success was

"All Should Go and Go to All"

due to thorough preparation and a mastery of Scripture.[6] From then on Pierson began to be a spokesperson for missions on a national level, and in 1886 he wrote a best-selling book that sealed his fate as a mission mobilizer. The book was called *The Crisis of Missions.*

In the summer of 1886, Pierson received a telegram from Luther Wishard and D. L. Moody inviting him to come to the Mount Hermon summer project to help with the speaking. Pierson immediately traveled to the project in order to give lectures on the Bible and prophecy. During that summer, Robert Wilder approached Pierson and suggested that he give a message on missions. Since the morning sessions were already scheduled, Wilder arranged an extra evening session to have Pierson speak. Pierson's chosen title was "All Should Go and Go to All" and during the lecture he drew a map of the world on the chalkboard and shared a strategy for world evangelization.[7] This was another tipping point that influenced many of the one hundred students at Mount Hermon to sign a declaration committing to be foreign missionaries.

The more he traveled and spoke on missions the more he wrestled with his own growing desire to go as a

---

[6] Delavan Leonard Pierson, 109.

[7] Robert P. Wilder, *The Great Commission: The Missionary Response of the Student Volunteer Movement in North America and Europe; Some Personal Reminiscences* (London: Oliphants Publishers, 1936), 20.

missionary. He applied with the Presbyterian Board but was denied because he was fifty years old and had a wife and seven children. So he devoted the rest of his life to rousing missionary commitment by being a spokesman for the lost around the world. He resigned from his church and became a full-time itinerate preacher, stating, "I feel myself called to somewhat peculiar work in behalf of world-wide missions... At present I have no definite plans save to hold myself open to divine leading and to go where God shows me the way."[8]

There can be no doubt that A. T. Pierson served as a father figure for the Student Volunteer Movement. He wrote over fifty books, traveled on the road for twenty years, and never lost his passion to challenge the Church in her obligation to evangelize the world. He died on June 3, 1911 at age seventy-four. On his gravestone is a globe depicting a map of the world and an open Bible on which are carved the words "Go ye into all the world, and preach the gospel to every creature" (Mark 16:15, KJV).[9]

---

[8] Robert, 176.

[9] Delavan Leonard Pierson, 332.

Grace Wilder

CHAPTER 6
GRACE WILDER

G race Wilder has impacted my wife so much that we decided to name our daughter after her. Grace was a trailblazer for all women who desire to work in some of the hardest regions of the world. My wife says, "The most beautiful thing to me about Grace is her hiddenness. She poured herself out into others and into prayer, neither of which afforded her any praise for herself... and she wouldn't have had it any other way."

She poured herself out into others and into prayer.

Royal and Eliza Wilder had five children. One of their daughters, Mary, died at a young age while two boys, Edward and William, returned to America from India for their education. This left Robert in a foreign country with one sibling to grow up with—Grace. Grace and he were close companions. She was older than Robert by two years and although born in Saratoga Springs, New York, on May 27, 1861, she spent most of her youth in Kolhapur, India.

Due to Royal's ill health, the family returned to the States and Grace attended college at the all-women's school Mount Holyoke College in South Hadley, Massachusetts. As a student there, in the class of 1883, she led the Mount Holyoke Missionary Association. She and her father crafted a declaration of missions commitment that Grace then used as a requirement to participate in her small group women's Bible study. The commitment those female students made was, "We hold ourselves willing and desirous to do the Lord's work wherever He may call us, even if it be in a foreign land." It was under her leadership that thirty-four women at Mount Holyoke signed this pledge.[1] This declaration and the concept of signing it formed the basis of Robert's recruitment strategy at Princeton and the pivotal Mount Hermon summer project.

It is apparent that her encouragement to Robert was one of the main things that enabled the beginning of the Student Volunteer Movement. In the early days, Robert was trying to find his voice in mobilization and he confided in Grace

---

[1] Robert P. Wilder, *The Great Commission: The Missionary Response of the Student Volunteer Movement in North America and Europe; Some Personal Reminiscences* (London: Oliphants Publishers, 1936), 16.

that he felt like a failure because he was afraid to speak in public. Grace took him aside and encouraged him that "with God nothing is impossible." This proved to embolden Robert, as from that time forward he began to speak with confidence.[2]

After her graduation, Grace returned to Princeton to help care for her sick father and it was during this season (1885-1886) that she and her brother and a handful of others saturated the nights with prayer. They begged God that a widespread missionary movement would sweep through the colleges and universities of America. They agreed together and asked God to raise up 1,000 volunteers that would go from the universities to the foreign mission field. During these countless hours that Grace, Robert, and their peers spent on their knees, the revival of missionary zeal soon to become the Student Volunteer Movement was birthed.

When Robert originally declined Luther Wishard's invitation to the summer project, it was Grace's vision that persuaded Robert to accept the invitation. Robert recalls that fateful conversation with his sister:

> At first I demurred as I had recently graduated, and it seemed more reasonable to send undergraduates who could return the following year to college to put into practice what they had learned. However, she insisted on my going. Before leaving, my sister said to me: "I believe our prayers will be answered at Mount Hermon and that there our Princeton

---

[2] Ruth Wilder Braisted, *In This Generation: The Story of Robert P. Wilder* (New York: Friendship Press, 1941), 13.

beginnings will become intercollegiate." She also prophesied, as I remember it, that there would be a hundred volunteers enlisted there.[3]

As a vision for missions spread through the lives of the students that July at Mount Hermon, exactly one hundred men signed the pledge proving that indeed God had laid those exact words on Grace's heart. When the student leaders decided to travel to campuses to continue spreading this vision, Robert was tempted to withdraw his commitment. His father was near death and Robert felt it his duty to stay at home and help. Once more Grace came alongside Robert and urged him to travel to the various campuses with the words, "Nothing worthwhile is ever accomplished without surmounting great obstacles."[4] Her encouragement to Robert continued as he traveled, "I almost envy you young men when I think of the host of girls which might be enlisted also."[5] Grace's words rang true as that year 550 young women enlisted as volunteers.

In light of her experience growing up in India and mobilizing girls at Mount Holyoke, the S.V.M. leadership looked to Grace for help in following up these female volunteers. Grace did what she loved to do, she took to the pen. She wrote a short pamphlet called *Shall I Go?* which dealt with reasons women should go to the field in spite of excuses that they face.

Following her father's death in November 1887, Grace was appointed, at age twenty-six, by the Presbyte-

---

[3] Wilder, 18.
[4] Braisted, 33.
[5] Braisted, 35.

rian Board to India and sailed on Thanksgiving Day of that year with her widowed mother.[6] The two lived together in various villages and Grace was appointed principal of a boys' school. Both Grace and her mother went on furlough in the U.S. from 1897-1898. During her furlough she spent time on college campuses speaking to and mobilizing female students to India. She challenged her audience with the needs of India and the needed work among villages, "We need workers who will live in a simple way for the people among the people... In a few months I expect to go back to the villages of India. It is my earnest hope that God may lead some here into this work."[7]

When she went back to India after her furlough she brought five women with her to establish the work in a village! On April 18, 1911, less than a year after the death of her mother, Grace Wilder passed away at age fifty and is buried near her old home in Kolhapur, India.[8] At her memorial service held at New York City Park Presbyterian Church, Rev. Stanley White spoke of her absolute surrender, quietness, and confidence, and how God used her and her brother to start the Student Volunteer Movement.

> In closing I am privileged to mention what is known to but very few, namely, Miss Wilder's relation to the Student Volunteer Movement.... Others are receiving the praise for this Movement. We should not forget that God redeemed his promise of answering prayer, and that it was the faithful and effectual

---

[6] Seventy-Fifth Anniversary. Western India Mission of the Presbyterian Church in the United States of America, Presbyterian Church, U.S.A., 1929, 11.

[7] The Student Missionary Appeal: Addresses at the Third International Convention of the Student Volunteer Movement for Foreign Missions, Cleveland, Ohio, Feb. 23-27, 1898 (New York: Student Volunteer Movement for Foreign Missions,1898), 310.

[8] Seventy-Fifth Anniversary: Western India Mission of the Presbyterian Church, 11.

They all had other options... but they all had one final thing in common; they allowed God to interrupt their lives.

prayer of Miss Wilder and her brother, which, humanly speaking, began this work.[9]

WHAT ABOUT YOU?

It is said you either *study* history, *watch* history, or *make* history. Grace's prayers literally changed the world's landscape. Robert's speaking influenced thousands. Mott's leadership gave structure to the greatest mobilization movement in history. A. T. Pierson and Luther Wishard's mentorship helped the younger generation stay the course. They all had some things in common. They were all students. They all had other options and the abilities to be very successful. Mark my words, had they continued on their own course, they may have been highly notable men and women who collected every accolade this world has to offer. But they all had one final thing in common; they allowed God to interrupt their lives. Will you be next to surrender and let Him change history through you?

---

[9] Stanley White, *In Memoriam: Miss Grace E. Wilder* (New York: Board of Foreign Mission of the Presbyterian Church, 1911), 14-15.

THEOLOGY
THEN AND NOW

"The years teach much which the days never know."

— Ralph Waldo Emerson

CHAPTER 7
SALVATION

My grandmother Mary Ahrend never met a Buddhist. She never met a Muslim. She was a product of her generation. People who followed these religions simply existed in extremely small numbers in the United States. She never left the country; I don't even think she left the state. Today, we have a new normal. My daughter's best friend is a Muslim and before her first birthday she had already flown around the world—literally.

In 1910 there were virtually no international students on college campuses. Today, over 38 percent of UCLA is of Asian descent. We live in a completely different world where the nations are at our door. The result is that many Christians struggle to understand what their own personal beliefs mean in the context of these world religions. When a person has no exposure to religious diversity, it is easy to adhere to the religion of the masses assuming it's the ultimate answer to the God question. However, what happens when a Christian encounters a Hindu who is more devout than himself? Or a Muslim who prays more than him? Or a Buddhist who sincerely feels he is on the threshold of enlightenment? How will his faith respond and what doubts will creep in? It is easy to say someone is lost without Christ if they are on the other side of the ocean, but what if they are on the other side of the lawn? This forces us to ask some crucial questions: Is salvation exclusively found in a person who was born 2,000 years ago in a small corner of the world? Or is authentic, sincere faith enough to save regardless of its object? Our 21st-century pluralistic society answers the latter question, yes!

The Church in the late 1800s was not facing a pluralistic paradigm. It was not an issue the Student Volunteer Movement was forced to deal with. To them, the heathen were the Mohammedans (Muslims), Hindus, and Buddhists on the other side of the ocean. The average college student never met a Hindu unless he traveled across land and sea to intentionally do so. In light of this there was no reluctance to exhort the students, no matter the venue, that those across the ocean were without Christ and thus without hope. It wasn't uncommon to hear this kind of teaching from the main stage in a large group setting:

The false religions give no answer to the question, "what must I do to be saved?" There is not another religion on earth, and never has been one, that has proposed any rational plan of justification... Find me anything like the cross in any other religion... If other religions are true there is no room for our religion on the earth. If there are other plans of salvation than the death of Christ was an awful waste of divine resource.

But, indeed, there is none other name given under heaven or among men whereby we must be saved.[1]

In all of the resources they produced there was no hesitation to boast the great superiority of Christianity over the non-Christian religions. The Student Volunteer Movement freely used terms and phrases that in today's student setting would, no doubt, cause many to raise their hand in protest. Robert Speer, a spokesman involved in the Movement unashamedly affirms:

Not only are the non-Christian religions destitute of our Lord's great teaching about God and man, but they do not have in them those fundamental moral principles which Christ brought into the world, and over which He poured a whole flood of illuminating glory from God. Take Christ's great ethical conceptions, such as truth and duty and purity and love and righteousness, and where can you find in any of the non-Christian religions any great moral conceptions corresponding to, or that anywhere approach the great moral idea which Jesus Christ brought into the world and which He both taught and lived?[2]

In contrast to the college students of 1880-1920 who had little access to cultures outside of their own, today's students need only to walk on campus to encounter other cultures! From coffee shops to the classroom, from the doctor's office to the dormitory we find the nations in our own

---

[1] The Student Missionary Appeal: Addresses at the Third International Convention of the Student Volunteer Movement for Foreign Missions, Cleveland, Ohio, Feb. 23-27, 1898. (New York: Student Volunteer Movement for Foreign Missions, 1898), 38-39.

[2] Robert Speer, *The Deity of Christ* (New York: Young Men's Christian Association Press, 1909), 29.

backyard. One very influential factor in this change is the migration of peoples. From 1880-1890 there were approximately 5 million immigrants in the United States. This may seem like a fair amount until you consider the fact that over 90 percent of them were Europeans in search of a better life.[3] The year 1965 marked a major turning point in migration as the government instituted a new policy called the Immigration and Naturalization Act. This act removed any quotas from immigration that were based on national origins. The result was a major rise in immigration from Asian and Latin American countries.[4]

Today there are over 30 million immigrants making up 11 percent of the total population of the U.S. If numbers stay the projected course, there will be 80 million immigrants in the United States by 2050.[5]

This migration of peoples has played an incredible role in Christian students' understanding of salvation as they now rub shoulders daily with people of other faiths. When they move into the dorms with people from all over the world they find themselves living with Chinese, Indians, Jordanians, and others. One friend of mine was so excited to reach his roommate for Christ before the semester even started. He soon found out that his roommate was a Muslim named Abdullah. My friend began to realize Abdullah was more dedicated to Islam than he was to his own faith. He said, "I don't pray five times a day! I don't even fast for a few days. Abdullah must love God more than I do, who am I to condemn him?"

---

[3] Roger Daniels, *Coming to America: A History of Immigration and Ethnicity in American Life*, 2nd ed. (New York: Harper Perennial, 2002), 122, 124.

[4] James P. Smith, *The New Americans: Economic, Demographic, and Fiscal Effect of Immigration* (Washington, DC: National Academies Press, 1997), 2.

[5] Smith, 3.

Another factor that has influenced our view of salvation is our desire to be politically correct. More and more commonly in the United States, you are viewed as backward, ignorant, extremely arrogant, and shallow if you hold that Christ is the only way. This creates enormous pressure on the college student looking for a potential program or to the job market. These environments make it feel wrong to be anything other than open.

A third influence is that in today's pop culture it is becoming in-vogue to be humanitarian. In the past if I wanted to dig a well in sub-Saharan Africa there was one word used to describe me—missionary. In contrast, today I would be seen as keeping up with the latest trendy charity, sponsored by some paparazzi-laden star. Thus, what used to be seen as distinctively Christian is today done by those with no Christian motive or understanding at all. Interestingly, the secular world has shown more compassion than the Western Church in some ways. Examples: *American Idol* hosted a special called "Idol Gives Back." Its first year, this one-hour episode managed to raise $64 million on behalf of various charities around the world.[6] Take a second example: Oprah. She decided to put much of her energy and money into a school that will house 450 of the poorest girls in all of Africa so that, for the first time, they can get an education. Her total financial contribution to date is $45 million.[7] So, the acts of compassion and love that ought to set Christianity apart as unique now only keep us on par with the secular world. Christian students begin

---

[6] ABC News, "Idol Gives Back Over $64 Million to Charities," Nov. 12, 2008. Available from abcnews.go.com.

[7] CNN News, "Koinange: Oprah School Opens Hearts, Minds in S. Africa," August 25, 2006. Available from cnn.com.

to question, "How is Christianity better than the rest of them?" The result is that Christians today struggle to understand what their personal beliefs mean in the context of these world religions. Take for example this e-mail I received from a Christian student who is a leader in his campus ministry:

> *I have a question and I figured your experience in Christianity and religion may give some clues to the answer. How can others find peace and spirituality in other religions? From observation, I find that Hindus, Muslims, and Buddhists have found peace and spirituality in their religions. The largest religions in the world stress the same basic points of life. It seems that it is the people who follow religions that make each religion different, but the messages are the same.*
> *This is the question that stands out in my mind. – Chris, Ohio State University*

THREE PARADIGMS

Today's Christian students have a choice to make as to how they will respond to the various religions they encounter on campus. The three major perspectives a Christian is forced to choose from are: *pluralism*, *inclusivism*, and *exclusivism*. As we begin this dialogue, let me say upfront that I am an exclusivist. I have attempted here to deal fairly with all of the perspectives and to present the cases for pluralism and inclusivism as they would have themselves.

Undoubtedly, the most prolific writer for the propagation of *pluralism* is John Hick. As an 18-year-old attending college in the UK, Hick experienced a powerful evangelical conversion.[8] He joined a campus ministry and set out to transform the campus. After a few years, however, difficult questions began to confront him and Hick found himself drifting away from the conservative, evangelical campus ministry and toward a pluralistic paradigm. He says:

> My departure from it was gradual and was partly the result of further reflection prompted by a philosophical training, partly of reading the works of the New Testament scholars, and partly of trying to preach the gospel in a way that made sense to ordinary twentieth-century men and women, both young and old. My conversion experience, with its powerful awareness of divine presence that was both profoundly challenging and at the same time profoundly creative and life-giving, remains basic; but the particular fundamentalist intellectual package that came with it has long since crumbled and disappeared.[9]

The pluralist identifies three tenets as true: 1) there is a religious ultimate reality—the Real—to which the major religions are all legitimate responses.[10] The reason they use the word Real instead of God is to not offend the Buddhists or Taoists. 2) All religions are historically and culturally conditioned interpretations of this divine reality.[11] This means that the resurrection of the dead was not an idea familiar to

---

[8] John Hick, *God Has Many Names* (Philadelphia, PA: The Westminster Press, 1980), 14.

[9] Stanley Gundry, *Four Views on Salvation in a Pluralistic World* (Grand Rapids, MI: Zondervan, 1995), 33.

the culture and experience of Siddhartha Gautama (the founder of Buddhism), but it was a culturally acceptable idea to the first Jewish Jesus-followers. Each culture, within their culture, has their own understanding of how to experience faith and relate to the Real. 3) Salvation and transformation are occurring roughly to the same extent across the major religions.[12] John Hick suggests,

> God is known in the synagogues as *Adonai*, the Lord God of Abraham, Isaac, and Jacob; in the mosques as *Allah rahman rahim*, God beneficent and merciful; in the Sikh gurudwaras as God, who is Father, Lover, Master, and the Great Giver, referred to as *war guru*; and in the Hindu temples as Vishnu, Krishna, Rama, Shiva, and many other gods and goddesses, all of whom, however, are seen as manifestations of the ultimate reality of Brahman; and in the Christian churches as the triune God, Father, Son, and Holy Spirit. And yet all these communities agree that there can ultimately only be one God![13]

There is a famous story found in Hinduism that pluralists use to try to drive home their point.[14] A king invites into his court five blind men and leads them to stand beside an elephant. The king instructs these five men to reach out and touch what is in front of them and then to describe it. One grabs the tail, the other a leg, another man feels the elephant's side, another an ear, and the fifth man grabs a tusk. Each began to describe what it was they were holding.

[10] John Hick, *The Metaphor of God Incarnate: Christology in a Pluralistic Age*, 2nd ed. (Louisville, KY: Westminster John Knox Press, 2005), 140.

[11] Hick, *God Has Many Names*, 45-46.

[12] Hick, *God Has Many Names*, 66.

[13] Gundry, 38.

[14] Premraj Dharmanand, *Your Questions Our Answers*, vol. 1 (Uttaranchai, India: Premraj Dharmanand, 2003), 33.

The one who grabbed the tail insisted it was a rope. The one who touched the leg claimed he was touching a tree; the one who touched the side described it as a mud-baked wall. The blind man who had held an ear was sure he held a banana leaf. Finally, the man holding a tusk confidently asserted that he indeed held a sword.

Pluralists use this story to illustrate that even though various religions may seem contradictory, they all point to a common goal. Hindus hold the proverbial tail; Buddhists feel the side, Christians grab the tusk, and so on. The point is that no view errs until it claims that what they hold is the whole truth. As long as each religion recognizes they hold but a part of the puzzle, a mere aspect of the truth, it maintains its place in the proper, equal balance among other paths in the pursuit of truth.

In the pluralistic worldview, even though each one of us approaches the Real differently, we are all actually chasing the same thing. The Christian appeals to the Bible; the Muslim favors the Qur'an; the Buddhist claims direct access through the enlightenment; the Hindu appeals to the Upanishads; and so on.[15] Thus, the world's religions provide independent access to salvation and Christianity is just one among many religions having no unique claim as the final or authoritative truth.

How do pluralists who consider themselves Christian reconcile this view with passages that are commonly interpreted as claims of exclusivity such as: "For there is one God, and there is one mediator between God and men, the

---

[15] David W. Baker, ed., *Biblical Faith and Other Religions: An Evangelical Assessment* (Grand Rapids, MI: Kregel, 2004), 22-23.

man Christ Jesus" (1 Timothy 2:5, ESV); "Salvation is found in no one else, for there is no other name under heaven given to men by which we must be saved" (Acts 4:12); and, "Jesus said to him, 'I am the way, and the truth, and the life. No one comes to the Father except through me'" (John 14:6, ESV)? Paul Knitter, an outspoken advocate and author for the pluralist view, explains:

> Exclusivist Christological language is much like the language a husband would use of his wife (or vice versa): "You are the most beautiful woman in the world... you are the only woman for me." Such statements, in the context of the marital relationship and especially in intimate moments, are certainly true. But the husband would balk if asked to take an oath that there is absolutely no other woman in the world as beautiful as his wife... That would be transforming love language into scientific or philosophical language. Christian dogmatic definitions, in the way they have been understood and used, have perhaps done just that to the love language of the early church. The languages of the heart and the head are not necessarily contradictory, but they are different. And their differences must be respected.[16]

The suggested answer is that biblical authors, like all Christians, were excited about Jesus and wanted others to experience Him as intimately as they had. These statements are more *descriptive* of their love for this Man rather than *prescriptive* in condemning all other saviors. According to

---

[16] Paul Knitter, *No Other Name? A Critical Survey of Christian Attitudes toward the World Religions* (Maryknoll, NY: Orbis Books, 2005), 185-186.

pluralism, Jesus did not *need* to go to the cross. He may have been a *type* of Messiah, but was certainly not *the* Messiah.

Surprisingly, it seems as though the majority of evangelicals are beginning to embrace a pluralist worldview as evidenced by a recent survey. Approximately two-thirds of evangelicals (64 percent) think there are multiple paths to salvation. In mainline Protestantism the statistic is as high as 73 percent.[17]

If the pluralistic paradigm seems too radical for some Christians to embrace, a second option is *inclusivism*. Inclusivism affirms without qualification that Jesus Christ is the definitive and authoritative revelation of God and that Christ's work on the cross is central, without which no one can be saved—sounds good so far![18] It also affirms that the death of Jesus Christ, God's Son, on the cross was absolutely necessary for salvation—I still like it! It qualifies this truth, however, by adding that it is unnecessary for an individual to know personally about Christ or His cross in order to benefit from the saving grace that He offers.[19] In other words, adherents of other faiths might not know the story of Jesus Christ, but if they have been true to their own faith (Islam, Hinduism, Buddhism, and so on) it is counted as faithfulness to Christ. So inclusivism claims that all acts of spirituality and devotion done in the name of any religion are ricocheted to the cross. Though these devotees would not call themselves "Christians," they are "believers" and thus

---

[17] The Pew Forum on Religion and Public Life, "Many Americans Say Other Faiths Can Lead to Eternal Life," Dec. 18, 2008. Available from pewforum.org.

[18] Timothy Tennent, *Christianity at the Religious Roundtable: Evangelicalism in Conversation with Hinduism, Buddhism, and Islam* (Grand Rapids, MI: Baker Academic, 2002), 20.

[19] Clark Pinnock, *A Wideness in God's Mercy* (Grand Rapids, MI: Zondervan Publishing, 1992), 75.

IN THIS GENERATION

saved by God's work in Christ just like every other believer.[20] Since this specific knowledge of Christ is non-existent in many parts of the non-Western world, inclusivists skirt the non-Christians' condemnation by making sincerity the issue. Here are two of the passages that inclusivists frequently reference,

Approximately two-thirds of evangelicals think there are multiple paths to salvation.

> The Lord is not slow in keeping his promise, as some understand slowness. He is patient with you, not wanting anyone to perish, but everyone to come to repentance (2 Peter 3:9).

> One day at about three in the afternoon he had a vision. He distinctly saw an angel of God, who came to him and said, "Cornelius!" Cornelius stared at him in fear. "What is it, Lord?" he asked. The angel answered, "Your prayers and gifts to the poor have come up as a memorial offering before God" (Acts 10:3-4).[21]

Clark Pinnock, an inclusivist, exposes the fact that the heart and motive of many inclusivists is compassion for the lost; a hope to emulate God's desire that none should perish. He states:

---

[20] John G. Stackhouse Jr., ed., *No Other Gods Before Me? Evangelicals and the Challenge of World Religions* (Grand Rapids, MI: Baker Academic, 2001), 196.

[21] This verse is used by inclusivists to support their claims because Cornelius is a Gentile whose worship is accepted by God *before* Peter arrives to give him specific knowledge of Christ.

75

To put it out in the open, I want evangelicals to move away from the attitude of pessimism based upon bad news to the attitude of hopefulness based upon Good News, from restrictivism to openness, from exclusivism to generosity. If we could but recover the scope of God's love, our lives and not just our theology of religions could be transformed.[22]

The third view to consider is *exclusivism*. Exclusivists affirm that the unique authority of Jesus Christ is the apex of revelation and that He is the only Savior.[23] Next, exclusivists insist that the Christian faith centers upon the "historical death and resurrection of Jesus Christ as the decisive event in human history."[24] Finally, and what ultimately separates them from inclusivists is that explicit faith in Jesus Christ is absolutely necessary for salvation and a person cannot be saved without an act of repentance. The passages exclusivists turn to are:

Whoever believes in the Son has eternal life; whoever does not obey the Son shall not see life, but the wrath of God remains on him (John 3:36, ESV).

All this is from God, who through Christ reconciled us to himself and gave us the ministry of reconciliation; that is, in Christ God was reconciling the world to himself, not counting their trespasses against them, and entrusting to us the message of reconciliation (2 Cor. 5:18-19, ESV).

---

[22] Pinnock, 20.
[23] Ronald Nash, *Is Jesus the Only Savior?* (Grand Rapids, MI: Zondervan Publishing, 1994), 11.
[24] Tennent, 17.

> And he said to them, "Go into all the world and proclaim the gospel to the whole creation. Whoever believes and is baptized will be saved, but whoever does not believe will be condemned" (Mark 16:15-16, ESV).

The exclusivist is adamant that Scripture defines salvation as a non-relative issue, even in the case of those who have no exposure to Christ since "faith comes from hearing the message, and the message is heard through the word of Christ" (Romans 10:17).[25] Those who do not have access to the message are without Christ and therefore without hope both in this life and in the next.

The exclusivist position causes the pluralist to cringe at its implications for the majority of humanity. This position incites such questions as "If God made Himself known in only Jesus, why then are there so many different religions?" "Why is it true that relatively few people of all time past, present, and future will ever hear about this particular person?" "How can Christianity claim exclusivity and uniqueness when in Hinduism, the Vedas, some of the first spiritual writings, were written before the Hebrew Scriptures?"[26] Paul Knitter, a pluralist, would then argue, "The only thing Christians could tell the other religions would be that 'the sun of God's grace fell on us, not you. Even though there may be no evident differences between our religion and yours, we have the truth and you do not.'"[27] An exclusivist, Robertson McQuilkin, answers such opposition in his book *The Great Omission*. He explains,

---

[25] Robertson McQuilkin, *The Great Omission* (Grand Rapids, MI: Baker Book House, 1984), 45.
[26] Knitter, 34.
[27] Knitter, 95.

If there is an alternative, God has not told us of it. If God in His revelation felt it mandatory not to offer such a hope, how much more should we refrain from such theorizing. It may or may not be morally right for me to think there may be another way and to hope there is some other escape. But for me to propose it to other believers, to discuss it as a possibility, is certainly dangerous, if not immoral… So long as the truth revealed to us identifies only one way of escape, this is what we must live by and proclaim.[28]

REFLECTING ON WHAT'S RIGHT

In terms of its dealing with Scripture, exclusivism's stance on salvation and its integrity in relation to the world religions make it the purest approach to salvation. Most evangelical theologians have historically been in this camp and, as an exclusivist myself, I think it takes Christ's claim at face value. Let us turn our attention now to evaluating pluralism and inclusivism from the perspective of exclusivism.

In pluralism, God is nebulous as He is swallowed up by human experience as the overarching standard of truth. Truth is everything and therefore it is nothing. This model gives us a God who is unknown and unknowable and about whom no definitive descriptive statement can be made. In regards to the compelling story about the five blind men and the elephant, the entire thing is built on one assumed premise; that there really is an elephant (truth).[29] But from where does absolute knowledge of the elephant come? From the

---

[28] McQuilkin, 50-51.
[29] Dharmanand, 34.

sixth man in the room, the all-seeing king (God who guides our interpretations and leads us into truth)!

I was once told the joke, "What do you get when you cross a Jehovah's Witness with a pluralist?" "Someone who knocks on your door for no real reason!" It illustrates the point perfectly. Pluralists have nothing in particular to offer.

> Despite what some modernists suggest, the world religions are not simply the guise that the one, hidden religion wears. Also suspect is the modern notion that all the so-called religions are in the end seeking the same goal. The world's religions may be attempting to prove answers to the human predicament, but they understand that predicament—and hence its solution—quite differently.[30]

In regards to inclusivism, Scripture is clear that a response is required of the hearer. The word *believe* is used over sixty-five times in the gospel of John alone. Paul says in Acts 20:21, "I have declared to both the Jews and Greeks that they must turn to God in repentance and have faith in our Lord Jesus." Furthermore, we must consider the strong possibility that devotees of other faiths do not wish for the mercy of Christ to be imposed upon them. They would potentially be quite insulted by the notion of their Brahman worship being ricocheted toward Christ. "Ethical Muslims do not suppose that they are on the path toward Christianity, and they can be expected to resent the suggestion that they are."[31]

---

[30] Stackhouse, 107.
[31] Gundry, 137.

As we have seen, the religious, cultural lay of the land looks quite different today than it did one hundred years ago. Exclusivism is facing some challenges today that it was not forced to face before. The inevitable pitfall that many Christians will succumb to (given that the majority of Christians are buying into pluralism and inclusivism) is that of inactivity when it comes to missions. Some are becoming hostile to the idea of missions. In light of today's world, it is not enough to be exclusivists; we need to be *engaged exclusivists*.[32] This fresh approach recognizes that God is and has been doing something in the world—even in non-Christian lands. This disarms any fear, pride, or the temptation to withdraw that almost seems inherent in exclusivism.

Arguably, the church's greatest challenge in the next century will be the problem of the scandal of particularity. More than ever before Christians will need to explain why they follow Jesus and not the Buddha or Confucius or Krishna or Muhammad. But if not while relating their faith to the faiths, Christians treat non-Christian religions as netherworlds of unmixed darkness, the church's message will be a scandal not of particularity but of arrogant obscurantism.[33]

There are three ways that today's Christian student must embrace an engaged exclusivist lifestyle: to be informed, be conversant, and to be evangelistic. In light of the fact that one out of every six people on planet Earth call the Qur'an their holy book, Christians need to be familiar with

---

[32] Tennent, 26.
[33] Gerald McDermott, *Can Evangelicals Learn from World Religions? Jesus, Revelation, and Religious Traditions* (Downers Grove, IL: InterVarsity Press, 2000), 10.

it. We need not stop with the Qur'an but should pursue at least a basic understanding of key religious texts like *The Bhagavad Gita*, *The Tao te Ching*, *The Dhammapada* and *The Adi Granth*. Students can pursue an engaged lifestyle by informing themselves of the world around

In light of today's world, it is not enough to be exclusivists

them. The second way is to be conversant. For those who do not have friends from other religious backgrounds it is time to learn how to initiate with internationals. In dialoguing with those of other faiths, a student's faith and doctrine are challenged, and a more complete appreciation and Christian understanding is gained along with a deeper appreciation and understanding for the other faiths. We see a great example of this in Acts 17. Paul did not get angry with the men at Athens, but actually affirmed their spiritual quest while trying to mature it. You can also see how he observed, complemented, and even quoted from their texts as he tried to enhance their understanding.

> Paul then stood up in the meeting of the Areopagus and said: "Men of Athens! I see that in every way you are very religious. For as I walked around and looked carefully at your objects of worship, I even found an altar with this inscription: To an unknown God. Now what you worship as something unknown

I am going to proclaim to you.... 'For in him we live and move and have our being.' As some of your own poets have said, 'We are his offspring'" (Acts 17: 22-28).

Finally, Christian students need to be evangelistic. It is clear that in Scripture we are asked to believe in a specific, historic Person who gave His life on our behalf. No one can be saved without an explicit act of repentance and faith based on the knowledge of Christ.

The Student Volunteer Movement never had to ask the question, "Why do we need to reach them?" Their "them" were heathen across the ocean. Our "them" live next door to us. They are our friends; we play intramurals with them; we sit by them in class. Today, the lines between us and them are blurred as we rub shoulders with the world's religions daily, often wishing some of their religious devotion would rub off on us. As we look back to gain a more informed approach to reaching the world today, we must realize some significant shifts have taken place in the realm of salvation. The consequence of not recognizing the chasm between our day and the S.V.M.'s day with regard to salvation may be a generation lost to confusion and paralysis. May we respond to our current muddle with a greater determination to live as engaged exclusivists.

CHAPTER 8
CHURCH

It is not odd to ask a Christian student where they go to church and get a blank stare in response. Another common reply is the name of the campus ministry they attend. Has this always been an issue? Definitions of church these days are becoming more and more varied. What do you think of when you think of the church? Some picture pews and a pulpit while others think of an elementary school gym where they gather weekly for encouragement. Some think of a cell group and still others might think of a few friends who get together in their living room for prayer and singing. What are the ramifications for this generation who are increasingly losing touch with and even devaluing the local church? One of the major shifts of the last one hundred years has been the way college students identify what church is.

One of the major shifts of the last one hundred years has been the way college students identify what church is.

Ralph Winter, the founder of the U.S. Center for World Mission, has contributed greatly to our understanding of the church and missions. He identifies the two biblical structures that God uses in missions, the modality and the sodality. The modality refers to the New Testament church, what people today commonly call their local church. He writes, "On the one hand, the structure we call the New Testament Church is a prototype of all subsequent Christian fellowships where old and young, male and female are gathered together as normal biological families."[1] The second structure, the sodality, was started when Paul was commissioned from the church in Antioch (the modality) in Acts 13 to work alongside of the church. Once away from the church at Antioch he had a measure of independence from them and the parachurch (sodality) was born. Winter continues, "On the other hand, Paul's *missionary band* can be considered a prototype of all subsequent missionary endeavors organized out of committed, experienced workers who affiliate themselves as a second decision beyond membership in the first structure."[2]

The key marks that define the local church (modality) are pure preaching of the Word, right administration of the sacraments, and the proper exercise of church discipline.[3] In contrast, the parachurch (sodality) works outside of and across denominations and exists primarily for a specific religious activity in a very specialized role (Campus Crusade for Christ, InterVarsity, Young Life, Fellowship of Christian Athletes, Operation Mobilization, Wycliffe Bible Translators, and so on).[4]

---

[1] Ralph Winter and Steven Hawthorne, *Perspectives on the World Christian Movement,* 4th ed. (Pasadena, CA: William Carey Library, 2009), 245.

[2] Winter and Hawthorne, 245.

[3] Charles Van Engen, *God's Missionary People: Rethinking the Purpose of the Local Church* (Grand Rapids, MI: Baker Book House, 1991), 63.

[4] Darrell L. Guder, ed., *Missional Church: A Vision for the Sending of the Church in North America* (Grand Rapids, MI: Eerdmans Publishing, 1998), 74.

In Scripture these are two separate entities, but we can see how the church and parachurch work closely together in commissioning, accountability, and involvement. Paul and Barnabas were "sent out" by the church at Antioch in a commissioning event. It was as the leadership of this church was praying that the Holy Spirit exhorted them to "set apart for me Barnabas and Saul for the work to which I have called them" (Acts 13:2). After the 800-mile journey throughout modern-day Turkey, Scripture says that Paul and Barnabas went back to those who had sent them out: "They sailed to Antioch, where they had been commended to the grace of God for the work that they had fulfilled. And when they arrived and gathered the church together, they declared all that God had done with them, and how he had opened a door of faith to the Gentiles" (Acts 14:26-27, ESV). Not only did they get "sent out" and "report to" the church at Antioch, but they also worked hand in hand in the theological struggles that accompanied missionary work. In Acts 15 when some were suggesting that circumcision was necessary for salvation, you again see Paul and Barnabas going to the apostles and elders (Acts 15:2-3).

During the medieval period the church was greatly aided by the parachurch in the form of specialized houses called monasteries.[5] As the Protestant Reformation began, however, Martin Luther was discontent with this seeming polarization between the two groups and abandoned the parachurch.[6] Ralph Winter comments on the disastrous

---

[5] Winter and Hawthorne, 248.

[6] Robert Blincoe, "The Strange Structure of Mission Agencies, Part 1: Still Two Structures After All These Years?" *International Journal of Frontier Missions* 19:1 (Spring 2002): 6.

ramifications of Luther's decision to forsake the monastic institution of his day. He states, "This omission, in my evaluation, represents the greatest error of the reformation and the greatest weakness of the resulting Protestant tradition."[7]

Many factors influenced the Protestant silence in missions over the next 250 years. Luther's rejection of the parachurch certainly contributed.[8] Even if they had considered missions, they lacked a mechanism for it.

It was William Carey who broke the 250-year parachurch silence that Luther began when Carey developed a sending agency that was patterned after the business world. This decision was counter to Protestant culture since a missions organization had not existed for 250 years and also because the church of his day held very tight reins on what could be pursued in evangelistic work. Thus, his organization allowed Carey and others to have freedoms in ministry that the church would not have allowed for.[9] Carey defends the missions organization to his skeptical church leaders in his book *An Enquiry*:

> Suppose a company of serious Christians, ministers and private persons, were to form themselves into a society, and make a number of rules respecting the regulation of the plan, and the persons who are to be employed as missionaries... This society must consist of persons whose hearts are in the work, men of serious religions, and possessing a spirit of perseverance.[10]

---

[7] Winter and Hawthorne, 250.

[8] Other factors influencing the Protestant silence regarding missions were: exploration was just beginning so there was very limited knowledge of the world beyond Europe, errant application of Calvinism led to the conclusion that the unexposed to the gospel were elected to be damned, the preoccupation with problems "at home" (both theological and physical with the end of the so-called Dark Ages) kept the European Church looking inward, and finally, some of the reformers actually believed that the Great Commission applied to and was fulfilled by the first-century apostles.

[9] Richard Tiplady, *World of Difference: Global Mission at the Pic-n-Mix Counter* (Waynesboro, GA: Paternoster Press, 2003), 78.

The development of this parachurch to work along-side the local church by William Carey provided the much-needed outlet for world outreach and allowed new missions agencies of all kinds to surface in the years to come.

CHURCH AND THE COLLEGE STUDENT OF OLD

At the turn of the 20th century when the Student Volunteer Movement was on the mobilization scene, the church context looked much different than it does today. When they stood up to address Christian students they did not attempt to convince them of the importance of church membership; it was understood.[11] In some cases, it was even required that the faculty of the universities they visited to be a member of a church.[12] Not only was involvement in the local church normative during this time, but church denominational boards also served as the primary sending agent even in the midst of other existent missions agencies. Bottom line, it was just accepted that Christians were at least members if not active participants in a local congregation.

Though the Student Volunteer Movement, as a parchurch organization, was focused primarily on strength-ening the missions vision on the campuses in America, they by no means ignored the church. They pushed for and taught on the mutuality of the relationship between the church and students. Both the church and the S.V.M. had an obligation to serve one another and both sought to be

---

[10] William Carey, *An Enquiry into the Obligation of Christians to Use Means for the Conversion of the Heathen* (England: Ann Ireland, 1792), reprint edition (Dallas, TX: Criswell Publications, 1988), 62.

[11] William R. Hutchison, ed., *Between the Times: The Travail of the Protestant Establishment in America, 1900-1960* (Cambridge: Cambridge University Press, 1990), 4-5.

[12] George M. Marsden, *The Soul of the American University* (New York: Oxford University Press, 1994), 22.

consequently blessed by the other. The church would fund, resource, and commission the mobilization movement and ideally confirm its message from the pulpit. In return they would be blessed with the trained student manpower to effectively carry out the church's vision for missions. The church also received encouragement and training in the form of books and messages from the S.V.M.'s leaders. Conversely, the S.V.M. was blessed by the church's resources and teaching.

John Mott, in his first book published in 1901, understood the power and benefits behind close cooperation between the local church and the missions agency.

> Among the greatest resources of the Church are the missionary societies, together with their workers and agencies on the foreign field... Without doubt there are missionary organizations in sufficient number and possessing sufficient strength and experience to guide an enterprise indefinitely larger than the pressing missionary operations of the Church.[13]

As we will soon see, some suggest today that if the local church was doing its job we would not have a need for parachurch organizations. However, what we see from history is quite the opposite. History shows us that it is when the local church is doing its job there is an incredible increase in parachurch growth. In 1904, John Mott wrote *The Pastor and Modern Missions* specifically to encourage and train pastors in passing on a missions vision.

---

[13] John R. Mott, *The Evangelization of the World in This Generation* (New York: The Student Volunteer Movement, 1901), 120.

The pastor is the director general of the Christian forces. He should regard his church not alone as a field to be cultivated, but also and more especially as a force to be wielded on behalf of the evangelization of the world.... The pastor is not only a leader of his members at home, but an advocate for the people abroad. If he does not plead their cause, who will? The multitude of the distant nations cannot come to seek for themselves, even were they conscious of their need. Nor can the missionary do so. The missionary visitor may arouse temporary interest. But it is the missionary pastor who makes a church a missionary power the year through.[14]

The Student Volunteer Movement supported and promoted the role of the local church in mobilization and understood the pastor to be the central recruiting figure of the church. The Movement sought the aid of the church in moving students from zero to zealot in missions. It was believed that if pastors across America were regularly presenting the needs of the world and challenging their congregations to move away from indifference and toward involvement, the job of the Student Volunteer Movement would be much easier. While it was hoped that the church would cooperate and pave the way for recruitment on campus, the S.V.M. desired that the church would recognize the blessing this mobilization movement was to them.

Without question there is need that the Church of Christ rise up in her might and enter into the heritage which God has

---

[14] John R. Mott, *The Pastor and Modern Missions: A Plea for Leadership in World Evangelization* (New York: Student Volunteer Movement, 1904), 52-53.

prepared for her as a result of the Student Volunteer Movement. This student missionary uprising presents to her an irresistible challenge and appeal to devise and to undertake great things for this generation. God grant that she may not fail to recognize the day of her visitation.[15]

God desires to use these two structures, the local church and the parachurch, in dynamic ways, but we need to heed a caution from history. We are beginning to see Protestant history repeat itself in that some local churches are looking to act independently from the parachurch, claiming they do not need it. The number of churches that desire and attempt to do missions independently is rapidly growing. Few have succeeded because, tragically, many have not counted the cost of carrying the full load of the work. They fall terribly short in pre-field training, missionary care, and casting vision for future work. The local church has a difficult time in sending and sustaining without the parachurch.[16]

THE CHURCHLESS CHRISTIAN

Over the past twenty-five years church attendance has changed. One report suggests, "Mainline Protestant churches have lost millions of members over the past three decades, and growth at evangelical Protestant churches has not been nearly large enough to offset those losses."[17]

---

[15] The Report of the Toronto Convention 1902: Missionary Campaign Library No. 1, Toronto, Feb. 26-March 2, 1902 (Chicago: Student Missionary Campaign Library, 1902), 58.

[16] Blincoe, 6.

[17] "Church Attendance on the Decline," *Christian Century*, Sept. 11, 1996. Available from findarticles.com.

These statistics reflect the growing trend among Christian students to place a higher value on parachurch ministry than the local church.

More and more Christian students have a hard time plugging into a local church as they enter college because they find their community solely among peers in the parachurch ministry. Students spend four to six years in college and these campus ministries are a natural fit to plug wholeheartedly into while church seems not quite as fun or relatable. Church music is not always as contextual, the pastor and congregation may not wear jeans, and it might start as early as 9 a.m.! Some will graduate and continue to ignore it and will battle spiritual stagnancy while they mourn their sudden lack of fellowship. Others graduate and will face a seemingly unnatural, awkward transition as they build the habit of church attendance into their lives. Either way students eventually experience a considerable adjustment period for their disregard of the church. Obviously, no good thing comes from avoiding the church.

There are six major issues that result from the local church being neglected. First, the parachurch is normally a homogenous group. The makeup includes similar age, ethnicity, and social class so that like attracts like. Though mentorship occurs in these communities, the loss is in the multigenerational landscape where the younger are learning from the older. Titus 2:3-5 (ESV) gives us this principle:

Older men are to be sober-minded, dignified, self-controlled, sound in faith, in love, and in steadfastness. Older women likewise are to be reverent in behavior, not slanderers or slaves to much wine. They are to teach what is good, and so train the young women to love their husbands and children, to be self-controlled, pure, working at home, kind, and submissive to their own husbands, that the word of God may not be reviled.

The homogenous group misses wisdom because everyone involved looks alike, talks alike, and has the same interests. The broader, diverse community is absent because sameness is prioritized.

Second, the parachurch tends to be more action-oriented, putting emphasis on doing versus being. To use a simple illustration, the local church is called to be a hospital and an army. In contrast, the parachurch has the luxury of being simply an army and focusing in on a specific mission or task. The result is they can be more selective in what they engage in doing and they do not have to care for every person who desires to be involved. They can simply move with the movers, and any individuals who have high needs can be sloughed off to the local church. For example, in some campus groups, if a student is seen as a potential leader, he is given many opportunities for growth and involvement and is offered a position with that particular ministry. Opposite that, if the student is perceived to be more of a social outcast and high maintenance, the campus ministry does not have to offer them the same opportunities for involvement or leadership. These are left for the church to deal with.

Third, though some parachurch organizations may at times exercise traditions historically associated with the local church (known as the *means of grace*; namely baptism and the Lord's Supper) they usually do not practice them with the same consistency. Because these sacred rituals are mandated by Christ, they are activities that God uses to deepen our Christian experience as we obediently and regularly engage in them. There are a growing number of new Christians in college who never experience baptism or the Lord's Supper. They are brought to Christ by the parachurch ministry who does not see these two actions as their primary function. Typically, it is these two that parachurch ministries have reserved for the local church. The result of this for college students who participate exclusively in the parachurch is that they miss out on the grace to be found in these practices.

Fourth, the parachurch is not self-supporting and therefore needs outside funding. Students who do not involve themselves in a local church while in college find it very difficult to raise adequate support to go overseas or be in full-time parachurch ministry. They have a small community of peers, but have not taken the time to cultivate relationships on multigenerational levels. It is difficult to aproach businessmen and other professionals regarding financial giving when you don't know any.

Fifth is the role of church discipline. Jesus taught the disciples how to deal with a brother in sin in Matthew 18:15-17. Church discipline revolves around witnesses and ultimately the local church.

> If your brother sins against you, go and show him his fault, just between the two of you. If he listens to you, you have won your brother over. But if he will not listen, take one or two others along, so that 'every matter may be established by the testimony of two or three witnesses.' If he refuses to listen to them, tell it to the church; and if he refuses to listen even to the church, treat him as you would a pagan or a tax collector.

This type of discipline does not exist in the parachurch to the same degree that it does in the local church—it cannot! Though parachurch ministries have a standard of leadership and are governed by moral codes, it is still connected in many cases with a college or university. So, instead of having liberty to act as a strictly religious institution, it is forced to consider the rules and limitations of the public university they are in connection with. Since the local church does not have this association, it is more able and more equipped to carry out the discipline that helps guide and correct members, both young and old, who have strayed off the path. Also, as far as biblical confrontation, correction, and rebuke go, the church's foundation of established authority may make it more capable of acting with wisdom and influence than the transient student ministry.

It is hard to plant a church if you don't know what one looks like.

Sixth, the church experience is not only important in the equipping and sending processes; it is also important in the end product. The church defines that which mobilization ultimately seeks to accomplish. In other words, students also need to be participating in the church from the practical standpoint that it is what they will be seeking to establish in areas where there is none. Matthew 16:18 states, "On this rock I will build my church, and the gates of Hades will not overcome it." The mission of God in the world and the church go hand in hand. It is hard to plant a church if you don't know what one looks like. Ramifications will be seen on the front end when one seeks to be sent out and on the back end when one has no model to reproduce. It is illegitimate to consider missions occurring healthily when the two have been separated. Prioritizing the parachurch over the local church should be avoided.

Today, we must have a balanced approach in regards to the local church and parachurch. Both the pastor and parachurch leader need to understand that when they can mutually encourage, pray for, and build each other, they will both be mutually stimulated. The church should count it a blessing to see entrepreneurial members raised up from within to launch various ministries. The local church needs to take advantage of the structures that are in place within parachurch groups and understand that they are a strategic way to advance the kingdom of God. On the other hand, parachurch groups need the local church for manpower and resources in order to be effective. Both benefit greatly when they seek to serve each other.

As we look to the past to reach the present, it's easy to recognize that there is much wisdom in how the Student Volunteer Movement's generation approached church. Today, there is much power in the presence of parachurch ministries. May we learn from history how to prioritize the church, God's ordained institution; especially as we pursue participation in missions! And, together with today's para-church organizations, may we create an atmosphere of co-labor in accomplishing the task before us.

CHAPTER 9
TRUTH

33 percent of self-defined Christians agreed that the Bible, Qur'an, and Book of Mormon teach the same truths.

In 1936, Harvard University did something that most universities never dare to do—they changed their seal. It was an obvious act to distance themselves from Christ as the source of knowledge and truth.

In George Barna's most recent survey of what Christians believe, 33 percent of self-defined Christians agreed that the Bible, Qur'an, and Book of Mormon teach the same truths, even though these three sacred books have different ideas about God, salvation, and truth.[1] For the university student holding a Christian paradigm this concept of truth erodes their ability to think systematically or logically. An example of this may be a postmodern Christian who affirms both the established doctrines of the Church yet embraces classically non-Christian ideas like reincarnation or karma.[2]

In John 18:33-38 we read a conversation between Pilate and Jesus. Pilate's personal and political agenda is

---

[1] Barna Group, "Most American Christians Do Not Believe That Satan or the Holy Spirit Exist," April 10, 2009. Available from barna.org.

[2] Stanley J. Grenz, *A Primer on Postmodernism* (Grand Rapids, MI: Eerdmans, 1996), 15.

confronted by Jesus' larger mission to bear witness to the truth. The conclusion of this conversation is Pilate's questioning "What is truth?" Today, this question could not be any more relevant. Over the past one hundred years we have seen a significant alteration in the way the West has viewed truth. During the time of the Student Volunteer Movement the climate of the American university was much different. Spirituality was obviously more on the forefront of daily life. In the 1890s, for example, most state universities had a required chapel.[3] Many had pastor-presidents who taught courses that defended the truth of Christianity and even encouraged campus revivals. One example of this is the University of Michigan. James Angell was president of the University from 1871-1909 and made the spread of Christianity on campus his highest priority. "Angell made Christianity in the University a major cause. He spoke about it, conducted surveys on it, wrote articles and edited a book on Christianity, facilitated the growth of campus ministries, and continued through the first decade of the twentieth century to preach Christ to Michigan."[4] This is a far cry from a university president today!

In 1884 Harvard University's seal had the Latin word *Veritas*, "Truth," at its center. Around the shield read the words *Christo et Ecclesiae*, "for Christ and the Church."[5] During this time, it was believed that these two ideas were compatible.

---

[3] George M. Marsden, *The Soul of the American University* (New York: Oxford University Press, 1994), 3.

[4] Marsden, 167.

[5] Julie A. Reuben, *The Making of the Modern University* (Chicago: The University of Chicago Press, 1996), 1.

The Harvard officials' views about truth represented the beliefs of most educated Americans at that time. In the late nineteenth century intellectuals assumed that truth had spiritual, moral, and cognitive dimensions… the broad conception of truth, referred to then as the "unity of truth," was institutionalized into the structure of higher education.[6]

When the Student Volunteer Movement's leadership spoke at conferences and conventions they could easily assume that every college student in the auditorium felt that truth was knowable. Truth was something one could possess, enabling the Christian to confidently assert, "The Bible is right and you are wrong." One college professor, Henry Drummond, challenged students in 1887 regarding absolute truth:

> Truth is not to be found in what I have been taught. That is not truth. If it were so, that would apply to the Mormon, it would apply to the Brahmin, it would apply to the Buddhist. Therefore let us dismiss from our minds that predisposition to regard that which we have been brought up in as being necessarily the truth. If that were the definition of truth, truth would be just what one's parents were—it would be a thing of hereditary transmission, and not a thing absolute in itself.[7]

In that day and age, if something was seen as true, the opposite was consequently false; if morally something was right, then the opposite was wrong.[8] Because of this

---

[6] Reuben, 2-3.

[7] T. J. Shanks, *A College of Colleges: Led by D. L. Moody* (New York: Fleming H. Revell, 1887), 31.

there was a definite conviction that truth exists absolutely; that Christians possess it and that they need to tell others.

When D. L. Moody spoke at Yale University in 1898, he was pleased with the campus's spiritual health, "I have been pretty well acquainted with Yale for twenty years, and I have never seen the University in so good a condition religiously as it is now."[9] Quite a compliment from one of America's leading religious figures!

However, in only the few subsequent decades a paradigm shift occurred in the academic world that targeted Christianity's claim of absolute truth.

> **While Moody's enthusiasm for the vigor of the voluntary religion of young men at Yale was understandable, the winds were already blowing that would eliminate Christianity as an effective force at the centers of American academic life. During the next sixty years these winds of modernity would reach gale force, so that even a generation of men dedicated to "evangelization of the world in this generation" could only ride the storm.[10]**

In 1951, William Buckley wrote a book entitled *God and Man at Yale*. Himself a graduate of Yale, he sought to criticize the faculty for abandoning the notion of truth. He writes, "There is surely not a department at Yale... that is uncontaminated with the absolute that there are no absolutes, no intrinsic rights, no ultimate truths."[11]

---

[8] Millard J. Erickson, *Postmodernizing the Faith: Evangelical Responses to the Challenge of Postmodernism* (Grand Rapids, MI: Baker Books, 1998), 64.

[9] H. B. Wright, *Two Centuries of Christian Activity at Yale* (New York: The Knickerbocker Press, 1901), 115.

[10] Marsden, 20.

At least one of the origins of this shift was the failure of religious studies to be integrated into intellectual life. The result was, religious truth was viewed as distinct from "factual," scientific truth. Religion was reduced to emotional and moral conviction void of any intellectual worth.[12] This is what caused Harvard to change its seal. They dropped the words *Christo et Ecclesiae,* "for Christ and the Church," so that the seal simply read, *Veritas*, "Truth." This marked the death of Harvard's ideal of truth as grounded in the Person of Christ.[13]

ABSENCE OF ABSOLUTES

Today, this understanding of religious truth as different from "factual," scientific truth is even more obvious on the college campus. The growing perspective is that absolute truth is simply nonexistent. Ravi Zacharias shows how this transition took place starting at the university level.

> The principal means to accomplish this was to take control of the intellectual strongholds, our universities, and under a steady barrage of "scholarly" attack change the plausibility structure for belief in God so that God was no longer a plausible entity in scholastic settings. This assault on religious belief was carried out in the name of political or academic freedom while the actual intent was to vanquish philosophically anything that smacked of moral restraint. Unblushingly, the full brunt of the attack has been leveled against Christianity as

---

[11] William Buckley, *God and Man at Yale* (Washington, DC: Regency Publishing, 1951), 8.

[12] Reuben, 5.

[13] Reuben, 15.

Eastern religions enjoy a patronizing nod and the protection of mystical license.[14]

Truth is no longer seen as objective and is no longer limited to its rational dimension. Now, truth is viewed as subjective and one is free to tap into emotions and intuition to find it. In light of this, there is no compromise in saying that a plurality of truths can exist alongside each other.

The postmodern worldview operates with a community-based understanding of truth. It affirms that whatever we accept as truth and even the way we envision truth are dependent on the community in which we participate. Further, and far more radically, the postmodern worldview affirms that this relativity extends beyond our *perception* of truth to its essence: there is no absolute truth; rather, truth is relative to the community in which we participate.[15]

In the past one could not hold to two truth claims that were incompatible. To say that Jesus was only a man and to also affirm that He was God incarnate would have created a predicament: The truth claims conflict and therefore one view must be false. Today, on the college campus, propositional truth has taken a backseat to personal truth. Propositional truth asserts that our truth claims can be stated and analyzed into logic, otherwise they are false.[16] Thus, the statement "I got married on May 8th" is true only if my actual wedding day occurred on May 8th.

---

[14] Ravi Zacharias, *Can Man Live Without God?* (Dallas, TX: Word Publishing, 1994), xiv.
[15] Grenz, 8.
[16] Harold A. Netland, *Dissonant Voices: Religious Pluralism and the Question of Truth* (Vancouver: Regent Publishing, 1991), 115.

Propositions are either true or false. Over the last one hundred years, propositional truth has been forced to submit itself to personal truth in the minds of many.

Wilfred Cantwell Smith, Harvard historian of religion, has been a leading proponent in this priority shift from objective to subjective. Especially in the religious arena Smith espouses that one's personal faith is of greatest importance. Therefore, doctrines are secondary to one's individual beliefs and one should not be concerned with propositional truth. In his mind, religious truth is of a different nature than truth found in the sciences. In contending for personal truth Smith suggests that statements and beliefs in Christianity may at the same time be true for one person and false for another.[17] Regarding religious tradition he states that it "becomes more or less true in the case of particular persons as it informs their lives and their groups and shapes and nurtures their faith."[18] Smith suggests that truth is not static and unchanging, but is dynamic; constantly in flux. The result is that today spirituality is more of a consumer product instead of a collection of consistent, reliable statements of fact.

If Smith's perspective is correct, then no two people can ever disagree over religious truth-claims. This means that, in the present day, truth is irrelevant to the concerns of most religious devotees in the world. This leads to a problem. Millions of Buddhists, Hindus, and Muslims oppose this overly user-friendly definition of truth in light of their commitment to a set of propositions. My Muslim friend would be highly

---

[17] Netland, 119.
[18] Wilfred Cantwell Smith, *Towards a World Theology* (Philadelphia: Westminster, 1981), 187.

offended if I told him that he and the Buddhist are both correct. They both adhere to their system because, in it, they believe the truth is found. The answer to conflicting truth claims is not to rebuff the idea of absolutes, but to instead find out what those absolutes are. Thus it is imperative to understand that the foundation of Christianity is its claim to truth.[19]

The Bible has much to say about truth and the nature of truth. The Old Testament word for truth is 'emet and it appears 127 times in the Scripture. It literally translates as "truth, right, or faithful."[20] Passages that use this Hebrew word include, "Your righteousness is everlasting and your law is true" (Psalm 119:142). "My mouth speaks what is true, for my lips detest wickedness" (Proverbs 8:7). "Now I know that you are a man of God and that the word of the LORD from your mouth is the truth" (1 Kings 17:24).

The Greek New Testament's understanding of truth mirrors that of the Old Testament. The Greek word, *aletheia*, retains the Hebrew idea found in 'emet. The meaning behind this is not merely ethical truth, but truth in all its fullness and scope, as embodied in Jesus.[21] In the New Testament, the Word of God is seen as truth (John 17:17), the Holy Spirit is called "the Spirit of truth" (John 14:17), the Church is said to be the pillar and foundation of truth (1 Timothy 3:15), and those who deny God are seen as oppressing the truth (Romans 1:18). Roger Nicole, a contemporary advocate for the unchanging nature of absolute truth states, "The biblical view of truth (*emet–aletheia*) is like a rope with several inter-

---

[19] Douglas Groothuis, *Truth Decay: Defending Christianity against the Challenges of Postmodernism* (Downers Grove, IL: InterVarsity Press, 2000), 81.

[20] W. E. Vine, Merrill Unger, and William White, eds., *Vine's Complete Expository Dictionary of Old and New Testament Words* (Nashville, TN: Thomas Nelson Publishers, 1985), 16.

[21] Vine, Unger, and White, 645.

twined strands… it involves factuality, faithfulness, and completeness."[22]

WINDOWS OF OPPORTUNITY

My Muslim friend would be highly offended if I told him that he and the Buddhist are both correct.

Many university students today see truth as adjustable to one's needs. Truth has been redefined in pragmatic terms; reduced to what works for me and my social group. The result of an understanding of truth void of absolutes is that it leaves no comprehensive categories of experience or knowledge. Because it rejects the idea of a singular grand story—a metanarrative—that explains what is true and gives meaning to all life, there is no overarching purpose wherein one's own experience can fit and find meaning. Instead, one's own experience is the only absolute.

Christopher Wright, in his book *The Mission of God,* clearly sums up how we find our mission in the metanarrative. He centers the grand story on Luke 24:45-47, "Then he opened their minds so they could understand the Scriptures. He told them, 'This is what is written: The Christ will suffer and rise from the dead on the third day, and repentance and

---

[22] Roger Nicole, "The Biblical Concept of Truth," in *Scripture and Truth*, eds. D.A. Carson and John D. Woodbridge (Grand Rapids, MI: Zondervan, 1983), 296.

forgiveness of sins will be preached in his name to all nations, beginning at Jerusalem.'" Wright suggests:

> Jesus' whole sentence comes under the rubric "this is what is written." Luke does not present Jesus as quoting any specific verse from the Old Testament, but he claims that the mission of preaching repentance and forgiveness to the nations in his name is "what is written." He seems to be saying that the whole of the Scripture... finds its focus and fulfillment *both* in the life and death and resurrection of Israel's Messiah, *and* in the mission to all nations, which flows out from that event.[23]

When one suppresses the story of God, he is left with a smaller story that is self-centered, self-absorbed, and has no mission. One of the tragedies of the 21st century is that this very popular belief system leaves little to live for. Ravi Zacharias states:

> There is no center to hold things together. Or to put it differently, there is no metanarrative to life, no overarching story by which all the particulars can be interpreted.... Life needs a story to understand the details. Life needs to hold tighter at the center if we are to reach to distant horizons. But our culture neither owns a story nor holds at the center.[24]

While the truth situation is urgent and Christian students are not immune to this paradigm, not everyone in the

---

[23] Christopher J. H. Wright, *The Mission of God* (Downers Grove, IL: InterVarsity Press, 2006), 29-30.

[24] D. A. Carson, ed., *Telling the Truth: Evangelizing Postmoderns* (Grand Rapids, MI: Zondervan, 2000), 23.

21st century has believed the lie. Many Christian students still uphold the absolute truth that is the Word of God. These students hold at the center; these students will reach to distant horizons. But they need encouragement. It is crucial that Christian leaders of our day come alongside students and affirm them in the Word of God, in absolute truth, and in the comprehensive meaning of life into which theirs fits. This is the understanding that will bolster one's belief that truth, purpose, and mission are tied together.

> Christianity contends that revelational truth is intelligible, expressible in valid propositions, and universally communicable. Christianity does not profess to communicate a meaning that is significant only within a particular community or culture. It expects men of all cultures and nations to comprehend its claims about God and insists that men everywhere ought to acknowledge and appropriate them.[25]

Truth is not only absolute; it is knowable, comprehensive, and found in Scripture. Students who embrace this view of truth *will* have a relevant message—their peers need not settle for a lesser story, and their lives *will* be missional—they will join in the spirit of the Student Volunteer Movement in proclaiming God's truth to fellow students and around the world.

---

[25] Carl F. H. Henry, *God, Revelation, and Authority,* vol. 1 (Waco, TX: Word, 1976), 229.

CHAPTER 10
NATIONS

In a recent survey almost 40 percent of Americans could not point to North America on a map.[1] That's hard to believe! That means if they were kidnapped by aliens, taken to outer space, and had to take a space taxi back home, they could not find their continent. It is hard to imagine lacking knowledge so central to life and identity. As Christians, the equivalent of locating one's home country might be the ability to identify God's purpose of reaching all nations. It is vital info to our identity as Christ-followers, yet if I had been kidnapped by aliens in college, transported to outer space, and needed to take a space taxi to an unreached part of the world, I would not have been able to locate one. I would have been equally embarrassed. When it comes to our making disciples of all the nations, many of us have been just as illiterate of our world as 40 percent of Americans are about their country.

In 1792, just before sailing to India, William Carey wrote a book that would become a catalyst of missions activity for centuries to come, known as *An Enquiry*. One key component in this eighty-six-page book is how Carey viewed the world. He divided the planet into four parts (Europe, Asia,

---

[1] Steven Shehori, "37% of Americans Unable to Locate America on a Map," Dec. 15, 2008. Available from huffingtonpost.com.

Africa, and America) and looked at their respective populations, civilizations, and religions.[2] He labeled the major religions as Christian, Jewish, Mahometan (Muslims), and Pagan. In trying to identify the cumulative population Carey writes:

> The inhabitants of the world according to this calculation amount to about seven hundred and thirty one million; four hundred and twenty million of whom are still in pagan darkness; a hundred and thirty million followers of Mahomet; a hundred million Catholics; forty-four million Protestants; thirty million of the Greek and Armenian churches, and perhaps seven million Jews.[3]

Amazingly, his calculations were quite accurate. Carey's goal through *An Enquiry* was to awaken the Church to the major religious blocs of the world and motivate it to action.

One hundred years later, though the world could still be defined in terms similar to the ones that Carey used, large parts of the world had begun to open their doors to the gospel. During this time the Student Volunteer Movement was thriving and it seized this opportunity to encourage people to look at the world as ready for harvest. A. T. Pierson describes the difference between the time of William Carey and the year the Student Volunteer Movement began:

> When, in 1792, [William Carey] led in the formation of that first British society, and when, in 1793, he himself went forth

---

[2] William Carey, *An Enquiry into the Obligation of Christians to Use Means for the Conversion of the Heathen* (England: Ann Ireland, 1792), Reprint edition. Dallas, TX: Criswell Publications, 1988, 62.

[3] Carey, 49.

as the first foreign missionary from English shores, the whole world was comparatively locked against missionary enterprise; there was scarce one real opening into pagan, papal, or Moslem lands to preach the gospel in its purity or win converts... Now the whole aspect of the world is changed, and there is scarce one closed door, or community where the preacher may not go with the open Bible... And yet these are but a part of the changes which make this nineteenth century the most conspicuous in history for the progress of missions.[4]

John Mott also was sensitive to this unique climate of the world when many countries were open to the gospel. "We can all remember the time when the larger part of inner Africa was regarded as inaccessible... Yesterday Africa was the continent of history, of mystery, and of tragedy; today it is the continent of opportunity."[5]

One major reason they could perceive the world as being so open was that they viewed it through a purely geographic lens. The predominant question they were asking was, "What countries do not have the gospel yet?" Because they were country-driven they were able to show students that roads had been opened into virtually every corner of the earth. This brought a sense of excitement to mobilization. At the close of the famous Mount Hermon summer project of 1886, the one hundred students who dedicated themselves to missions wrote down the country God was sending them to beside their signature.[6] They were geographically driven.

---

[4] A. T. Pierson, *Crisis of Missions* (New York: Baker and Taylor Co., 1886), 2.

[5] John R. Mott, *The Pastor and Modern Missions* (New York: SVM, 1904), 6.

[6] C. Howard Hopkins, *20th Century Ecumenical Statesman John R. Mott: 1865-1955* (New York: Eerdmans Publishing Company, 1979), 27.

Because every aspect of the Student Volunteer Movement interpreted the world through this lens, they were diligent to get up-to-date country information out to the students. They created resources for those wanting to go overseas in order to enhance their understanding of what God was doing around the world. These materials almost always dealt with the issues from a country paradigm.[7]

On one hand, this view made mobilization efficient. The amount of material that was geared to specific places or religious groups was quickly produced and dispersed. On the other hand, missionaries would collect in the same areas of a country while other parts of that country were left untargeted, because at least they were in the country—their strategy went no further.

The leadership of the S.V.M. became aware of this and sought to counter it, but it was not an easy task. One of the means employed to correct this error was the pen. The Student Volunteer Movement's gifted writers advocated for those parts of each country that still did not have an adequate witness. Their goal was to help believers see that though missionaries were present in a country, their distribution was still a matter of concern to ensure effectiveness and thoroughness.

The term *unoccupied fields* was adopted to counter this geographically driven perspective. It represented places in countries where there were few to no workers and was used as a means of highlighting various cities that were untouched by the gospel. An example of this can be seen

---

[7] Some of the more popular titles used were: *South American Problem; Islam, Geography and Atlas of Protestant Missions;* and *World Atlas of Christian Missions.* John R. Mott, *Addresses and Papers of John R. Mott Volume 1: The Student Volunteer Movement for Foreign Missions* (New York: Association Press, 1946), 178.

in the writings of Samuel Zwemer, product of the Student Volunteer Movement and pioneer missionary to the Middle East. As he reviews several areas that would fall into this category he says, "Before leaving the survey of the unoccupied fields in Asia we cross over once more from the East to the extreme West. Arabia, the cradle of Islam, is still a challenge to Christendom... The present missionary force is wholly limited to the East coast and the vicinity of Aden."[8] James Barton, in his book *The Unfinished Task* published by the Student Volunteer Movement in 1908, also honed in on this concept of unoccupied fields and sought to highlight the great work that still remained. He sounded a warning to not oversaturate certain cities.

> Much has already been done in the way of world evangelization. Owing to the unequal distribution of the world, the impression may have been made that the unevangelized portions of the world have been pretty well covered already, and that it but remains for us to maintain the present forces on the ground until they accomplish the task that has been set for them to do. But the fact is far otherwise and those who are planning to go out as missionaries, as well as the missionary societies themselves... ought to know where the greatest needs are, that the unevangelized world may be adequately covered.[9]

Barton goes on to show that while countries like India, Japan, and China were receiving missionaries, the

---

[8] Samuel Zwemer, *The Unoccupied Mission Fields of Africa and Asia* (New York: Laymen's Missionary Movement, 1911), 23.
[9] James L. Barton, *The Unfinished Task* (New York: Student Volunteer Movement, 1908), 39-40.

problem lay in their distribution. They all worked in the same cities: Calcutta, Madras, Bombay, Tokyo, and Shanghai. Missionaries needed to spread out from these cities to the rest of the country. Barton's challenge in showing the unoccupied fields was to shed light on large sections within each country that received no workers at all.

THE NEW LENS

The 1930s began a slow transition process in terms of how Christians viewed the world. Through men like Cameron Townsend and Donald McGavran (products of the Student Volunteer Movement) several observations were made that would affect missions thinking for years to come. Townsend worked in Guatemala distributing Bibles in Spanish and it was soon pointed out to him that the indigenous populations did not speak Spanish. Furthermore, they could only be reached in their own language.[10] This so motivated Townsend that he gave the rest of his life to translating Scripture for these indigenous peoples. Meanwhile in India, McGavran recognized through his church-planting efforts the social and cultural barriers that were present. He wrote:

> Every nation is made up of various layers or strata of society. In many nations each stratum is clearly separated from every other... Individuals of one stratum, possibly close neighbors, may become Christians or Communists without that stratum

---

[10] James and Marti Hefley, *Uncle Cam* (Huntington Beach, CA: Wycliffe Bible Translators, 1984), 39.

being much concerned. But when individuals of their own kind start becoming Christians, that touches their very lives.[11]

McGavran realized that "people become Christians as a wave of decisions for Christ sweeps through the group mind."[12] He called this process a "People Movement" and became the proponent of a new way of understanding and thinking about missions. After these two men paved the way, there were pockets of people who began seeing the same thing.[13] However, this new paradigm was fully introduced and explained in 1974.

In 1974, when Billy Graham hosted a world evangelization conference in Lausanne, Switzerland, Christians from all over the world met for an international discussion about reaching the world. Ralph Winter challenged the participants through a paper entitled, "The Highest Priority: Cross-Cultural Evangelism" and showed that if anyone considered the world to be reached it was because they were looking through the wrong lens. He asserted that it is false and misleading to proclaim that the world has been evangelized simply because a church exists in every country. Dr. Winter's influence at this convention went on to ignite the Congress to an understanding of what he called the "hidden peoples" of the world — those that have no access to the gospel.

I'm afraid that all our exultation about the fact that every *country* of the world has been penetrated has allowed many

---

[11] Donald McGavran, *Bridges of God* (London: World Dominion Press, 1957), 1.

[12] McGavran, 12.

[13] In 1963 Leslie Lyall of Overseas Missionary Fellowship wrote a world survey called *Missionary Opportunity Today*. In 1968 another global survey identifying unreached peoples by Missions Advanced Research and Communications Center was released and in 1972 Patrick Johnstone wrote *Operation World*. Patrick Johnstone, *The Church Is Bigger Than You Think* (Great Britain: Christian Focus Publications, 1998), 91-92.

to suppose that every *culture* has by now been penetrated. This misunderstanding is a malady so widespread that it deserves a special name, let us call it "people blindness" that is, blindness to the existence of separate *peoples* within *countries.*[14]

This congress helped erect a new foundation stone that would eventually become the hallmark of missions thinking. Following the Congress, Dr. Winter and others agreed to use the term "unreached peoples" in describing the ethnolinguistic groups that were not yet reached.[15] The emergence of several publications on the issue resulted in a precise definition of what was once a vague idea: *unreached people* — "a people group within which there is no indigenous community of believing Christians with adequate numbers and resources to evangelize this people group without outside (cross-cultural) assistance."[16]

It is false and misleading to proclaim that the world has been evangelized simply because a church exists in every country.

Missions was no longer described in terms of countries and geopolitical boundaries as it had been with the

---

[14] J. D. Douglas, *Let the Earth Hear His Voice: International Congress on World Evangelization Lausanne, Switzerland* (Minnesota: World Wide Publications, 1975), 221.

[15] Johnstone, 103.

[16] Ralph Winter, "Momentum Is Building! Many Voices Discuss Completing the Task by 2000 A.D.," *International Journal of Frontier Missions* 3, no. 1-4 (1986): 71.

Student Volunteer Movement and the preceding generations, but rather in the new language of ethnolinguistic
groups. With this new understanding came the use of terms
that today seem to be taken for granted. *Ethne* is one such
term and its use in Scripture began to take on a more explicit definition.[17] It became important to look at the Bible
and see if it had a deeper connotation than just "all countries." Winter's address at Lausanne helps us on this point:

> The "nations" to which Jesus often referred were mainly eth-
> nic groups within the single political structure of the Roman
> government. The various nations represented on the day of
> Pentecost were for the most part not *countries* but *peoples*.
> In the Great Commission as it is found in Matthew, the phrase
> "make disciples of all *ethne* (peoples)" does not let us off the
> hook once we have a church in every country—God wants a
> strong church within every people![18]

John Piper has done one of the most thorough works
on the use of the word *ethne* in his book *Let the Nations Be
Glad*. He contends that most of the 18 times the phrase
panta ta ethne (all the nations) is used in the New Testament
it favors the idea of people groups.[19] He points back to the
promise given to Abraham in Genesis 12:3, ESV, (and by you
all the families of the earth shall be blessed) to show the Hebrew word *Mishpaha* can be, and usually is, even smaller
than a tribe. This, Piper says, proves that the blessing of

[17] Ralph Winter and Steven Hawthorne, *Perspectives on the World Christian Movement,*
4th ed. (Pasadena, CA: William Carey Library, 2009), 275.
[18] Douglas, 221.
[19] John Piper, *Let the Nations Be Glad* (Grand Rapids, MI: Baker House, 1993), 180-
182.

Abraham was meant to reach small groupings of people. Based on his evidence he concludes that to view Matthew 28:19 in light of people groups is a solid interpretation.

The scope of the task changes as it becomes more clearly defined.

The singular use of *ethnos* in the New Testament always refers to a people group. The plural use of *ethnos* sometimes must be a people group and sometimes must refer to Gentile individuals, but usually can go either way… The combination of these results suggests that the meaning of *panta ta ethne* leans heavily in the direction of "all the nations (people groups)."[20]

Piper writes, "Dr. Winter reached up and pulled the unseen rope called 'unreached peoples' that rang a bell which reverberates to this day."[21]

FROM WHERE TO WHOM

The implication of this people group understanding for today's mobilizer is that strategy must be a higher priority. The responsibility to preach the gospel is constant but the scope of the task changes as it becomes more clearly defined.[22] Today, missions mobilizers have focused in on

---

[20] Piper, 180.

[21] John Piper, "Personal Tribute to the Late Ralph Winter." Available from desiringgod.org.

[22] Alan Johnson, "The Frontier Mission Movement's Understanding of the Modern Mission Era," *International Journal of Frontier Missions* 18, no. 2 (Spring 2001): 82.

what exactly is the task remaining—enabling us to see with clarity where the workers are, who is yet to have a witness, and where to send those whose desire is to be frontline workers. India is an example of this. In the past, if God laid on someone's heart to go to India, they could end up anywhere in the country. In fact, this is exactly what happened. Though they might have known where pockets of Hindus, Sikhs, and Christians were, they had no idea the number of existent people groups or how to strategize to get teams of workers into each of them. Today, because of our paradigm shift, we now focus our efforts on the 2,500-plus distinct people groups speaking 438 languages instead of on India as a whole.[23] We can tell with amazing accuracy where the missionaries are located and who has yet to have a church planted among them.

During the S.V.M.'s conferences students stood up to tell where they were going as missionaries in the next twelve months. One at a time, all across the room, students arose and said, for example, "to India," "to Sudan," "to Korea," or "to Brazil."[24] Today, however, in the same setting, you might hear students announce their intentions to go "to the Uighurs," "to the Hausas," "to the Ansaris," or "to the Betawis." In the past the question may have been posed, "*To where* are you going?" but currently it is more appropriate to say, "*To whom* are you going?" Alan Johnson expounds on this shift well when he says:

---

[23] For more information on people groups see joshuaproject.net or thetravelingteam.org/stateworld. Patrick Johnstone and Jason Mandryk, *Operation World*, 6th ed. (Waynesboro, GA: Authentic Media, 2006), 309-310.

[24] John R. Mott, *Student Mission Power: Report of the First International Convention of the Student Volunteer Movement for Foreign Missions* (Pasadena, CA: William Carey Library, 1891), 178.

From the charts and maps of Carey, to the cry of the Student Volunteer Movement, down to the work of McGavran and Townsend, there was continual sense of need for a fine-tuning of the picture of the remaining task. As the gospel penetrated deeper and deeper into the various countries, national boundaries and divisions of humanity, there was a rather natural progression to begin to see the task in terms of peoples rather than geo-political nations... The stage was being set for the articulation of a new paradigm for viewing the missionary task.[25]

May this be the generation to bring God glory not only in every country, but in every people group!

---

[25] Johnson, 86.

METHODS
THEN AND NOW

"A generation which ignores history has no past and no future."

— Robert Heinlein

CHAPTER 11
STATEMENTS OF COMMITMENT

Looking back to when missions became a reality to me, there were various hooks on which I was able to hang my missions conviction. First, were the books and stories of those who had gone before me. There is power in the printed page. Another method of growth for me was listening to and being challenged by the lives of those who spoke about missions. I was finding missional models for my own life. I can remember when I showed up at a Bible study and a world map was placed in the middle of the floor and we just spent time praying for the world. Each hook secured and mobilized my vision for missions in a deeper way. But the first and strongest hook was the decision I made in my college dorm room. My friend challenged me to sign the proverbial dotted line—to put my "yes" on the table and allow God to put it on the map! It set the course of my life and held me to it in the face of many more decisions and distractions.

It is amazing to step back and look at the achievement of the Student Volunteer Movement; the sheer mass of students they enlisted! There was a definite sense that God's hand was present as young men and women surrendered their lives to follow the Lord in His purposes for all nations. The leadership of the S.V.M. acknowledged early on that, while God was responsible to stir the heart, they were responsible to utilize the appropriate tools to ensure that students who began the journey toward missions could faithfully complete it. Thus they used several methods or hooks to recruit, train, and secure Christian students' involvement in missions.

Many of the current methods we use in missions mobilization are a mirror image of those employed by the S.V.M. In addition, new methods have emerged to mobilize students in our present generation. We will explore both methods—past and present—to arrive at an accurate frame of reference for what God has used throughout the years. We begin with the first method: statements of commitment.

The first method that the S.V.M. utilized was bringing students to a decisive moment, much like mine in college. These well-crafted commitment statements were intended to enlist and keep the volunteers on track. These statements were actually printed on cards with a line for the student's signature. A student could not even embark on the initial phases of involvement within the Movement without being immersed in the very essence and purpose of the S.V.M. which were encapsulated in two such statements: the Volunteer Declaration and the Watchword. These represented the heartbeat of the Movement.

The first of these commitment statements was the Volunteer Declaration, adapted from Robert Wilder's Princeton Pledge, and (in its final form) it read, *"It is my purpose, if God permit, to become a foreign missionary."* This was the declaration that each of the Mount Hermon One Hundred signed and as such it became the DNA of the S.V.M. when it was officially organized in 1888. The Volunteer Declaration helped each student who signed it understand the life-altering effect that the missions decision was intended to have.

> A man who signs the Volunteer Declaration signifies by this act that with the light that he then has he forms the definite and clear-cut decision that he will be a foreign missionary. To this end, he turns his face in that direction. He not only decided, and turns his face, but he begins to adapt his course of study and special outside work to his newly chosen lifework.[1]

It was repeatedly emphasized, in order not to manipulate the college student, that the declaration should be used only under the manifest guidance of the Spirit. The Volunteer Declaration was meant to be balanced in the mind of the signer with a decided pursuit of missionary work on the one hand and a willingness to be redirected by God on the other. Robert Wilder brings a healthy balance to the declaration:

> We do not wish to take our lives in our own hands to the extent of dictating to God. Hence we have put in the words,

---

[1] John R. Mott, *Addresses and Papers of John R. Mott Volume 1: The Student Volunteer Movement for Foreign Missions* (New York: Association Press, 1946), 40.

"if God permit."… It is true, is it not, that the majority of students take the position, "We will stay where we are unless God thrusts us out." We who signed the card put it the other way, "We will go abroad unless God stops us."[2]

DECLARATION CARD

Student Volunteer Movement for Foreign Missions

IT IS MY PURPOSE, IF GOD PERMIT, TO BECOME A FOREIGN MISSIONARY

Signature

Institution

Location of Institution

Permanent Address

Date _____ 19____

IF SIGNED, RETURN TO
STUDENT VOLUNTEER MOVEMENT, 25 MADISON AVENUE, NEW YORK CITY

Volunteer Declaration Card

The benefits of the Volunteer Declaration were manifested in many ways. It put the issue of missionary service in front of the student in such a confrontational way that students had no choice but to face it. Also, because the declaration card called for a decision, younger students had the opportunity to use their college years following that decision by pursuing greater preparation in language and

---

[2] "North American Students and World Advance," Addresses Delivered at the Eighth International Convention of the Student Volunteer Movement for Foreign Missions, Des Moines, Iowa, Dec. 31, 1919 – Jan. 4, 1920, 311-312.

culture. John Mott states, "It leads men to make a definite decision because it helps to hold men who have decided; because it puts a man in a position to do more for missions while he is securing his preparation than he possibly would or could do otherwise; because it puts a deep central purpose into his life which means greater power."[3]

One of the ways in which the S.V.M. measured their success was by the Volunteer Declaration, for it allowed them to put a number on those who had joined the Student Volunteer ranks. By 1891, the young men and women who had signed the declaration numbered *6,000*. By that time, at least 320 of them had already gone to the foreign field. Mott called it the "keystone of the Movement." He goes on to say that:

> **Without this solid, binding factor the Movement long ago would have crumbled. It cannot be too strongly emphasized that there would have been no continuous Volunteer Movement with its ever-expanding numbers, had it not been for this clear-cut, unequivocal statement of personal purpose. This is it which enabled students to burn the bridges behind them and to press forward with undiscourageable resolution across the seas and over the mountains of difficulty.[4]**

The second statement used to recruit students was the Watchword or rallying cry created to stir vision and passion in the heart of students. It read, "*The evangelization of the world in this generation*," and eventually became even

---

[3] Mott, *Addresses and Papers*, 41.
[4] John R. Mott, *Five Decades and a Forward View* (New York: Harper and Brothers, 1939), 22.

more closely associated to the heart of the S.V.M.; A. T. Pierson is credited for creating the Watchword from a verse in the book of Acts: "For David, after he had served the purpose of God in his own generation, fell asleep and was laid with his fathers" (Acts 13:36, ESV). The force of the Watchword is attested to in the mass amount of volunteers that it inspired throughout its history.

The force of the Watchword is attested to in the mass amount of volunteers that it inspired throughout its history.

Robert Wilder said, "The Student Volunteer Movement did not so much produce the Watchword, as the Watchword—or rather the thought behind it—helped to bring into being the Student Volunteer Movement."[5] Even at the Mount Hermon summer project "the evangelization of the world in this generation" was used in many addresses and was another reason for the enlistment of the initial one hundred in 1886.[6] It created a sense of urgency for the student and showed that world evangelization was a real possibility in the near future.

The fact that it is a startling phrase, calling for explanation, has arrested the attention of earnest men and stimulated

---

[5] Robert P. Wilder, *The Great Commission: The Missionary Response of the Student Volunteer Movement in North America and Europe; Some Personal Reminiscences* (London: Oliphants Publishers, 1936), 84.

[6] Wilder, 84.

their thought regarding Christ's great program for the world. It has emphasized as has no other one thing the urgency of the world's evangelization... It is a stirring reminder that our plan must embrace the whole world and that we must act without delay.[7]

This saying not only aided the formation of the S.V.M., it had profound impact on students nationwide by laying the pressing burden of missions upon their shoulders and offering a certain hope of the fact that their goal could be accomplished if they unified themselves around these truths. It was believed that there was no place in the world that was out of reach of the gospel if only students would listen and respond to the message of the Watchword. They looked at the improvements in transportation and communication, the industrial age, and worldwide exploration as "signs of the times" that God was about to complete something.[8]

Another powerful element of the Watchword was that it suggested the hope of fulfillment. Students truly believed that they would finish the task that was commanded by Jesus and that this would hasten "the day of the Lord" (1 Thessalonians 5:2).[9] For them there was a direct correlation between the entire world hearing the gospel and the return of Christ. This concise statement summarized both Christian responsibility and the achievability of the desired end; making it a potent, yet doable challenge.

The Watchword was such a success because it purposefully stayed free from dates and timelines. There was

---

[7] Mott, *Five Decades and a Forward View,* 25.

[8] Timothy C. Wallstrom, *The Creation of a Student Movement to Evangelize the World* (Pasadena, CA: William Carey International University Press, 1980), 68.

[9] "Now, brothers, about times and dates we do not need to write to you, for you know very well that the day of the Lord will come like a thief in the night" (1 Thessalonians 5:1-2).

no proposed end date, e.g., "The evangelization of the world by 1900." This gave the motto an immortal, universal application to successive generations as long as the world remained unevangelized. John Mott explains:

> If the Gospel is to be preached to all men it obviously must be done while they are living. The evangelization of the world in this generation therefore, means the preaching of the Gospel to those who are now living. To us who are responsible for preaching the Gospel it means in our lifetime; to those to whom it is to be preached it means in their lifetime... the phrase "in this generation" therefore, strictly speaking has a different meaning for each person.[10]

It is amazing to listen in to the student testimonies regarding the Watchword's impact:

> In my life the Watchword has become a passion and a controlling force. It has kept me from confining my prayers and efforts to any one country.[11]

> The Watchword has, I think, been the strongest call to consecration that has ever come to me. It does not of course set before us any standard or make upon us any demands which are not to be found in the love and commands of Jesus Christ. We cannot reflect upon it without being startled from our apathy.[12]

---

[10] John R. Mott, *The Evangelization of the World in This Generation* (New York: S.V.M, 1900), 6.

[11] Mott, *The Evangelization of the World in This Generation*, 201.

[12] Mott, *The Evangelization of the World in This Generation*, 201.

It breaks down denominational and national barriers and makes me feel a part of a great and united army of young missionaries who are working for a common end under a common Master. It is a spur to attempt great things for God.[13]

I wish to bear emphatic testimony to the influence of the Watchword of the Student Volunteer Movement upon my own life. It was not possible for me to get to the foreign field within over fourteen years after my decision to go. During these long years of waiting there was no end of forces to weaken one's conviction of duty to the unevangelized world. This conviction the Watchword, on the other hand, intensified and did much to make a permanent and the controlling influence in my life.[14]

From these testimonies it's obvious the Watchword was a force for the Movement, the power of which was released by students' ownership of it and submission to it. John Mott said in 1924, "Next to the decision to take Christ as the Leader and Lord of my life, the Watchword has had more influence than all other ideals and objectives combined to widen my horizon and enlarge my conception of the kingdom of God."[15] In the same vein, Robert Wilder, when he looked back fifty years later regarding how the Watchword had helped shape the S.V.M., stated emphatically:

What have been some of the results of the Watchword where it has been proclaimed and most widely accepted? It has

---

[13] Mott, *The Evangelization of the World in This Generation*, 202-203.
[14] Mott, *The Evangelization of the World in This Generation*, 203.
[15] Wilder, 90.

arrested the attention of earnest men and compelled them to consider the claims of world-wide missions; it has emphasized as has no other one thing the urgency of the task of world evangelization; it has called out the latent energies of the students of our days as has no other challenge that has been presented to them; it has led to a larger discovery of God and a deepening acquaintance with Him, and has for an increasing number lifted the whole missionary enterprise to the superhuman plane.[16]

> *Evangelizing the world was man's part, but conversion of the world was God's part.*

The leadership of the Movement worked hard to fend off critics who misinterpreted the Watchword to mean the conversion of the world. Evangelizing the world was man's part, but conversion of the world was God's part. Robert Speer explains:

We do mean, however, that every intelligent, thoughtful, sincere volunteer believes in and prays for the evangelization of the world before we die, and that by that simple phrase is meant simply this: the presenting of the Gospel in such a manner to every soul in this world that the responsibility for what is done with it shall no longer rest upon the Christian

---

[16] Wilder, 85.

Church, or on any individual Christian, but shall rest on each man's head for himself.[17]

THE POWER OF A STATEMENT

There can be no doubt that God used these statements of commitment in the lives of students during this era. The confrontational nature of them proved to bring young people to such a point of decision that, indeed, the rest of their lives was spent with great resolve toward the nations. It is arguable to say that not only was the landscape of the entire world completely affected by these statements, but that most of that generation was highly influenced by being given the opportunity to encounter the high calling that these statements asked of them.

Ministry today is extremely diversified, and you might be wondering, what is today's Volunteer Declaration? What is our Watchword or rallying cry? What banner can we unite under in our generation? In contrast to the one single student ministry in existence a hundred years ago (the Y.M.C.A.) so many organizations are present on today's college campuses. Of course with a single organization a single Watchword was achievable; but what about now? God is still at work drawing students to a place of total surrender and He's using statements of commitment! It obviously looks different and we are responsible to know our generation and how this method of mobilization is reflected today. We see the same momentum building; the same power of

---

[17] John R. Mott, *Student Mission Power: Report of the First International Convention of the Student Volunteer Movement for Foreign Missions* (Pasadena, CA: William Carey Library, 1891), 74.

commitment is influencing masses of students. The secret is that these statements of commitment have infiltrated *each* individual campus ministry. Campus Crusade's powerful rallying cry is "Win, build, send." Passion's theme has attracted hundreds of thousands: "Your name and renown are the desire of our souls." The Navigators unite under "To know Christ and to make Him known." Each of these organizations has recognized, as the S.V.M. did, the power behind a challenging, transferable slogan to serve as a guide for ministries and their participants. However, the power of these slogans today lies in the individual nature of each one, not in a single, overarching watchword.

Every campus ministry has a specific niche, something they do particularly well, some certain personality type that they attract; each has their own objective. Because of this, when they stick to what they do well, they emulate the body of Christ. The cumulative effort of these ministries will have a far-reaching effect on this generation. Despite our diversity we are still believers who sharpen and challenge each other and who are more complete when we live in fellowship. The Volunteer Declaration and Watchword were dynamic in their day. Today, let each ministry follow God with confidence as to what their rallying cry should be and let us passionately invite the students of this generation to buy in. As Claude Hickman says, "The next Student Volunteer Movement may not be a tsunami, but a thousand rivers." May we anticipate the Lord's powerful moving through the varied student organizations that exist to uniquely serve this generation.

CHAPTER 12
THE PRINTED PAGE AND OTHER MATERIALS

I n the past, websites were called books! I know it's hard to believe in this day and age, but people actually survived without Google. On a serious note, the next method of the six major methods that the S.V.M. utilized is the printed page. They were constantly using existing material and creating their own innovative publications across the spectrum—from the newest and most up-to-date missions magazines to books and even simple pamphlets. In the first five years of the Movement's existence, it had already sold over 84,000 books.[1]

The printed page to the S.V.M. was its own force in recruitment, able to "inform the ignorant, to convince the skeptical, to strengthen the faint-hearted."[2] Periodicals, charts, and books were expected to stir people to action or they were deemed useless. F. P. Haggard, a pastor and missions speaker, stated emphatically, "Missionary literature that will not burn—I mean that will not burn somebody, that

---

[1] Michael Parker, *The Kingdom of Character: The Student Volunteer Movement for Foreign Missions 1886-1926*, 2nd ed. (Pasadena, CA: William Carey Library, 2008), 265.
[2] The Report of the Toronto Convention 1902: Missionary Campaign Library No. 1, Toronto, Feb. 26-March 2, 1902 (Chicago: Student Missionary Campaign Library, 1902), 114.

will not arouse missionary ardor and enthusiasm, that will not lead to missionary doing and giving—is worthless."[3]

Although they utilized all forms of print material, pamphlets and periodicals were the most popular and the most focused upon simply because of their accessibility. By 1890, there were eleven major pamphlets for students that had surfaced. Topics ranged from the history of the S.V.M. to an explanation of the Volunteer Declaration to maintaining missions vision as a member of the local church. Also, many times new pamphlets would be created to expose students to the needs overseas.

Magazines were also a popular resource. Luther Wishard used *The College Bulletin* to spread missions vision even before the Mount Hermon summer project and the *Bulletin* became a major source for missionary news.[4] *The Watchman* was the national magazine of the Y.M.C.A. and by 1896 reached a circulation of 100,000 people.[5]

Another magazine that found its way into the hands of students was called *The Student Volunteer*. This magazine originated in 1891 when a minister suggested the great potential of a monthly magazine that would specifically keep all the volunteers networked.[6] *The Student Volunteer* went out to thousands of students and became one of the most useful agencies employed by the S.V.M. to stay connected with the volunteers.[7] The S.V.M. used it to keep the aims, methods, and

---

[3] The Students and the Modern Missionary Crusade, addresses delivered before the Fifth International Convention of the Student Volunteer Movement for Foreign Missions, Nashville, Tennessee, Feb. 28- March 4, 1906, 170.

[4] Parker, 7.

[5] After several years its name was changed to *The Young Men's Era*. Howard C. Hopkins, *History of the YMCA in North America* (New York: Associated Press, 1951), 137-138.

[6] John R. Mott, *Addresses and Papers of John R. Mott Volume 1: The Student Volunteer Movement for Foreign Missions* (New York: Association Press, 1946), 37.

[7] Fred L. Norton, *A College of Colleges: Led by D. L. Moody* (New York: Fleming H. Revell, 1889), 11.

results of the Movement before the church and to cultivate interest among students. John Mott referred to it as the "unifying force" or the "constant guide and inspiration" to the entire membership of the Movement and to the larger number of students interested in Christian missions.[8] One of the remarkable things about this Movement is that without

We owe much to the literature of that era which is still serving to mobilize people toward the nations.

the use of modern technology for communication, it was able to maintain correspondence with students to the degree that mobilization and encouragement continued well after missions speakers had left a campus. Their strategic use of the pamphlets and *The Student Volunteer* is primarily responsible for sustaining this connection.

Another important magazine was known as *The Missionary Review of the World*. Though not limited in scope to college students and campus happenings, this was an incredible tool used in the hands of the volunteers. The magazine had been initiated under Royal Wilder, father of Grace and Robert Wilder. In describing Royal's focus with the magazine, A. T. Pierson said, "He emphasized the biblical and spiritual basis of missions, the need of generous and sanctified giving, and suggested the best methods for awakening the church to accept her responsibility."[9]

---

[8] Mott, 58.

[9] Delavan Leonard Pierson, *Arthur T. Pierson: A Biography* (London: James Nisbet and Co, 1912), 201.

There can be no doubt that print literature was a strategic method of mobilization that the S.V.M. sought to capitalize on. In a day when connection was not nearly as convenient as it is today, the printed page served this movement well. It allowed the influence of the volunteers to go far beyond any large group presentation or one-to-one meeting. Indeed, it allowed their influence to extend even into our own day. We owe much to the literature of that era which is still serving to mobilize people toward the nations.

THE INFORMATION GENERATION

In 1990, over one hundred years after the Student Volunteer Movement was birthed, a milestone of immeasurable proportions was reached when a precedent-setting tool was created that enabled the access of a world of information from the fingertips: the Internet! Mobilizers of the past relied solely on print literature; today there are endless pages that are ready to be employed as creatively as the imagination will allow. This has by no means negated the use of print resources to mobilize others, but it has exponentially increased the capacity for distributing information. Today, just as in the days of the S.V.M., we have an incredible reservoir of printed resources to draw from for mobilizing others.[10] Many have sought to capitalize on both print and Web-based material to move students further along in their World Christian journey.[11] Out of the many

---

[10] There are some wonderful selections of books to increase world vision available today, too many to include. For a fuller list go to thetravelingteam.org/personalhelps.

[11] There is a social networking phenomenon that has been on the rise over the past few years. It includes such venues as Facebook, blogs, and Twitter. Mobilizers are increasingly utilizing these tools for God's kingdom. Facebook claims over 100 million users and in one month it was reported that there were over 26 million tweets a day on Twitter. It may be a missions organization creating a cause online that attracts users, students inviting other students to an event or informing them of a resource; it may be an agency checking profiles before they accept potential applicants, but one thing is clear—the use of social networking will only continue to grow in the future. For more information see Andrew LaVallee, "Facebook to Nonprofits: More Pages, Fewer Apps," *Wall Street Journal*, August 28, 2009.

resources available today I have chosen the following materials for their easy access and community-friendly quality.

College students all across the country, no matter what campus ministry they are affiliated with, have the opportunity to be involved in small groups. In light of this, missions mobilizers have endeavored to create *missions-based studies* that are a perfect fit for this format. Jeff Lewis, professor of intercultural studies at California Baptist, created an eight-week study that can easily be incorporated into any small group or personal devotion. *God's Heart for the Nations* walks students through the biblical theme of missions. Following each lesson there are people-group profiles that challenge the reader to connect the Word of God with praying for those who have no access. In explaining his intention for writing, Lewis states:

> The purpose of this study is to help create an awareness of one of the most ignored themes of the Bible—God's global purpose: His desire and activity of redeeming mankind: the nations—to Himself... This study will reveal how the themes of God's blessing and His global purpose are beautifully woven together in Scripture.[12]

Another excellent resource by Paul Borthwick entitled, *Missions: God's Heart for the World*, takes a student to a deeper understanding of God's heart for lost people after only nine lessons. Borthwick intentionally avoids the more common missions texts of Scripture because his purpose is

---

[12] Jeff Lewis, *God's Heart for the Nations* (Riverside, CA: The Global Center California Baptist University, 2000), 1.

to prove that the entire missionary enterprise does not rest on one isolated passage in Matthew 28.[13] Instead he draws the reader to verses such as 2 Corinthians 5:11-12, Philippians 2:1-11, and Hebrews 11:1–12:3.

Every Ethne is a ministry whose purpose is to engage, equip, and connect college students to their most strategic role in completing the Great Commission. The ministry created a mobilization tool called *XPlore*, a six-lesson series designed to unveil God's global heart. The student who works through this study will not only learn significant missions passages, but will also be introduced to foundational terms such as the "10-40 window" and "unreached people groups."[14] The student will also be challenged to live a missional lifestyle on campus through praying, welcoming internationals, giving, and mobilizing other students.

I can think of no one in today's culture who is sounding the missions alarm from the spoken and written word with greater intensity than John Piper. Lead pastor at Bethlehem Baptist Church in Minneapolis and prolific author, his book *Let the Nations be Glad* has challenged thousands of people to consider giving their lives to foreign missions. His books are proof of the power of the printed page. His writings have almost single-handedly transformed our current perspective on missions. Piper's mantra, "Missions exists because worship doesn't," has literally become the new answer to the question, *Why missions*?[15]

Another noteworthy piece of print literature written with college students in mind is Claude Hickman's book,

---

[13] Paul Borthwick, *Missions: God's Heart for the World* (Downers Grove, IL: InterVarsity Press, 2000), 6.

[14] Every Ethne, *XPlore: God's Heart for the Nations* (Fayetteville, AR: U.S. Center for World Missions, 2007). Also see everyethne.org.

[15] John Piper, *Let the Nations Be Glad: The Supremacy of God in Missions* (Grand Rapids, MI: Baker House, 1993), 11.

Live Life on Purpose.[16] This book communicates well the point of the Bible as the metanarrative by illustrating our desire for a road map when His Word is a compass, pointing believers in the direction of the nations. He effectively challenges his readers that the question *What is God's will?* should always come before the question we are often consumed with, *What is God's will for my life?*

"Missions exists because worship doesn't" has literally become the new answer to the question, why missions?

No doubt, the book that influenced me the most as a college student was Bob Sjogren's *Unveiled at Last.*[17] Sjogren's premise is to prove that the character of God is missional and, therefore, His people ought to be characterized by this missions objective. What set this book apart for me was that, by the time I'd finished reading it, I was reading the Bible in a different way. Sjogren trains his readers to see that when God blesses His people, they have a corresponding responsibility to the nations; in so doing, he counters our typical me-centered way of reading the Scriptures.

Today's top missions magazine is *Mission Frontiers,* published by the U.S. Center for World Mission, and it is the most widely circulated publication of its kind, with over

---

[16] Claude Hickman, *Live Life on Purpose* (Enumclaw, WA: WinePress Publishing, 2003).

[17] Bob Sjogren, *Unveiled at Last: Discover God's Hidden Message from Genesis to Revelation* (Seattle, WA: YWAM Publishing, 1988).

80,000 subscribers in over 160 countries.[18] Each edition deals with the latest missions issues and anyone at any level can benefit from this publication.

One of the most in-depth and thorough World Christian websites geared toward students and mobilizers alike is that of The Traveling Team.[19] It is over a thousand pages of information for every interest level—Bible studies, talks, interactive lessons, and lists of ideas for personal application and mobilization. Because The Traveling Team is not affiliated with any missions agency or campus ministry, the site exists purely for equipping and establishing the vision of missions for World Christians.

More than half a million international students are enrolled at U.S. college campuses. International Students Incorporated, a ministry focused on internationals, is seeking to equip believers with resources to reach them.[20] Its website is a helpful source of practical tools for sharing Christ with the world at our door.

My intention in this chapter is not to present an exhaustive list of resources available today; that would not even be possible! No, my hope is simply to show that historically and currently, practical resources have contributed mightily to the furtherance of the missions cause. The S.V.M. utilized them with great efficiency, even creating their own for specific needs. Today, we have an overabundance of material at our disposal. Let us recognize the role and capacity that the printed page and other material have in mobilizing our generation to involvement in missions.

---

[18] missionfrontiers.org
[19] thetravelingteam.org
[20] isionline.org

CHAPTER 13
TRAVELING TEAMS

Someone once said that speakers are considered professionals on their topic if they drive farther than eighty miles to speak. There is something about the outside voice. For some reason, when it comes to spiritual issues, the outside voice is often more readily heard than the steady, consistent encouragement of someone familiar. I personally know campus ministers who regularly feed their students with opportunities and information about the world, yet, when the guest speaker comes to talk about missions, students are jolted out of their current complacency on the issue.

The Mount Hermon summer project of 1886 ended with a resolve to send a few graduates from campus to campus all across the United States in order to further enlist volunteers and to rouse missions interest on the campuses. Another goal of these travelers was to unite those who had signed the Volunteer Declaration. These men and women were called the Traveling Secretaries. You may be picturing travelers who go around filing papers and answering phones, but nothing could be further from the truth! Harlan Beach, the director of the Student Volunteer Movement's Mission Study Department, describes the Traveling Secretary position:

> Their work consists in presenting the claims of foreign mission to the institutions visited, in organizing classes for the study of missions, in conferring with missionary committees and officers of associations as how to best awaken and promote missionary interest, in recommending plans and methods which will increase the giving, praying, and working for missions in the colleges, and in interviewing students with reference to devoting their lives to foreign service.[1]

Basically, these men and women were itinerant speakers whose subject was always the promotion of interest and involvement in missions and whose audience was always Christian students.

The role of the Traveling Secretaries was strategic because of their connection to the students. John Mott explains, "This agency is the most potent because the Traveling Secretary comes in personal contact with the field. It has been employed since the inception of the Movement in 1886."[2] It is interesting to note here that Mott calls the students of his generation "the field." He means it in a totally distinct way than he would refer to the overseas mission field. In fact, the Traveling Secretary position was usually held by recent graduates who would travel for about a year and then go themselves as missionaries. At the heart of this organization was an urgency to mediate between the two

[1] Harlan P. Beach, "Sketch of the Student Volunteer Movement for Foreign Missions," *The Intercollegian* 24, no. 3, Fourth Series (December 1901): 56.
[2] John R. Mott, *Addresses and Papers of John R. Mott Volume 1: The Student Volunteer Movement for Foreign Missions* (New York: Association Press, 1946), 35-36.

"fields," raising up students to go to the harvest. The Traveling Secretaries were the most direct link and this is one of the reasons they saw such impact. Another significant reason for the potency of the Traveling Secretaries is the personal connection they made with their

The man who apologizes for foreign missions apologizes for his own conversion.

message. They owned a conviction for missions and consequently they spoke with convincing power to the minds and hearts of students wherever they went. Robert Wilder once said, "The man who apologizes for foreign missions apologizes for his own conversion. We would have been heathen this afternoon had not foreign missions come to our ancestors in northern Europe."[3]

They believed that missionary work is the most important theme of the Bible because many of them were also students whose lives had been dramatically interrupted by God's heart for the world. Robert Speer was one such student turned Traveling Secretary after a life-altering conversation when the travelers came to his campus. He recalls his own experience:

> This Missionary Movement has quite a different meaning to us. We look back to that hour when perhaps for the first time in our lives there was a hand laid upon our shoulder that once

[3] John R. Mott, *Student Mission Power: Report of the First International Convention of the Student Volunteer Movement for Foreign Missions* (Pasadena, CA: William Carey Library, 1891), 108.

was nailed to the Cross, and there was lifted up before our eyes the vision of a new and larger life, and there came a new Heaven and a new earth for us. This Movement has a definite and vivid meaning to those of us who look to its first call to us as the spring of the richest and largest blessing of our lives. I can see still the little room in the North Middle Reunion at Princeton, where a little group of us met years ago in our sophomore year and faced this question, and one by one sat down at a table and wrote our names under the words: "I am willing and desirous, God permitting, to become a foreign missionary."[4]

The perceived effectiveness of Traveling Secretaries rested on whether they could convince their audience of the global Christian imperative. And because the message they taught came out of deep, personal conviction they quickened missionary interest in every audience without fail.

Not only was it the most strategic position, but it was the most strenuous. Robert Wilder and John

Robert Speer

---

[4] W. Reginald Wheeler, *A Man Sent from God* (Westwood N.J: Revell Publishing, 1956), 53.

Forman were the first Traveling Secretaries in the year 1886-1887. They visited 162 colleges and saw 2,106 students volunteer. During the first year of traveling Robert Wilder collapsed completely under the strain and doctors advised him to give up the tour or risk breakdown. After a brief period of rest he resumed.[5] From there, the average yearly travel schedule was just as rigorous and as fruitful. Because the Traveling Secretaries submitted to the pains of constant travel, students' lives by the hundreds were interrupted as they signed the Volunteer Declaration. The Traveling Secretary was the position that constituted the most self-sacrifice yet had the most enduring spiritual results.[6]

Now that we have established the strategic nature of this position and the undeniable difficulty of it, let's take a more intimate look at the details of a Traveling Secretary's ministry. E. B. Haskell of Oberlin Theological Seminary explains how the Traveling Secretaries would attempt to enlist students: "Just a word as to how to get volunteers. I would

---

[5] Robert P. Wilder, *The Great Commission: The Missionary Response of the Student Volunteer Movement in North America and Europe; Some Personal Reminiscences* (London: Oliphants Publishers, 1936), 24.

[6] A list of the S.V.M. Traveling Secretaries for the first twelve years of the Movement follows: 1886-1887 Robert Wilder and John Forman of Princeton; 1887-1888 None; 1888-1889 Robert Wilder of Princeton (enrolled 600 new recruits and visited 93 institutions); 1889-1990 Robert Speer of Princeton; 1890-1892 W. H. Cossum of Colgate College added 300 volunteers and extended the Movement to Eastern Canada, then he himself left for China. Miss Lucy E. Guinness of London, England, traveled for three months on women's colleges and added 240 volunteers; 1892-1893 J. C. White of Wooster College visited one hundred institutions then left for India; 1893-1894 F. A. Keller of Yale; 1894-1895 Sherwood Eddy, H. W. Luce, and H. T. Pitkin, Misses Agnes G. Hill and Abbie M. Lyon. These were the most famous and influential of the Traveling Secretaries as Eddy was a powerful speaker, Pitkin was the Movement's first martyr, and Luce became the founder of *Time* magazine; 1895-1896 W. J. Wanless, John L. Marshall, J. M. Brodnax, Miss Clarissa H. Spencer; 1896-1897 R. E. Lewis, H. W. Luce, Miss Nellie Allen; 1897-1898 F. S. Brockman, R. E. Lewis, R. R. Gailey. For more information see John Mott, *Addresses and Papers of John R. Mott Volume 1*, 25, 36, 57. Also see Michael Parker, *The Kingdom of Character: The Student Volunteer Movement for Foreign Missions 1886-1926,* 2nd ed. (Pasadena, CA: William Carey Library, 2008), 18.

pray over it; I would reach them in just the same way I would try to get people to be Christian. Be courteous, be candid, be careful in your statements, with their objections, above all, never get angry at their stupid or frivolous excuses, or anything of the kind."[7]

Every presentation, whether formal or informal, was meant to be a challenge to global service for Christ. They were to teach through sharing their experiences. The Traveling Secretaries were taught to be straightforward, forcible,

I was surrounded by scores of Christian students who, like me, had little to no knowledge of how God could use them to impact the nations.

and, above all, scriptural. They were trained to not be long-winded, but to take half an hour for preaching and the next half hour for questions and answers. Their perspective was that stories should be told to achieve a climax and illustrations should contribute to the total effectiveness of the speaker with humor interspersed into the presentation. After a presentation was given to a group of students, a major part of the Traveling Secretary's job was to meet the following day with interested students. In these fifty-minute sessions they would assess the student's emotional stability, academic pro-

---

[7] Mott, *Student Mission Power*, 107.

ficiency, and spiritual dedication. At each of these appointments an interview record was filled out. It included questions about the student's date of graduation, field preference, experience in Christian activities, and personal problems. The Traveling Secretary wanted to make the student sitting across the table feel like he or she were the only reason they came to visit that particular campus. The S.V.M.'s ministry did not end there. Remarkably, this is only the beginning of their follow-up with students as their home office continued the process. Based on their commitment to thorough interactions with every interested student on every campus that would open its doors, it is no wonder that this ministry saw the unparalleled fruit that it did. Without the Traveling Secretaries, the Student Volunteer Movement would not have seen the breadth of impact or the depth of commitment that characterized the entire Movement.

MY JOURNEY "THE TRAVELING TEAM"

As a college student who had just been fired up for missions by a type of "traveling secretary" that came to visit my own campus ministry, I cultivated my newfound passion by educating myself about the world. I devoured books and sought out every conference and speaker in a driveable range whose topic was missions. Those who influenced me the most during this season had their own vision shaped by the Student Volunteer Movement. They passed on to me a deep respect and zeal for this awesome historical Movement.

While God was deepening my commitment to serve His global cause, He was also opening my eyes to see that He desired to use every Christian in some way to further the spread of the gospel worldwide. I realized that I was surrounded by scores of Christian students who, like me, had little to no knowledge of how God could use them to impact the nations. From my own study and exposure, I began to create resources that would promote their understanding, challenge them to some of the very things that had encouraged me on the journey, and give presentations to communicate a biblical foundation for involvement in missions. Within the circles of my own campus ministry, I found regular avenues for this type of missions emphasis. This drove me to continued study and personal dedication to the mobilization cause. I soon recognized that there were Christian students with incredible potential, mobility, and availability who were underchallenged in this area not only on my campus, but all over the country. My conviction was that each student had a vital role to play in God's global agenda.

In 1999, I created a mobilization ministry that focused on casting vision to every Christian student to help move them from ignorant to obedient. I decided also to specifically target college students because they are teachable and mobile as they pursue a growing independence. This four- to six-year period has the potential to be life-changing because it is so transitional. My aim in starting this ministry was to seize the openness of this season in students' lives and inspire them to live for something greater.

In the spirit of the Student Volunteer Movement, I launched The Traveling Team, a mobilization ministry focused on raising up college students to be World Christians. The purpose of The Traveling Team is to educate and equip college students to become World Christians who fulfill their responsibility in world evangelization. Existing campus ministries host the teams and therefore The Traveling Team is enabled to recruit to a vision rather than to an organization. It is fairly common that The Traveling Team's presentation is a college student's first exposure to this grand story or first challenge to live a World Christian lifestyle. There is power in the outside voice.

The result is transformation as hundreds of students each year contact The Traveling Team to share their story,

Hi, I was a student last year in college and heard you speak. As a result of God working through that experience, I am presently in China serving with a ministry. I am doing their one-year teaching program. Through conversations with my teammates, I discovered that 4 out of 6 of us are here as a result of The Traveling Team. Thank you. –Amber

I was a student at University of North Carolina several years ago when The Traveling Team came through with their van and two couples. They spoke at our weekly meeting that Thursday night and it was possibly one of the best meetings of the year.

What a great ministry that you have and what fertile soil you'll find in the hearts of students soon to graduate college. Your presentation and the Lord's leading helped send me over to East Asia for a year, which ended up being two years. I am actually going back overseas long-term. I think often about the clarity with which you present the biblical basis for missions.
–Graham

Louie Giglio, founder of the Passion movement, says, "The Traveling Team has been circling the U.S., challenging college students to live out of the box for the Glory of God among the nations. I cheer them on as they are one of the most strategic mobilization movements of this generation."

The Traveling Team visits approximately eighty to one hundred ministry meetings per semester to share the biblical theme of missions. Starting in Genesis with the call of Abraham (Genesis 12), the presentation moves through the Old Testament highlighting specific passages that emphasize God's heart for the world (Deuteronomy 4:5-6; Joshua 2:9-10; 1 Kings 4:34; Daniel 3:29; 6:26). The goal is to show that the story of God's redemption does not begin with Christ in the gospels but reaches all the way back to the beginning of Genesis. After highlighting the Old Testament, the New Testament is emphasized with passages such as Matthew 24:14; 28:18-20; Mark 11:15-17; 16:15; Luke 24:46-48; John 20:21; and Revelation 7:9. The presentations are high impact and the testimonies of the young adult staff team offer a fresh approach to communicating the overarching purpose of God.

At the conclusion of the presentation students are invited to meet with the staff the following day for more resources on the major world religions, the biblical basis for missions, and practical ways to pursue World Christian habits both here and overseas. Every student is walked through a transferable tool that diagrams the difference between the Christian who is seeking his or her own purpose and the Christian seeking God's. This written resource is a powerful illustration of why and how a student should focus on three areas: God's Word, God's World, and God's Work. Students are challenged to memorize Scripture, pray for the world, reach out to internationals on campus, and mobilize others using resources such as books, Bible studies, and Web-based material.

Since The Traveling Team's focus is to educate and equip students, and since our time on each campus is limited to about one day, the staff has invested much time and energy in developing a sizable website full of material. These range from articles, Bible studies, maps of the world, and missions talks.[8]

Each summer The Traveling Team hosts the I.T. Project (Intensive Training). Students are invited out to Los Angeles, California, for seven weeks, where they will be exposed to a more in-depth study of missions. The students spend the summer listening to missions speakers from all over the world as well as visiting the temples and mosques

---

[8] thetravelingteam.org

to get face-to-face with the world's major religions. Missionaries working in each of these religious groups come and equip the participants with evangelistic tools. Missions agencies to each major block also come and share with the students. Interacting with Hare Krishnas, conversing with the imam at the mosque, listening to a devotee at the Buddhist temple, meeting seasoned missionaries to the tribal world, and getting connected to peoples and opportunities abroad leave students not only incredibly impacted, but equipped with the practical information they need to follow through with their own next step! The last week of the project is designed to prepare them to go back to campus. Plans are made to implement world vision in their campus ministries and small- group studies. The student who attends the I.T. Project not only goes deeper on a personal level, but is ready to mobilize other believers to be World Christians.

The Traveling Team values going overseas and understands the imperative that more laborers must be sent out. In our globalized society, however, we would be missing the mark if our message on campus mirrored the Traveling Secretaries' in solely focusing on a challenge to go. So our ministry raises a high bar for students to give their lives overseas, but also rightly incorporates all aspects of the World Christian lifestyle in recruitment. The result is that students are equipped to be businessmen who live missionally at work, nurses who use their vacation time sacrificially overseas, churchgoers who teach God's global purpose to the junior high class, and families who reach out to their Afghan neighbor.

Ralph Winter, founder of the U.S. Center for World Mission, was a fan of The Traveling Team. He stated, "They are invading campuses with real impact. I know of no other approach that is this serious. This kind of activity was the very essence of the famous Student Volunteer Movement." The Traveling Team is convinced with John Mott that our purpose is to mediate between the students of today and the world. May God use this ministry to the degree that He used the Traveling Secretaries of old. And may the students of this generation allow God to interrupt their lives to the end that they engage in reaching the nations.

CHAPTER 14
CONVENTIONS AND CONFERENCES

I wish I had been there, but I didn't go. A friend who went to the conference said he sat among a sea of four thousand students and, with tears in his eyes, he watched as fully one thousand of them responded to a challenge to spend a year on the mission field. The image of hundreds and hundreds of students lining up to obey God convinced me of the incredible gravitational pull toward obedience that occurs when you get Christians together to focus on God. Gathering like-minded Christian peers in a worshipful environment where encouragement, challenge, and praise are the steady diet for a solid four days or more can be life-changing. It's an experience that stays with you, often serving as a pivotal point; a life landmark where big decisions were made. It's as true today as it was in the late 1800s for the Student Volunteer Movement. As God blessed the growth of the Student Volunteer Movement, the leadership felt the need to establish another key mobilization method, the *conventions*. By way of comparison, what we will see in the next few pages is that an S.V.M. convention would look almost identical to a modern-day conference, complete with an appealing location, four to five days in length, large-group sessions, big-name speakers, moving worship sets, practical workshops in between main events, and lasting change made in the hearts of participants. Though the layout is the same between the two, the content is very different. God used this particular instrument of change in the past, but He is working in a new and unique way through it today.

The S.V.M. decided to host the First International Convention in Cleveland, Ohio, in 1891 and 680 students attended. That's a lot of students for that time period, but now consider the fact that at this time, the Student Volunteer Movement was a mere four and a half years old.[1] The success and impact of this event would lead them to host conventions every four years (Quadrennials), which were very strategic for the organization. They were usually held over a weekend, beginning Thursday night with morning, afternoon, and evening sessions each day and open to any students, professors, or missions agency representatives. Even though the early Mount Hermon gatherings were for men only, the conventions were open to women as well. A listing of the conventions in the early years highlights the incredible growth that they experienced:

---

[1] John R. Mott, *Addresses and Papers of John R. Mott Volume 1: The Student Volunteer Movement for Foreign Missions* (New York: Association Press, 1946), 10-11, 34, 55, 73, 94, 121, 141, 173, 233, 247.

CONVENTIONS AND CONFERENCES

Place	Year	Attendance
Cleveland, OH	1891	680
Detroit, MI	1894	1,325
Cleveland, OH	1898	2,221
Toronto, Canada	1902	2,957
Nashville, TN	1906	4,235
Rochester, NY	1910	3,747
Kansas City, KS	1914	5,031
Des Moines, IA	1920	6,890
Indianapolis, IN	1924	6,195
Detroit, MI	1928	3,363

The 1920 Convent

These numbers are significant because the majority of those in attendance were already mobilized! The convention audience, though large, was narrow in that these students were there because they were excited about going to serve overseas. In their lives, the conventions served a purpose of *equipping* and *preparing*, not *stimulating* initial interest.

Though the conventions served the S.V.M. on other fronts—they enabled the leadership to track organizational growth and promote unity among the students—the primary purpose of the conventions was to encourage those students who were going and rally them behind the Watchword, "The evangelization of the world in this generation." Listen to the opening appeal at the 1898 convention:

> What purpose has brought us together? Surely we have not come merely for a short pleasure trip, for a few days' rest from our studies, for a railroad excursion and the delightful entertainment, which a hospitable and liberal city like this affords. Nor have we come merely to enjoy those delightful spiritual emotions, which a gathering such as this is sure to engender. I take it we have come for this clearly defined purpose—to consider the problem of the evangelization of the world, and unitedly to resolve to undertake greater things for the extension of His kingdom.[2]

The records kept from these conventions make it clear that they sought to address two areas: The needs of

---

[2] The Student Missionary Appeal: Addresses at the Third International Convention of the Student Volunteer Movement for Foreign Missions, Cleveland, Ohio, Feb. 23-27, 1898. (New York: Student Volunteer Movement for Foreign Missions, 1898), 25-26.

the world and the need to enlist more volunteers to go. All areas of instruction were incredibly applicable toward these ends.

At every convention it seems like there was no corner of the world left unmentioned. Workshop titles were simply: India, China, Africa, Japan, Turkey, and so on. The next day's workshops might be entitled: Phases of Missionary Work—Medical, Educational, or Evangelistic. Foreign missionaries came from all over the world to speak to the students. So the reports were fresh and effective in recruiting the attendees to immediate service. Rev. A. J. Gordon exhorted the students at the 1891 convention:

> I was looking over this great company this afternoon, wondering what would be the history of these young men and women. There is one thing, dear friends, that I have to say— that it does not matter what our history is if we are consecrated to the Lord Jesus Christ. That is one of the joys of missionary service, that our reward does not depend upon success. The Master does not say, "Well done, good and successful servant," but "Well done, good and faithful servant."[3]

The conventions also placed a priority on women in

---

[3] It is important to note that the opening speaker at the first convention on Feb. 26, 1891, was A. J. Gordon, pastor of Clarendon Baptist Church and the president of the American Baptist Missionary Union. His topic was *The Holy Spirit in Missions*. In 1889 he realized the need to train more missionaries and opened the Boston Missionary Training College (BMTC). This would eventually develop into Gordon Divinity School. By 1967 over 1,000 of its students would become missionaries. See John R. Mott, *Student Mission Power: Report of the First International Convention of the Student Volunteer Movement for Foreign Missions* (Pasadena, CA: William Carey Library, 1891), 7, 72. Also see Klaus Fiedler, *The Story of Faith Missions from Hudson Taylor to Present Day Africa* (Oxford: Regnum Books International, 1994), 43, 61. Also A. J. Gordon, *The Holy Spirit in Missions* (New York: Fleming H. Revell Company, 1893).

missions. The first convention held in Cleveland had no less than twelve female speakers to address the audience on various subjects! Nettie Dunn, who served as one of three on the Executive Committee of the S.V.M. (alongside John Mott and Robert Wilder) challenged the women in the audience, "Thirty years ago there were no women's missionary societies on this continent; today there are forty-three different societies in different churches, and these societies are working in all the fields of the world."[4]

> *The Master does not say, "Well done, good and successful servant," but "Well done, good and faithful servant."*

The Student Volunteer Movement raised the standard on each issue addressed and students rose to meet that standard. After the 1891 convention John Mott asked students to stand, state their university, and tell the dominant impression the convention had made upon them. Here are a few of the responses:

> "Oberlin. Go to India."
> "Syracuse University. An indefinite purpose to give my life to foreign missionary work changed to a definite purpose for that work."
> "Yale University. The immense power of prayer."

---

[4] Mott, *Student Mission Power*, 111.

"Bucknell University. I am convinced of the fact that the motto of the Volunteer Movement can be realized."

"Olivet. Have decided that I will hand in my name to the Student Volunteer Movement."[5]

Poster in Exhibit Hall

[5] Mott, *Student Mission Power*, 180.

Yes, there is an overwhelming sense of the intensity that rang forth from these gatherings! It is safe to say that missions, in its every detail, was unquestionably the drive behind every address, every workshop, and all prayer time. It was *the* reason for gathering. If, for some crazy reason, an uninterested student

Even the most missions-minded attendee would have left the convention changed.

had haphazardly signed up for the convention hoping to meet a cute girl, he'd probably end up either swallowing the deposit and heading home or boarding a boat to China. As I have researched the conventions' records, I am challenged by the authority, passion, excellence, and thoroughness by which these conventions were carried out. They even went so far as to close the 1898 convention by replacing the usual concluding gavel with the hammer used by William Carey in his shoe cobbler days, whom they called the consecrated cobbler, urging the students to "let the hammer of the Spirit of God drive in the nail of your life in its appointed place."[6] Even the most missions-minded attendee would have left the convention changed. God used these gatherings to prepare the students to go, to solidify their commitment to service, and to further educate volunteers in mobilization and the status of the world.

[6] William Carey is considered the first Protestant missionary who launched out from England to India. He sailed in 1793. For more information regarding his life see John Brown Myers, *William Carey: The Shoemaker* (Scotland: John Ritchie Publishers, 1887). See also The Student Missionary Appeal: Addresses at the Third International Convention of the Student Volunteer Movement for Foreign Missions, Cleveland, Ohio, Feb. 23-27, 1898 (New York: Student Volunteer Movement for Foreign Missions, 1898), 269.

THE NEW FACES

Today there are several college ministries that are especially strategic in tapping into the effectiveness of this method of mobilization. Though their extreme popularity among students still holds, we will see that the nature of the conferences today and of the students who attend them are far removed from the conventions of old. The topics covered spanned the gamut. It's no stretch to see a conference bulletin with titles such as, *Why the Bible Is True, Is Jesus the Only Way?, How to Study the Bible, or Five Elements of a Personal Ministry* for the workshops and main sessions. The reason that subjects range in relevance from pre-Christian to mature believer is that this is the spectrum of students who are coming. Certainly missions is one of many options to be pursued at a given conference, but by no means does missions occupy the center stage as it did at S.V.M conventions, nor should it. Each generation's emphasis seems to match the need of the day. A hundred years ago, conferences encouraged the students who were missions-minded; today they encourage the students to come to Christ, allow Him to be Lord of their life, and *sometimes* to be missions-minded. Let's just say that if an uninterested student had haphazardly signed up for a conference today hoping to meet a cute girl, he'd probably be successful! But then again, he may have his life interrupted and go home a missions-minded change agent.

As we begin now to survey a couple conferences today, let me also make clear that I am speaking generally. Certainly some gatherings prioritize missions more heavily than others. My goal is not to be exhaustive, but rather to give a broad-brushed picture of how this instrument is used by God today.

No doubt the conference with the oldest roots is Urbana. The first Urbana conference took place at the University of Toronto in Canada in 1946 when 575 students from 151 colleges gathered to study God's Word and explore God's call to world evangelization.[7] Two years after the conference in Toronto, a second conference took place on the campus of the University of Illinois in Urbana, Illinois, and from that time on the conference was simply known as Urbana. The purpose of Urbana has always been to help students find God's place for them in world missions and in so doing to serve the church by strengthening its ministry.[8] Gordon MacDonald, former president of InterVarsity, captures the experience of the conference well when he says:

> Today there are scores of men and women serving Jesus Christ in a variety of ways who first made a commitment to respond to His call at Urbana... Not a few were gripped by the biblical exposition of a plenary session speaker and left the assembly hall with a renewed appetite to understand and

---

[7] Urbana flowed out of two existent campus ministries: InterVarsity Christian Fellowship (I.V.C.F.), which began in 1929 in England, and the Student Foreign Mission Fellowship (S.F.M.F.) organized by Dr. Robertson McQuilkin in 1936. These two groups eventually merged in 1945. David Howard, *Student Power in World Evangelism* (Downers Grove, IL: InterVarsity Press, 1970), 102-103.

[8] John Kyle, *Should I Not Be Concerned? A Mission Reader* (Downers Grove, IL: InterVarsity Press, 1987), 11.

obey the Word of God. From all the continents the students come, and almost no one leaves the same.[9]

It is estimated that over 200,000 students have been challenged by this great ministry.

Another ministry that utilizes conferences is the Passion movement. In 1985 Louie Giglio began a small Bible study on the campus of Baylor University. Over a ten-year period this study grew to over 1,400 students.[10] From this, he realized the spiritual need of millions of college students around the United States and in 1995 the vision of the Passion conference was born. Gathering students from all over the nation to seek God, Giglio's desire is to ignite students in a passionate pursuit of Jesus Christ and to spread His fame to everyone on earth.[11] From its inception, the purpose that drives and directs the movement has been Isaiah 26:8, "Yes, LORD, walking in the way of your laws, we wait for you; your name and renown are the desire of our hearts."[12]

Passion attracted 40,000 students outside Memphis in 2000 and averages between 18,000-23,000 at their annual Passion conferences. It is estimated that they have reached more than 500,000 students since their beginning.[13] Giglio was influenced by Samuel Mills and the Haystack Prayer Meeting of 1806 and explains why he wants the world to be a focus at the conferences: "God may love a well for a village in Africa way more than hearing us sing 'Holy Is the

---

[9] Kyle, 7.

[10] Passion Conferences, "About the Movement." Available from 268generation.com.

[11] Passion Conferences.

[12] For a greater understanding of Louie Giglio's vision, see Louie Giglio, *I Am Not but I Know I Am* (Sisters, OR: Multnomah Publishers, 2005).

[13] Collin Hansen, "Passion Takes it Higher," *Christianity Today*, March 3, 2007. Available from ctlibrary.com.

Lord' one more time… It's the redeemed making God happy, because we're doing the thing He wants most."[14]

Though Urbana and Passion represent the largest conferences, several smaller ones take place all over the country. Campus Crusade for Christ is a campus ministry founded by Bill Bright at UCLA in 1951. This ministry is represented on over 1,000 campuses in America and beyond.[15] Every year they host as many as ten regional conferences, each attended by 300-3,000 students. Participants can be expected to be challenged by Crusade's threefold vision of *winning* students to Christ, *building* into them, and then *sending* them out.

Numerous small- to medium-sized ministries are leveraging conferences to have a huge impact. Student Mobilization, headquartered in Arkansas, takes full advantage of its conference as a way to give practical steps in walking with Christ, challenge students to have a personal ministry on campus, and unashamedly recruit for missions.

For the last one hundred years, this method of mobilization has held steady and I see no reason for it to disappear anytime soon. As our culture continues to change, we need to model our approach to conferences in a way that most effectively communicates with those in attendance. May we use this opportunity to introduce some students to missions and to take others even deeper in their resolve for missions.

---

[14] Hansen.
[15] Campus Crusade for Christ, "About Us." Available from uscm.org.

CHAPTER 15
TRAINING

Try to talk to a single guy about keeping his apartment clean, shaving, his finances, or his personal hygiene and you will probably not get much response. It's just not a felt need. But as soon as he gets in a relationship, guess what—he is knocking on your door with deodorant. So what happened? He made a decision that exposed his immense knowledge gap and therefore made him extremely teachable—and deodorized. This is exactly what happens to those who gain a heart for the world. Suddenly they see their need and understand they must get training. The Student Volunteer Movement responded to the students' teachability and interest.

As thousands of students all over the country began to catch a vision for the nations and volunteered as missionaries, it became apparent that something was needed to sustain their interest during the one- to three-year window between their initial exposure and their ability to sail overseas. Obstacles and excuses sprang up rampantly during this time and were often effective in sidelining the once enthused volunteer. In 1894, the Student Volunteer Movement sought to answer the question of how to keep the students engaged by launching the "Mission Study Department." This was a division of the S.V.M. that was responsible to create and facilitate small-group meetings on colleges, universities, and seminaries all over the United States, in order to expose students to the best available missionary literature in a classroom setting. The department called these small-group studies the Mission Study Courses. The purpose of the courses was to provide a way to keep the volunteers enlisted, but another great by-product was that those who were not yet volunteers were drawn to the classes to see what the missionary commitment entailed. At one point, even, more non-volunteers were in these small groups than volunteers themselves. These small groups provided interested students a safe environment to grow in their understanding of missions. The courses served as follow-up for volunteers and a method of mobilization for new students. The Mission Study Courses (whose attendants were three-fifths women) sought to take all students to a deeper, more comprehensive and practical understanding of missions. John Mott stated:

> There are marked advantages in connection with this mission study work. It is developing an intelligent and strong missionary interest. It is doing much to make such interest permanent. It is an invaluable help in preparing missionary candidates for their lifework. It is making the conditions favorable for the multiplying of the number of capable volunteers. It is developing

right habits of praying and giving for missions. It is promoting reality in Christian experience.[1]

Harlan Beach, the leader over the Mission Study Courses, kept meticulous records of the classes and would report them to John Mott. For example:

Date	Classes	Attendance
1894-1895	144	1,400
1895-1896	217	2,156
1896-1897	267	2,361
1901-1902	325	4,797
1905-1906	1,049	12,629
1908-1909	2,084	25,208
1918-1919	3,000	47,666[2]

The result of the Mission Study Courses was that few people left college without having had the opportunity not only to be introduced to missions, but to take their interest to the greatest level of proficiency desired. As students were gaining their degrees and becoming professionals in their area of study, they were preparing themselves for life's work in a more critical way. The leaders of the Movement were recent graduates, which enabled them to understand the plight of those who err on thinking that the sole purpose of college is to simply get trained for secular work. On the contrary, these years are most fruitful when great priority is given to the study and practice of ministry. The S.V.M.'s high

---

[1] John R. Mott, *Addresses and Papers of John R. Mott Volume 1: The Student Volunteer Movement for Foreign Missions* (New York: Association Press, 1946), 102.

[2] Mott, *Addresses and Papers,* 59, 77, 126. Also see "North American Students and World Advance," Addresses Delivered at the Eighth International Convention of the Student Volunteer Movement for Foreign Missions, Des Moines, Iowa, Dec. 31, 1919 – Jan. 4, 1920, 64.

value of this concept is seen in the fact that they published twelve books for the sole purpose of being used in the Mission Study Courses.

The stated purpose of the Mission Study Courses was fourfold. First, create among their members missionary convictions. Second, help students form the habit of independent missions study. Next, train them to pass on their vision for missions to others. Fourth, challenge students to take world evangelization seriously, understanding that it deserves their greatest efforts.[3]

Courses were normally led by those who had previously taken them and who were in a position to influence others in the missionary cause, and in this way, mobilization was served again. The students allowed to lead may have been young and still in training, but teaching actually provided the needed opportunity to mature and equip them. "It may be urged that sophomores are apt to be immature. Still, a sophomore who has taken a course and has been chosen on account of demonstrated ability in practice work, is apt to make a better leader than a senior who has never studied the textbook nor had any practice in teaching it."[4] The commitment of both teacher and participant was quite high. The size was limited to around ten to ensure unity and good discussion, and each class usually met for no less than an hour and would last a few months at a time.[5] Here we see another opportunity that the S.V.M. gave students to rise to the occasion. They set the bar high without apology and the result was exceptionally capable volunteers.

---

[3] John R. Mott, *The Pastor and Modern Missions* (New York: SVM, 1904), 82.

[4] T. H. P. Sailer, "Suggestions as to Policy in Mission Study," *The Intercollegian* 28, no. 6, Fourth Series (March 1906): 145.

[5] Mott, *The Pastor and Modern Missions,* 84.

For John Mott, it was the Mission Study Department that represented the core strategy for enlisting more recruits for the Movement and, in turn, increasing the momentum of virtually every area of the S.V.M. For example, at a conference in 1909, nineteen hundred of the 1,930 delegates who attended were involved in Mission Study Courses. If initial exposure and missionary zeal had been left to the student to cultivate themselves, the fire would have faded quickly. This Movement would not have seen such extraordinary fruit had it not been for the Mission Study Courses.

THE SAME PERSPECTIVE TODAY

Dr. Ralph Winter often used this intense statement to enlist students: "Every major decision you make will be faulty until you see the whole world as God sees it."[6] Today, the modern component to the Mission Study Course is the Perspectives on the World Christian Movement course. This Course has been around for over thirty years and has a track record of effectiveness in mobilizing and training for world evangelization. The course was created by Winter, who after the Urbana Student Convention in 1973 perceived the need for follow-up for the thousands of aspiring missionaries who were headed back to campus with few resources.

In 1980 the course received its name from Ralph Winter and the first Perspectives book was released at Urbana '81.[7] The target of the course was not ordained clergy, but university students and laypeople.[8]

---

[6] Steve Hawthorne, "Perspectives," *Mission Frontiers*, May-August 2009, 28.
[7] Originally, in the summer of 1974, Ralph Winter called on various professors to collect their teachings and provide a basic introduction to God's global purpose. He called it *Summer Institute of International Studies* (S.I.I.S.). The first course was held in Wheaton, Illinois, over a nine-week period. This would eventually become the Perspectives course.

From the beginning, college students provided the much-needed momentum that allowed the Perspectives course to prosper. Mike Jordhal, the former National Director for The Navigators' collegiate division, states:

> During my years as a Campus Director with The Navigators, we routinely used Perspectives with the students in our ministry. Today, many of those students are engaged in missions around the globe! Without a doubt, Perspectives played a huge role in helping our student friends *develop an informed worldview, a deepened passion for Christ*, and *specific plans* to do their part in taking the good news of Christ into the nations![9] (italics mine)

If initial exposure and missionary zeal had been left to the student to cultivate themselves, the fire would have faded quickly.

The Perspectives course shares many things in common with the Mission Study Courses of old, but specifically, it is a source of first-time exposure, follow-up, and deepening education. This means that a student of any interest level can be involved in the course and gain much from it.

The companion book to the Perspectives course is a collection of writings from over 150 authors that are broken

---

[8] Hawthorne, 28.
[9] Perspectives on the World Christian Movement, "What Campus Ministries Are Saying." Available from perspectives.org.

down into four main sections: the Biblical, Historical, Cultural, and Strategic perspectives of missions. The Perspectives course exposes the participants to various articles over a fifteen-week period and facilitates weekly lectures by leading missions experts. This approach, which allows for instruction to go hand in hand with interaction, has been the recipe for dynamic life change since its inception. Over 80,000 people have taken the course in numerous countries, and the Perspectives book has sold over 150,000 copies.[10]

I have seen firsthand how college students have been impacted by Perspectives. A student named Megan from University of Oklahoma took the course and she was challenged by what she learned. After completing it she launched a class in her college town. Over fifty people participated, the majority of whom were students. From Megan's class, five other classes emerged in Oklahoma over the next few years. Megan's story is not unique. Rather, she represents hundreds of other university students who have been greatly impacted by this course. Iowa, Oregon, Kansas, Arkansas, and other states have similar history with college-student pioneers.

Today, the Perspectives movement is continuing to target university students, understanding how strategic this age group is. Thousands each year will take this life-changing course. Many mobilizers, campus ministers, and missions agencies are recognizing the potential and necessity for the kind of training that the Perspectives course

---

[10] Perspectives on the World Christian Movement, "History of Perspectives." Available from perspectives.org.

provides. The Student Volunteer Movement's Mission Study Courses and the Perspectives course convince me that true, sustained intentions to impact the world for Christ are supported by the hook of training. The result is that a greater ratio of students, no matter where they are geographically, will be engaged in the World

Training is where the heart's convictions are solidified. There is no substitute.

Christian lifestyle. Follow-up is what secures a student through difficult times when excuses and distractions are rampant. It allows a student to truly ready his heart and life to be used of God. Training is where the heart's convictions are solidified. There is no substitute.

CHAPTER 16
PRAYER

I f you could ask Jesus to teach you anything, what would it be? Personally, I would want to learn how He multiplied the bread to feed the 5,000! Can you imagine? It is interesting that in all of Scripture we see only one time when the disciples asked Jesus to teach them something. Their request, "Lord, teach us to pray" (Luke 11:1). It's telling that after following Jesus for a short time, their desire was to pattern His prayer life. Of course, Jesus goes on to model prayer for them and, from that time on, prayer was considered foundational to the Church itself (Acts 2:42).[1]

John Mott states, "A missionary movement which would evangelize the world in this generation must acquire great momentum; and this can result only from more Christians giving themselves to the ministry of intercession."[2] The most enduring method that mobilizers of all generations can avail themselves to is prayer. It is the only tactic with a pure, proven track record of success. If our aim is to raise up more missionaries for the fields of the world, then prayer is indeed our God-ordained course of action. "The harvest is plentiful, but the laborers are few; therefore pray earnestly to the Lord of the harvest to send out laborers into his harvest" (Matthew 9:37-38, ESV).

---

[1] "They devoted themselves to the apostles' teaching and to the fellowship, to the breaking of bread and to prayer" (Acts 2:42).

[2] John R. Mott, *The Evangelization of the World in This Generation* (New York: S.V.M., 1900), 208.

When the Student Volunteer Movement was experiencing colossal results as thousands of students lined up to enlist themselves to serve overseas, curiosity grew as to the source of its great success. From the top down the unanimous answer was prayer. Everyone involved credited prayer not only for the Movement's birth, but also for its sustaining influence. John Mott couldn't have stated more clearly, "The Student Volunteer Movement owes everything to prayer. It was conceived in days and nights of prayer at Mount Hermon. The missionary enthusiasm which it called forth all over the student field had its springs in prayer."[3]

In a prayer meeting the idea for conventions arose. The use of a Volunteer Declaration was adopted in a prayer meeting. The necessary funds for the Movement were raised in answer to prayer. The volunteers were sustained by prayer. If more volunteers were needed, the emphasis was not on recruiting more Traveling Secretaries, but on prayer. "Thus prayer—definite, fervent, importunate—has marked every important step in the development of the Movement from its origin down to the opening of the wonderful doors of opportunity of the present college year."[4] In fact, they considered the opposite to be true as well; all failure was attributed to a lack of prayer.

The S.V.M. challenged students, "How many laborers have you and I thrust out by our prayers? How often have we obeyed our Lord, and prayed that prayer in earnest? Are we obeying Him in asking Him that the laborers may go forth

[3] John R. Mott, *Addresses and Papers of John R. Mott Volume 1: The Student Volunteer Movement for Foreign Missions* (New York: Association Press, 1946), 358.
[4] Mott, *Addresses and Papers*, 358.

and that the Kingdom may come?"[5] Failure to pray meant failure in your undertakings:

> If the work of missions were purely a human enterprise, this neglect might be intelligible. But in a supernatural cause, resting on a supernatural charter, led on by an omnipotent Leader, with all His supernatural power pledged to its support on the conditions of consecration and prayer on the part of its human agents, a neglect of prayer is a denial of the Lord's leadership and a willful limitation of success.[6]

Failure to pray meant failure in your undertakings.

Each volunteer was encouraged to cultivate what was called the Morning Watch. This meant that upon waking every morning, the word and prayer were given first priority. John Mott encouraged students:

> Give prayer a large place in the Morning Watch. There needs to be prayer not only at the beginning and close of the hour, but the Bible study, meditation, and self-examination also should be conducted in the spirit of prayer... Only by filling the quiet hour with prayer can we keep out formalism and make the Morning Watch a great reality and force in our lives.[7]

---

[5] The Students and the Modern Missionary Crusade, Addresses Delivered before the Fifth International Convention of the Student Volunteer Movement for Foreign Missions, Nashville, Tennessee, Feb. 28-March 4, 1906, 31.

[6] Robert Speer, *Missionary Principles and Practice: A Discussion of Christian Missions and of Some Criticisms upon Them* (London: Fleming H. Revell Company, 1902), 467.

[7] The Student Missionary Appeal: Addresses at the Third International Convention of the Student Volunteer Movement for Foreign Missions, Cleveland, Ohio, Feb. 23-27, 1898 (New York: Student Volunteer Movement for Foreign Missions, 1898), 236.

The S.V.M. valued prayer resources that could aid the students in their endeavor. The leadership of the Movement asked all volunteers to read two resources specifically. One was a small pamphlet called *Prayer and Missions* by Robert Speer as well as the book *With Christ in the School of Prayer* by Andrew Murray. Another tool to help the volunteers to pray was called the *Cycle of Prayer of the Student Volunteer Movement*. This was developed for those who wanted to pray for worldwide missions. The S.V.M. provided these materials because they understood the preeminent place that prayer should be given and they sought to develop a rich love and habit of prayer. They had immense impact in solidifying and empowering the volunteers' own prayer lives as they incorporated them into their personal Morning Watch time.

Prayer and missions are as inseparable as faith and works; in fact prayer and missions are faith and works.

Missionary pioneers such as Paul the apostle, Nicholas Zinzendorf, William Carey, and Hudson Taylor all gave themselves to prayer and the volunteers modeled that. John Mott drives home the role of prayer for the Student Volunteer Movement:

Prayer and missions are as inseparable as faith and works; in fact prayer and missions are faith and works. Jesus Christ, by precept, by command, and by example, has shown with great clearness and force that he recognizes the greatest need of the enterprise of worldwide evangelization to be prayer. Before "give" and before "go" comes "pray." This is the divine order. Anything that reverses or alters it inevitably leads to loss or disaster.[8]

A list of sailed volunteers

PRACTICAL PRAYING

The average Christian today prays for two minutes a day while the average full-time minister prays for an average of three! When we consider the potential missionary force that this student generation represents, we ought to be encouraged to give greater priority to that which Jesus defined as *the* method for mobilization. What I like about the passage in Matthew 9:37-38 is that Jesus, in essence, says if

---

[8] The Report of the Toronto Convention 1902: Missionary Campaign Library No. 1, Toronto, Feb. 26-March 2, 1902. (Chicago: Student Missionary Campaign Library, 1902), 241.

you want to see people go, ask God about it. He cares about the lost. What it does not say is, if you want to see people go, host a huge conference; make a missions T-shirt; or yell more when you're preaching about it. I sense an eagerness to *do* something; and prayer doesn't always feel like we're doing anything. The unseen nature of prayer makes it a bit uncomfortable for many people. James Fraser, a missionary to China in the early 20th century, once said, "I used to think that prayer should have the first place and teaching the second. I now feel it would be truer to give prayer the first, second, and third places and teaching the fourth." I find it easy to identify with Fraser's initial sentiments; teaching is concrete, tangible, it's doing something. And yet God delights so in prayer's secrecy because then He receives more glory. We would do well in our generation to emulate the Student Volunteer Movement's constant emphasis and dependence on prayer. There is no excuse. We have been blessed with incredible resources to do so. The following are only two of the most useful guides to assist our efforts.

The Joshua Project is a Web-based research initiative that highlights unreached people groups of the world.[9] Anyone with access to the Internet is able to learn basic statistics and information on any unreached people group. One can survey based on country, people group, language, or religion. For example, the profile for Afghanistan reveals that there are seventy-six people groups representing 28.8 million people. From there one can click on any of the people groups and learn where they are located, percentage of the

---

[9] joshuaproject.net.

population that is Christian, and the progress scale which charts church-planting efforts among that particular people. The site is filled with presentations on the world, maps, photos, and informative articles that can be downloaded and utilized for prayer and mobilization. What a great tool! I know a worship leader who after a few songs shares information about an unreached people group from this site and asks the congregation to pray for them. Entering into that which is so close to the heart of God is such an addition to both personal and corporate worship.

One of the greatest resources for prayer is the book *Operation World*.[10] This tool guides the reader to pray for every country in the world utilizing its easy-to-follow calendar that allots various days for each country. *Operation World* presents important divisions of each country: people groups, languages, percentage of languages with Scripture, percentage of Christians, and statistics on missionaries present and missionaries sent. Several prayer points are listed with each country. The first *Operation World* was released in 1974 and since then has been translated into 14 languages and has sold over 2 million copies. The desired use of *Operation World* is twofold: prayer and mobilization. The statistics and requests are meant to enable the church to pray knowledgeably and specifically as well as to inform the church of facts about people groups. The originator of *Operation World*, Patrick Johnstone, states:

---

[10] Patrick Johnstone and Jason Mandryk, *Operation World*, 6th ed. (Waynesboro, GA: Authentic Media, 2006). See also operationworld.org.

The ministry of the children of God is not doing but praying, not strategizing, but prostrate before God seeking His will, not clever stratagems for manipulating people and events, but trusting in God who moves in the ears of even His most implacable enemies. Through prayer Nebuchadnezzar, and today's dictators get converted, Manasseh and today's persecutors repent and kingdoms of Babylon and Iron Curtains are torn down. We do not engage in ministry and pray for God's blessing on it, prayer *is* the ministry from which all other ministries must flow.[11]

We have the time, we have the resources, all we have to do now is to pray and watch God move.

When I look back on what God did through the Student Volunteer Movement, I picture a flood line. In real estate, a common gauge for the appeal of a piece of property is its 100-year flood line. For insurance purposes, a flood line is basically a measurement that predicts that in 100 years, there is only a one percent chance that any flood will exceed the line. When waters do rise above the mark it is considered an extreme anomaly. Perhaps we would pray larger prayers if we had a gauge of the spiritual flood line in history. At the height of the Student Volunteer Movement, one out of every thirty-seven students in the U.S. were recruited to be involved in missions in their generation—what a precedent; what a flood line! In a hundred years, the likelihood of a move like that ever occurring naturally must be less than one percent. Prayer is the force behind the fact

---

[11] Johnstone and Mandryk, xiii.

that this Movement not only exceeded what would naturally be possible, it blew everyone's expectations out of the water! What greater proof could we seek for the truth that God is "able to do far more abundantly than all that we ask or think, according to the power that works within us" (Ephesians 3:20, ESV). I began this book with a verse, "Elijah was a man with a nature like ours" (James 5:17, ESV). It's a comforting thought: we are all on a level playing field; all of us bound by the limitations of human nature. Elijah was human, Robert Wilder and John Mott were human; we are all flawed humans. But the verse goes on to say, "And he prayed fervently that it might not rain, and it did not rain on the earth." In our own limited nature we are not capable of producing the kind of results that will impact the world, but I truly believe that if this generation would ask God on behalf of the nations, we would see a demonstration of His regenerating power such as has not been paralleled in history. Andrew Murray says, "The person who mobilizes the church to pray will make the largest contribution in history to world evangelization."

Let it be this generation, Lord.

CHAPTER 17
SHORT-TERM TRIPS

Last week I flew to Germany to speak over the weekend. I was a little disappointed when my flight home through London got delayed. It meant I would get home two hours late and not make it for dinner. While sitting in the airport, starting to feel sorry for myself, I realized something—I probably wouldn't have survived if I'd lived in pioneer days, let's be honest. In 1793, William Carey, the father of modern missions, left England on a voyage from London to India that took five months.[1] Today we call that "long-term." Five months! If the average mission trip is six weeks, that would have put Carey about 400 yards off shore. In the time it takes us to get there, build a house, and get home, Carey could still have been waving good-bye and could easily have gone back for his wife's purse! Today, that same trip from London to India takes a mere nine hours.

This method of mobilization—the short-term mission trip—so prominent and so familiar in our own day, was simply not possible in the Student Volunteer Movement's day. Crossing an ocean today is no big deal, and this obviously has huge

---

[1] John Brown Myers, *William Carey: The Shoemaker* (Scotland: John Ritchie Publishers, 1887), 37.

advantages in quickly exposing students to the world. For these reasons, short-term mission trips have become a primary method in mobilizing students to world evangelization.

Over the past five decades the short-term missions movement has exploded. In light of how widespread and how diverse the involved groups are, it is impossible to finalize an exact number, but research approximates between one and four million short-term missionaries go out from North America each year.[2]

MAXIMIZING MOTIVATIONS

The next time you get a chance to talk to someone fresh off a short-term mission trip, ask them why they went. After a handful of people, you will realize the list of motivations is long. There are as many motivators as there are personalities and interests.

God commands it: For some students, biblical evidence of God's desire to reach the nations is all the argument they need to sign up and cross a culture to reach people for Christ.

Adventure: Brochures with college students riding camels across the Sahara Desert and trading goats with nomadic Muslims are eye-catching, depicting something most

---

[2] There are three types of short-term sending entities: churches, missions agencies, and schools. It is estimated that 10 percent of U.S. churches are doing short-term missions, which means around 35,000 churches are involved. If you approximate low and assume only twelve people per church are going short-term every year, that means you have 420,000 people. If you approximate high at 40 per church, you have 1.4 million in the church category. The second sending arm is the missions agency. It is estimated that U.S.-based missions agencies send 106,000 people annually on short-term missions. Finally, Christian high schools and colleges are a major sending entity. Between them, they are launching out thousands of students every year. Together, all three groups—the church, agency, and schools—account for between 1 and 4 million. Roger Peterson, Gordon Aeschliman, and R. Wayne Sneed, *Maximum Impact Short-Term Mission* (Minneapolis, MN: STEMPress, 2003), 243, 252- 253.

people never experience. I know of trips where students can bike the ancient Silk Road and share Christ in East Asia. Canoe excursions through the jungle to befriend remote tribesmen entice many young people, and so this is the way they are advertised. The more extreme the trip sounds, the more appealing it is to students.

Changed life: Over three-quarters of trip-goers report that the short-term experience altered their life in some way.[3] Those who have been on a short-term trip understand the life-changing event that it can be.

Making an impact: For some, it means deploying a quick-response team for tsunami victims, and for others it may mean passing out tracts in a Guatemalan village. Whatever the case may be, helping others is an enormous incentive for participating in short-term trips.

Compassion: Some are ready to sign on for a cause, especially one that brings aid to another in need. Their eagerness to meet practical needs is a wonderful, Christlike thing that is in no way opposed to the aims of short-term missions and should be channeled in a missional direction.

These all appeal to certain personality traits of this generation. On the whole, students are looking for a challenge—something to rise up to. It's almost as if they are begging, "Just give me something big enough to give my whole self to!" This is a generation of risk takers. If we can attach some purpose and meaning to those risks—it's almost irresistible.

---

[3] The Barna Group, "Despite Benefits, Few Americans Have Experienced Short-Term Mission Trips," Oct. 6, 2008. Available from barna.org.

BLESSINGS AFTER THE FACT

I know a guy who took a short-term trip to Senegal. He is now a high-school math teacher in Seattle. He never went back overseas after that summer trip, but he is different. He prays for the world; if he hears any news about that part of Africa, he listens a little more closely. If he meets someone from anywhere in West Africa, he strikes up a conversation. Students who are involved in short-term missions are impacted and benefited by the experience. There are several pros to short-term mission trips.

This is a generation of risk takers. If we can attach some purpose and meaning to those risks—it's almost irresistible.

Consider long-term: By giving them a look into the roles and responsibilities involved in short-term missions, students are encouraged to consider long-term missions. A four-year commitment to East Asia is more easily made under the persuasion of firsthand experience. A short-term mission trip is the door through which most long-termers will need to walk.

Informed: In relation to this, it helps students considering long-term involvement to know the right questions to ask. What training should I pursue? Where do I want to serve? What agency do I want to join? These questions can be answered more thoroughly after on-site exposure.

Peek into poverty: Short-term missions provide a healthy dose of reality for students today who have access to all the latest technology. They see their wealth against the backdrop of the rest of the world.

Life perspective: Short-term mission trips provide that needed incentive for students to change their lifestyles back home. Many come back and, altered by a newfound global paradigm, they desire all the more to alleviate their debt, raise the standard of their dating life, and fervently pursue the spiritual disciplines.

Personal ministry: Lastly, the short-term trip can generate incredible momentum for the student's ministry back on campus. Most likely there will be new understanding of reaching out to internationals, a fresh zeal for recruiting others to go, and a renewed energy for prayer and evangelism.

HYPOCRITE ON A TRIP?

There is a flip side. Short-term missions as a tool for long-term mobilization have received much criticism of late, and a lot of it is valid.[4] There are four major arguments against short-term missions that must be mentioned.

Stewardship: Approximately two billion dollars each year is spent for short-term missions. This means

---

[4] For more on the topic of the problems with short-term missions see Robert Priest and Kurt Ver Beek, "Are Short-Term Missions Good Stewardship?," *Christianity Today*, July 2005. Available from christianitytoday.com. See also Glenn Schwartz, "Two Awesome Problems: How Short-Term Missions Can Go Wrong," *International Journal of Frontier Missions* 20:4 (Winter 2003); Wes Widner, "Short-Term Mission Trips: Sanctified Vacations?," available from reasontostand.org; and Jim Lo, "Concerns Regarding Short-Term Missions," available from drurywriting.com.

that we as the American Church are spending as much on short-term trips as we are on supporting long-term missionaries.[5] A plane ticket to Africa, housing, food, and transportation can cost thousands of dollars. Imagine a team of twenty! This financial excess causes many to wonder if short-term trips are the best way to go about mobilization. David Maclure writes, "In passing quickly through a foreign culture on a short-term trip and returning two weeks later with photos to boot, the young short-termer can be left with a sense that his/her excursion abroad felt much like a package holiday."[6]

Self-focused: Most short-term mission trips focus predominantly on the benefit to those going rather than on the receiving country. Those trips that are between ten days and three months provide hardly enough time to really see significant ministry happen. The critique is that since the goal is changing this participant's life, the ministry is inherently self-centered. Jim Lo, in his article entitled *Concerns Regarding Short-Term Missions,* states, "Self-centered team members often times do not care if they destroy culture with their ethnocentric ways or insult nationals with their snide comments, since the aim is focused on what their own needs are."[7]

Unrealistic experience: Short-term participants do not get a real understanding of what life on the field is like because they leave so soon. They never leave the romance stage of first-time experience. As a result, even the most drudging activity is not clearly processed for what it is because it is executed with a camera in hand and is mentally

---

[5] Dana Bromley, ed., Mission Maker Magazine (Minneapolis, MN: STEM Press, 2009), 19.
[6] David Maclure, "Wholly Available? Missionary Motivation Where Consumer Choice Reigns," *Evangel* 20, no. 3 (Autumn 2002): 3.
[7] Lo, "Concerns Regarding Short-Term Missions."

filtered through a framework of what a great story it will make back home at church. I can remember being in China and eating three scorpions—my first two pictures were fuzzy!

Low return: In the midst of the short-term missions boom, long-term missionaries have been on the decline. In 1990 there were approximately 55,000 long-term missionaries from the United States. By 2006 that number had dropped to 35,000.[8] It would seem from this statistic that, while many justify short-term missions by calling it a tool to boost long-term commitment, actually, it has become an end in itself for many.

Short-term mission trips have their issues, to be sure, and have received their fair share of bad press. But we must remember that "if criticisms alone are enough reason to abandon the entire movement, then let's be consistent. Let's also abandon all career missions and support of nationals, because we're not short on criticism and bad behavior in those expressions of global missions either."[9] One thing seems definite: short-term missions is here to stay. If the terrorist attacks on September 11, 2001, did not slow this movement down, not much will. So we might as well focus on utilizing the short-term movement with cultural intelligence and sensitivity toward the receiving people group.

RETURNING TO REALITY

One of the greatest contributors to the life change that occurs through short-term trips takes place in intentional

---

[8] These statistics come from Bill Stearns (author of *Run with the Vision*), Patrick Johnstone (author of *Operation World*), and Steve Shadrach (U.S. Center for World Mission, Mobilization Division). Specific data cannot be found in any document; however, the essence of the data has been confirmed across the board.

[9] David A. Livermore, *Serving with Eyes Wide Open: Doing Short-Term Missions with Cultural Intelligence* (Grand Rapids, MI: Baker Book House, 2006), 110.

debriefing. In order to fully capitalize on this we need to proactively prepare short-termers to live more effectively back home. Amazingly, even when a group experiences a terrible trip, good follow-up has the potential to overcome any unmet expectations and send the group home with a vision to mobilize others. Sarah took a short-term trip to Uzbekistan. Not only was she on a terrible team, but it seemed like everything went wrong *all summer*! She had an emotional breakdown in the airport trying to get out of the country. Bottom line, she was miserable the entire summer. But she is actually back overseas long-term. Her debriefing helped her understand and appropriate the big picture of her short-term trip.

In order for follow-up to be effective, participants must be confronted with the question, *"How will this short-term mission trip alter my long-term vision for my life?"* This puts the trip in perspective as one in a myriad of experiences that God is using to redeem both the team members and the people of the world that they just encountered, not just a box to be checked off in one's spiritual pilgrimage. The students also need to be informed of the many other methods that God uses in order to cultivate their vision for the world. Engaging them with this mentality during debriefing is often where lifestyle changes are cemented, where an event mentality matures into consistency.[10]

---

[10] It is beyond the scope of this book to discuss ways of creating short-term trips with greater impact. For this topic see Livermore, *Serving with Eyes Wide Open*. Also Roger Peterson, Gordon Aeschliman, and R. Wayne Sneed, *Maximum Impact Short-Term Mission* (Minneapolis, MN: STEMPress, 2003); Duane Elmer, *Cross-Cultural Servanthood: Serving the World in Christlike Humility* (Downers Grove, IL: InterVarsity Press, 2006); Richard Tiplady, *World of Difference: Global Mission at the Pic-n-Mix Counter* (Waynesboro, GA: Paternoster Press, 2003); and H. Leon Greene, *A Guide to Short-Term Missions: A Comprehensive Manual for Planning an Effective Mission Trip* (Waynesboro, GA: Gabriel Publishing, 2003).

More laborers are an element of reaching the world that cannot be compromised.

The short-term missions boom is indeed a phenomenon, for better or for worse. It is enabled by our technological advances in travel and global networking and, as our culture grows only more advanced, I wouldn't expect this movement to be ending any time soon. As a mobilizer, I can sincerely affirm the remarkable addition short-term trips are to the World Christian panorama. Of course my desire is to see more people committing to long-term overseas work. It's necessary. More laborers are an element of reaching the world that cannot be compromised. No increase in the other World Christian habits of giving, reaching internationals, praying, or mobilizing could provide a substitute for going. That being said, the student who agrees to go short-term and, at the end of his summer, senses God's leading in a direction other than long-term work will still likely manifest a greater orientation to World Christianity for the rest of his or her life. It is still a huge win in my mind. I say let's keep sending students short-term, as many as will go! And may God finish His own good work in their hearts. Some will go back long-term; some will stay at home and live significantly different lives. In both cases, the nations will be impacted and the kingdom will be furthered.

ISSUES
THEN AND NOW

"He that is good for making excuses is seldom good for anything else."

— Benjamin Franklin

CHAPTER 18
FAMILY, FRIENDS, AND FIANCEES

Starting The Traveling Team ministry was one of the most rewarding things I have ever done. We got into a minivan and basically did not get out for seven years, traveling to state after state, campus after campus. During that time I heard some tough questions from students. Are those who have never heard the gospel really going to hell? What about the needs here? How do I raise support? My parents say I can't. Excuses arose every semester, on every campus, from almost every student. At times these were an obvious smoke screen—a lame attempt by the college student to justify lack of involvement which was really rooted in disinterest and apathy. At times they were valid struggles. In the last decade I have identified eight hurdles that seem to always rise to the surface as the predominant issues out of all the others. And once again, I found the Student Volunteer Movement to be a reliable guide to look back to for wisdom.

Robert Wilder, who sat down with thousands of students, says,

What is a valid excuse? This must be settled by each volunteer with God. But if after prayer he be convinced of his unfitness to go, he owes it to himself and to the Student Volunteer Movement for Foreign Missions that this unfitness be demonstrated; otherwise, he will be regarded as one who, "having put his hand to the plough," has looked back.[1]

Every volunteer worthy of a place on the foreign field has had obstacles in his path. In surmounting them, motives have been purified, faith has been disciplined and strengthened, men have been led to look beyond themselves to God, unworthy candidates have been kept out of the field, the fittest have survived and pressed to the front. The missionary enterprise does not want and does not need men who can be deflected from their purpose.[2]

Let's take a look at the few most common issues dealt with in history and in our own generation.

THOSE WHO LOVE US MOST

The opposition students felt from family and friends was the primary issue that paralyzed them when presented with missions. The S.V.M. knew all too well the gravitational pull that the family had on a new recruit; even John Mott's own parents tried to hold him back from going into the ministry. Mott was very aware of and sympathetic to the weight of influence that parents brought to bear on the

---

[1] John R. Mott, *Student Mission Power: Report of the First International Convention of the Student Volunteer Movement for Foreign Missions* (Pasadena, CA: William Carey Library, 1891), 33.

[2] "North American Students and World Advance," Addresses Delivered at the Eighth International Convention of the Student Volunteer Movement for Foreign Missions, Des Moines, Iowa, Dec. 31, 1919 – Jan. 4, 1920, 63.

decision-making process of their child, even as that student sought to follow God's will. He considered the family to be the principal obstacle standing in the way of the student's obedience.

> The opposition of parents and relatives prevents many a qualified young man or young woman from becoming a missionary. It is the testimony of the officers of the Volunteer Movement, based on the thousands of interviews with students by their Traveling Secretaries, that this has been the principal obstacle which prevents hundreds of students [from] volunteering.[3]

When encountering the obstacle of family and friends the S.V.M. constantly pointed back to the words of Jesus directed right at the heart of this issue—the proper place of loved ones on the list of loyalties: "Anyone who loves his father or mother more than me is not worthy of me; anyone who loves his son or daughter more than me is not worthy of me" (Matthew 10:37). Yet many students struggled to balance this teaching with another very difficult passage, "Children, obey your parents in the Lord, for this is right" (Ephesians 6:1). Robert Wilder suggests:

> The most serious peril under this head is that presented by home ties. The winds of opposition from father and mother have changed the course of many a man who has weathered other gales of fierce opposition. You say, are we not told,

---

[3] John R. Mott, *The Pastor and Modern Missions* (New York: SVM, 1904), 162.

"Children obey your parents?" Yes, but complete the verse; it reads, "obey your parents in the Lord." Are we obeying them in the Lord if they interfere with our doing the Lord's work? How did Christ deal with this subject? (Matt. 10:35-38; Matt. 12:46-50).[4]

Wilder, rather tongue-in-cheek, toyed with the audience at the 1898 convention and spoke of the ridiculous notion of skirting the problem of parents by targeting only orphans:

Possibly some of us feel we cannot leave friends and home. Think what Christ left for us!

Possibly some of us feel we cannot leave friends and home. Think what Christ left for us! I remember when we went through the colleges a few years ago nearly every man and woman we met told us that he or she had parents. Mr. Forman and I came to the conclusion that there were not enough orphans in the United States and Canada to evangelize the world. One day we came across a genuine orphan. We congratulated ourselves, and I shall never forget the eagerness with which we went to him, and our disappointment when he told us that there was someone in whom he was interested and therefore he could not go! If we seek for excuses to stay at home we can find plenty of them.[5]

---

[4] Mott, *Student Mission Power*, 167.

[5] The Student Missionary Appeal: Addresses at the Third International Convention of the Student Volunteer Movement for Foreign Missions, Cleveland, Ohio, Feb. 23-27, 1898 (New York: Student Volunteer Movement for Foreign Missions, 1898), 245.

The parents' complaint against their child's involvement in missions was that they had worked so hard to send their son or daughter off to college. Their opportunities for success upon completion were significantly greater than their own! The family perceived this as a squandered life, one that is thrown away in flippant disregard for the love, support, and sacrifice of so many in exchange for wasted efforts in a foreign land. Students were forced to choose between their earthly father and his faithful, physical support and their heavenly Father and the work He had entrusted to them.

> "If God permit," not if my parents permit. There are very few of us whose parents do permit; they rather must submit. I was talking to a young man less than a week ago, and he said, "The moment that I speak of going as a foreign missionary it seems to me that a thousand chords are pulling me back... my parents begin to plead with me; my friends begin to plead with me." It is not if man permit; it is if God permit.[6]

There were two primary ways in which the S.V.M. encouraged students to overcome the obstacles of friends and family. The first was to enlist the help of their pastor. Pastors could individually counsel the family and preach from the pulpit that missions was a viable option for students. John Mott even challenged pastors specifically to come to the students' aid: "Seek to influence parents through sermons and through personal conversation to be willing to facilitate

---

[6] Mott, *Student Mission Power*, 167.

their children devoting themselves to the service of Christ either at home or abroad."[7]

Second, the S.V.M. communicated that ultimately this was not their parents' decision, but it was a personal decision to follow the will of the Lord. Their encouragement was that as the student followed God to the field, God would deal with their parents at home.

> If God says "go," no home tie is strong enough to be valid. Should I not consult with my parents? (Gal. 1:15-17). Let God, not your parents, settle this question. You should pray for them and give them the facts. If consecrated they will in time feel the force of Christ's command as do you, and will bid you "God speed" in the work. If you are an only child with aged parents you are exempt. But if there are other children in the family, you are under no more obligation than they to support parents.[8]

Fiancées also had a track record for derailing would-be missionaries. Many students were in relationships when they signed the Volunteer Declaration, thereby committing to overseas missions. The student was counseled to break off the relationship immediately when their girlfriend or boyfriend was discovered to be uninterested in missionary work. This counsel came as a direct response to the fact that some women had intentionally deceived their fiancés by confessing their willingness to go. It was only after the marriage ceremony that they revealed and insisted upon

---

[7] Mott, *The Pastor and Modern Missions*, 167.
[8] Mott, *Student Mission Power*, 167.

their true desire—to live in close proximity to family. So, Robert Wilder would counsel engaged students to write a letter to their fiancée filled with the harsh reality of the field. He even went so far as to help them construct it:

> May this be the year in which you will take final leave of your relatives and native land, in which you will cross the wide ocean and dwell on the other side of the world among heathen people. We shall no more see our kind friends around us or enjoy conveniences of civilized life... the jargon of an unknown tongue will assail our ears. We shall see many dreary, disconsolate hours, and feel a sinking of spirits, anguish of mind, of which now we can form little conception.[9]

It was hoped the reality of his intended direction to go would sink in deep and her true character would surface. Wilder said, "Strong language, you say. Yes, write such a letter to your fiancée. If she be thoroughly consecrated, it will nerve her to new consecration. If she is unwilling to go, find out the fact as soon as possible, leave her, and thank God for your escape from a union which would defeat His plans."[10]

HONORING PARENTS

With all the advances that globalization and modernization offer, this generation varies only slightly on this issue. We have, for example, the advantage of going short-term.

---

[9] Mott, *Student Mission Power*, 168.
[10] Mott, *Student Mission Power*, 168.

When students present the idea of "going" to their parents, it is most often a short-term trip. This was not the case for the students that Robert Wilder was sitting across the table from. When that student decided to go, he had to face his mom, dad, and fiancée with an ultimatum.

We have another advantage on our side that was not available to the students in the S.V.M.'s day—loved ones can easily come and visit their child who has committed several years to the field. In a matter of hours, a student's parents can board a plane and be by their child's side, setting fears and curiosities to rest. One would think that these advances would alter today's state of affairs concerning parents, but they really haven't. Parents still present a major obstacle for students who desire to go overseas.

> When those in the emerging generation tell their parents that they want to go on a summer cross-cultural trip, a large percentage are not supported and are actually told that they cannot be involved. Surprisingly, it is not only unbelieving parents who respond in this way, but also Christian parents. If this is the response when faced with a short-term summer trip, imagine if these students told their parents that they wanted to [go] long-term.[11]

When I was a freshman in college I approached my parents about going on a summer project to learn practical ministry skills for college. They said no. I even explained to

---

[11] Ryan Shaw, *Waking the Giant: The Resurging Student Mission Movement* (Pasadena, CA: William Carey Library, 2006), 143.

them that this summer project was in Florida; I'd live in a condo on the beach. They still said no. I told them they could come and visit and I would call them once a week. Still no.

One student expressed in frustration, "You see, my parents only gave me three options. I could become a doctor, an engineer, or a businesswoman as long as I was a highly successful one. You talk about offering my career options to God. Well, I can't. I can only offer one of these three to my parents."[12] The possibility that Christian parents are the number one hindrance to world evangelization is truer than we would like to admit.

Parents are not always out of line in questioning their child's desire to go. They have watched their son or daughter make a string of bad decisions growing up—dating and breaking up with all the wrong people, speeding tickets, poor choice of friends and use of money, even changing majors two to three times; the list goes on. Then their child calls from college about the summer trip to Sudan they are considering! Mom and Dad assume this is just another bad idea. A few months before I asked my parents to go to the summer project in Florida, I had taken a 1,500-mile road trip with my fraternity brothers. The problem was that I wasn't exactly truthful about it. And I'd taken their car. Let's just say I wasn't in the greatest standing when I presented my grand condo-on-the-beach idea.

It has been my experience that there are two types of parents who resist their child's participation in a mission

---

[12] Jeanette Yep, ed., *Following Jesus Without Dishonoring Your Parents* (Downers Grove, IL: InterVarsity Press, 1998), 24.

trip—those who mean it and those who don't. There are some parents who say, "If you go on this mission trip don't bother coming home ever again and don't plan on us paying for your car and for college when you get back." In this case, it is advisable that the student wait until their parents are a little more softened to the idea. No matter how much information this type of parent receives or with how much maturity the student handles

The possibility that Christian parents are the number one hindrance to world evangelization is truer than we would like to admit.

this situation, these parents usually remain hostile to the idea. Students should honor the desires of their parents while under their authority. For the American culture it seems that authority and financial independence are linked so that the college student who is still dependent on their parents for funding is still in a position of submission.

The other type of parent says no initially, but gradually concedes as they see that their son or daughter is committed to going on the trip. The difference with this parent is that as they are informed, see their child taking responsible steps toward the trip and growing increasingly interested, they gain confidence in their son or daughter's decision and will eventually give their blessing. Most parents fall into this category. I sat down with my parents and showed them a video on the summer. I asked them to pray with me about it; they said maybe. I showed them my list of potential supporters. Eventually, they gave me their blessing to go!

There are two commands in Scripture that God desires us to keep in balance, and we must be careful not to be extreme and one-sided. The tension is between Exodus 20:12, "Honor your father and your mother," and Luke 14:26, "If anyone comes to me and does not hate his father and mother, his wife and children, his brothers and sisters—yes, even his own life—he cannot be my disciple." How do these two passages co-exist? The way to biblically heed both of these commands simultaneously is to listen to parents' advice, speak with them in an honorable way, but still follow God's will over our parents' will when the two are in contradiction. The late musician Keith Green said:

> **It is true that God wants us to honor our parents and love our friends, but He also made it clear in His Word that this honor and love must not exceed our love and obedience to Him and His call on our lives. We should always try our best to explain God's call to our families, lovingly and patiently, but the bottom line must be that we will obey Christ no matter what the cost (Mark 10:29).[13]**

Generally, the cultural transition point from submission to independence happens at college graduation.

---

[13] Keith Green, *Why You Should Go to the Mission Field.* WiseTracts from Last Days Ministries (Lindale, TX: Pretty Good Printing, 1982), 3.

Usually at this time a person is viewed as "on their own." It's rare to hear a 28-year-old saying, "I would go overseas, but my parents won't let me." By then they are making their own decisions. On one end of the spectrum are the high-school years when a student is most definitely under authority, and the other side would be post-college years and beyond, when one has transitioned to total independence. It is specifically the college years that represent a gray area on the authority/submission continuum. Each family will handle this rite of passage differently and at varying speeds. Therefore, this ground should be tread with sensitivity.

THE OTHER SIDE OF THE TABLE

The key is genuinely trying to understand this situation from a parent's perspective, namely that it is hard for them to let their son or daughter go into a potentially dangerous, seemingly irresponsible, and certainly expensive situation with their full consent! It is important that students respectfully discern God's path for them, spending much time before the Lord and seeking much counsel.[14] Campus Crusade for Christ put together a brochure to help students with a few practical steps to take when God says go but parents say no.

Reflect on the way you've represented your great ideas before. You've sounded certain about so many other things that you are no longer very interested in. Ask them to pray with

---

[14] For further study see the National Network of Parents of Missionaries available at pomnet.org. Also see Diane Stortz and Cheryl Savageau, *Parents of Missionaries: How to Thrive and Stay Connected When Your Children and Grandchildren Serve Cross-Culturally* (Colorado Springs, CO: Authentic Publishing, 2008).

you for several months about your plans. If your parents are Christians, say to them, "Can we both seek the guidance of God during the next six months?" Ask them why they feel as they do. And listen carefully! They may be right!... Let them know you haven't just dismissed their objections. Seek counsel from an older Christian who knows your family. The point may come when you must go in the face of parental opposition.[15]

There is nothing like the love parents have for their child. Throughout a child's life parents try their best to guide, nurture, and provide for them. They have big dreams of their child going on to do great things—medicine, law, engineering. Whatever they have imagined for the future, the majority of parents have no place in their paradigm for their child working among a people group in a war-torn country. This is also true for dedicated Christian parents. Most hope their son or daughter is obedient to the Lord, joins a church, plugs into a Bible study, meets and marries a godly person, and eventually moves back home to work. Then the dreaded phone call comes to the parent. Not that their child was in a car accident or dropped out of school, but that they are thinking of being a missionary. As these and other relational pressures surface today, it is helpful to remember that this issue has been around for over a hundred years (probably a few thousand)!

Throughout history, students have disagreed with their loved ones about the direction of their lives. In many

---

[15] Campus Crusade for Christ Midsouth Region, *When God Says "Go" and Parents Say "No"* (Orlando, FL: CCC, 2002), 1.

situations, God has used the conflict to reveal Himself more clearly to both sides. As we seek His will we must deal delicately and humbly with those who love us the most, boldly pursuing His desires above all else.

My wife and I invited our families to a very special dinner where we told them to expect a great announcement. In hindsight, I can totally see how they were thinking a grandchild was on the way, but for some reason, that never entered *my* mind. As I stood up to tell them the news, I saw my mom and my wife's mom exchange smiles. Did I mention we did this on Mother's Day? Expectations were high. "Thanks for coming, everybody; we are so excited to tell you that we are moving to the Middle East!" Honestly, I expected hugs; high fives maybe. Spontaneous, uncontrollable weeping I was not prepared for. That night was the first of many nights over the next few months that we spent consoling, explaining, and praying with them. And then we invited them to come see us for two weeks. They did not even own passports! Something crazy happened. They came. Their lives were impacted. If you walk in my dad's office, you'll see a picture of us in the Middle East on his desk. He still talks about it to this day. It changed their lives. Part of my journey was God's desire to mobilize them.

CHAPTER 19
I HAVE NO CALL

There has been no bigger tragedy, no bigger misunderstanding, and no bigger enemy in missions than the confusion of the missionary call. Just as J. Herbert Kane said, "No aspect of Christian mission is more puzzling than this problem of a call."[1]

Looking back to the Student Volunteer Movement's day, the prerequisite of a "special" call by God to preclude work in a foreign land was also a prominent idea held among college students. Their conclusions were based on the passage in Acts 13—Paul and Barnabas ministered to the church at Antioch and the Holy Spirit came upon the leadership and personally called these two men out for a special work. Students without this "mystical" experience defaulted into ministry at home. Therefore the S.V.M. dismantled this excuse by changing the question from "Am I called to the foreign field?" to, "Can I show sufficient cause for not going?"

Their attack on the idea that a "special call" was needed for missionary service was mounted on three fronts: the need abroad, the general obligation of believers, and the command of the Lord Jesus Christ.

A common analogy presented to illustrate the point of meeting needs abroad was that of a man standing on a

---

[1] J. Herbert Kane, *Understanding Christian Missions* (Grand Rapids, MI: Baker Book House, 1982), 39.

riverbank as he witnesses another man drowning. Does the man on the bank demand a special summons from anyone telling him to help the drowning man? Or is the fact that he sees the need and is in a position to help enough basis to act?[2] The need constituted the call! Robert Wilder looked out on the audience of students and challenged them with the need:

> The need was the call... Study the lives of missionaries. One after another have been led to the work by *reading* of the *need*... Do not wait for a special call to the foreign field. Do not wait for an avalanche to strike you, or for a sheet from Heaven to be let down... The millions in India, China, Japan, Africa are crying, "Come over and help us." Who are under more obligation to go than we? In the greater *need* abroad we hear the call of God.[3]

Testimony after testimony was evoked to break down the presumption about and expectation for a special call. Those who had signed the Volunteer Declaration explained to other students that they themselves had never experienced this elusive phenomenon, but were instead persuaded toward the foreign field in obedient response to sheer reality. One student confessed, "Even then I can remember the thought coming to me, 'You haven't had any definite call.' I don't think that even up to now I have ever felt any definite, clear-cut, dramatic call to the foreign field. I think what really

---

[2] Fennell Turner, "Student Volunteer Series: The Call, Qualifications and Preparation of Candidates for Foreign Missionary Service," *Papers by Missionaries and Other Authorities* 4, no. 4, (Oct. 1901), 5.

[3] T. J. Shanks, *A College of Colleges: Led by D. L. Moody* (New York: Fleming H. Revell, 1887), 201-202.

constituted the call in my case was an appreciation of the need. I think that the need constitutes the call."[4]

During a question-and-answer session at the 1891 convention, a student asked Robert Wilder how he would deal with a person who thinks that he is not called to missions. His response was straightforward: "I should tell him that there is nothing in the Bible to indicate that a man needs more of a call to take him to Africa than to Dakota. If a man can labor in Texas without a 'special call,' is it right to oppose his crossing the Rio Grande into Mexico unless he receives a 'special call'?"[5] The pamphlet that stirred people to understand this concept was written in 1901 by Robert Speer, entitled, *What Constitutes a Missionary Call?* In it he argues that there exists no distinction between the sacred and the secular.

> **If men are going to draw lines of division between different kinds of service, what preposterous reasoning leads them to think that it requires less divine sanction for a man to spend his life easily among Christians than it requires for him to go out as a missionary to the heathen? If men are to have special calls for anything, they ought to have special calls to go about their own business, to have a nice time all their lives, to choose the soft places, to make money, and to gratify their own ambitions? Is it not absurd to suggest that a special call is necessary to become a missionary, but no call is required to gratify his own will or personal ambitions?[6]**

---

[4] The Report of the Toronto Convention 1902: Missionary Campaign Library No. 1, Toronto, Feb. 26-March 2, 1902 (Chicago: Student Missionary Campaign Library, 1902), 305.

[5] John R. Mott, *Student Mission Power: Report of the First International Convention of the Student Volunteer Movement for Foreign Missions* (Pasadena, CA: William Carey Library, 1891), 33-34.

[6] Robert Speer, *What Constitutes a Missionary Call* (New York: Student Volunteer Movement, 1901), 1.

The next means used to break down this excuse was the teaching that believers have a general obligation to take the gospel to those who are without. The call of God ought to be sought equally from those who stay home and work and from those who go to the field for full-time Christian service. For Speer, the obligation was rooted in the command of Christ and it was therefore general in its application to all who claim to be Christian. He continues:

> There is a general obligation resting upon Christians to see that the Gospel of Jesus Christ is preached to the world. You and I need no special call to apply that general call of God to our lives. We do need a special call to exempt us from its application to our lives. In other words, every one of us stands under a presumptive obligation to give his life to the world unless we have some special exemption.[7]

If the student could justify himself enough to move, unaffected, past the need and the general obligation, a third tactic was used. This third appeal was an explanation that no personal, individual call was needed since Christ had already spoken the command in Scripture. The final words of

It was not God's responsibility to push anyone in a direction which He had already pointed.

---

[7] Speer, 1.

Christ commissioned His disciples to the nations and that has been passed down through all generations of Christians. It was not God's responsibility to push anyone in a direction which He had already pointed.[8] If you had given your life to Christ, you were no longer your own, you had been bought with a price. Therefore, you should be making your way to the nations.

> Missions, in this large sense is the response of Christian obedience to the explicit command of the risen Lord, "Go ye into all the world and preach the gospel to every creature." That order has never been countermanded; it determines forever the nature and the measure of the obligation of the Church. We have no right to hesitate in obeying it. True obedience will not go picking and choosing its way among the commandments of the Lord.[9]

A. T. Pierson advocated for simple obedience to the final command of Christ as the foundational argument for all to be involved in world evangelization. From his own initial involvement with the S.V.M. as a speaker at the Mount Hermon summer project in 1886 until his death, he believed the command of the Lord to be sufficient motivation to move out in faith:

> Our great captain has left us His marching orders: "Go ye into all the world and preach the gospel to every creature." Such a plain command makes all other motives comparatively

---

[8] Timothy C. Wallstrom, *The Creation of a Student Movement to Evangelize the World* (Pasadena, CA: William Carey International University Press, 1980), 18.
[9] The Report of the Toronto Convention 1902, 109.

unnecessary... Where there has been given a clear, divine word of authority, immediate, implicit submission and compliance will be yielded by every loyal, loving disciple. Even to hesitate, for the sake of asking a reason, savors the essence of rebellion.[10]

For those who, after hearing the arguments for the need, the general obligation, and the command of Christ, still refused to go without a valid reason to stay, the S.V.M. reserved some of their harshest words. At the 1906 convention in front of 4,235 students, speaker Donald Fraser said, "I wonder, my brothers, if the reason why you have not been hearing the call to the foreign field is not just this, that you have not got a salvation worth passing on."[11]

Did the S.V.M. see any justifiable reason for a student to stay behind, or were all students who stayed seen as disobedient? There were actually five reasons: 1) if they were personally disqualified due to sin; 2) if there were insurmountable hindrances; 3) if an opportunity on the home front proved more strategic than going; 4) if they had a physical or mental defect that kept them from going; 5) if they were unavoidably responsible for family duties. However, even to those, the warning rang out, "But woe to those who in this case give a false excuse, for He knows the inmost soul; He measures the validity of each excuse."[12] G. T. Manley was a professor at Cambridge University and a part of the S.V.M. in Britain. He challenged American university students about the men who had gone before them and the missionary call:

[10] Arthur T. Pierson, *Crisis of Missions* (New York: Robert Carter, 1886), 11-12.
[11] The Students and the Modern Missionary Crusade, Addresses Delivered before the Fifth International Convention of the Student Volunteer Movement for Foreign Missions, Nashville, Tennessee, Feb. 28-March 4, 1906, 255.
[12] Turner, 11-12.

Am I called to the mission field? I think it is possible that some of us have an exaggerated idea of the special nature of the call to the foreign field. I look back at some of the great historic missionaries. William Carey said that his call consisted of an open Bible before an open map of the world. That call comes to every one of us. Henry Martyn had the idea of the mission field first suggested to him by his own pastor, Charles Simeon, who said, "Martyn, aren't you the sort of man who might give your life to the evangelization of India?" and that was his call... David Livingstone said that he had no special call; he had no special enthusiasm for the mission field beyond what he describes as "a strong, overwhelming sense of duty."... And young Keith Falconer said, "A call, what is a call? A call is a need, a need made known, and the power to meet that need."[13]

The S.V.M.'s definition of the call was quite different from that of the students they were dealing with. They placed the burden of proof on each believer to convincingly articulate their viable "call to stay." If this was not possible, the only alternative was overseas work.

Today, this idea of calling is still a very prominent issue and equally confusing! It seems that a Christian student could easily hear counsel from both sides; one missions conference might promote the idea that a special call is necessary before going overseas. The student may have a heart for internationals on campus and a desire to serve God anywhere, but may feel paralyzed by this emphasis on

---

[13] The Students and the Modern Missionary Crusade, 246.

the abstract notion of a mysterious call. Another conference might say just the opposite—that students don't need a call but a kick in the pants! Keith Green would say:

> The truth is that God has already told you to go in His Word. In fact, He commands you to go (Mark 16:15)... If you don't go, you need a specific calling from God to stay home. Has God definitely told you *not to go* somewhere outside your country to preach the gospel? If He hasn't, then you'd better start praying about *where to go*, again, you're already called![14]

What if a call is as practical as reading a missions book... or having your heart broken by a statistic?

The obvious result is that we have countless students confused when it comes to the concept of calling. How should a student reconcile such contradictory advice?

WHAT EXACTLY IS A CALLING?

Have you ever thought about the question, "What would a call look like?" Most of us don't even know what to expect. We would not even recognize a call if it came. What

---

[14] Keith Green, *Why You Should Go to the Mission Field,* WiseTracts from Last Days Ministries (Lindale, TX: Pretty Good Printing, 1982), 2-3.

if a call is as practical as reading a missions book, having a map up on the wall that you can't get out of your mind, or having your heart broken by a statistic? One student who had committed to go to India after graduation explained:

> If you say your work is in this country, and wait for a call out there, you will never get that call… I got that little chart with the populations of the world, and I put it on my bedroom door, right at the foot of my bed… I have a map of Africa, and a map of China. I look at those maps, and the world's populations, and the commission of the Lord Jesus… It almost breaks my heart to think that there are so many millions waiting to hear of the Lord Jesus Christ, and so few who are willing to go—so many willing to stay at home.[15]

In the New Testament the word *call* is used many different ways. The major usage of the word is in reference to salvation (Romans 9:24-26).[16] The believers are called to be saints (Romans 1:7), called to grace (Galatians 1:6), and Paul was called to be an apostle (Romans 1:1). There are two passages that are most commonly thought of in reference to the missionary call. The first is found in Acts 13:2 (ESV), "While they were worshiping the Lord and fasting, the Holy Spirit said, 'Set apart for me Barnabas and Saul for the work to which I have called them.'" Here, the leaders of the church at Antioch, commanded by the Holy Spirit, sent out these two men on what would later be known as their first missionary journey.

[15] Shanks, 185-186.
[16] C. Gordon Olson, *What in the World Is God Doing?* 3rd ed. (Cedar Knolls, NJ: Global Gospel Publishers, 1988), 80.

The second passage has become known as the Macedonian call:

> When they came to the border of Mysia, they tried to enter Bithynia, but the Spirit of Jesus would not allow them to. So they passed by Mysia and went down to Troas. During the night Paul had a vision of a man of Macedonia standing and begging him, "Come over to Macedonia and help us." After Paul had seen the vision, we got ready at once to leave for Macedonia, concluding that God had called us to preach the gospel to them (Acts 16:7-10).

Keep in mind that when the Macedonian vision came to Paul and Silas they were already missionaries (this was their second missionary journey).

How do we deal with the notion of a call today? Just as the S.V.M. mounted a threefold attack on this excuse, Paul Borthwick has answered this question by breaking the New Testament "call" down into three categories. While we may attempt to use appeals to the logic of being called to stay and testimonies of others who are going with or without a "call," it seems students are particularly sensitive to feeling guilty. Unless we are very careful, these approaches will easily get interpreted as manipulation. I think you will find that Borthwick brings balance and biblical support to many types of experiences in a way that best communicates with this generation.[17]

---

[17] Bill Taylor and Steve Hoke, *Global Mission Handbook: A Guide for Cross-Cultural Service* (Downers Grove, IL: InterVarsity Press, 2009), 67.

The first category he suggests is the *mysterious call*. Here the call comes directly (even audibly at times) from God Himself. An example of this is when Peter saw a vision from God in Acts 10:10 or the Macedonian call (Acts 16:9). The second call is the *commissioned call*. It's found in Acts 13:1-3, when the leaders of the church in Jerusalem identify Paul and Barnabas and send them out as missionaries to Antioch. "In this case, there is not so much mystery; instead, it is the Holy Spirit speaking through the church leadership."[18] The third call is the *common sense call*. In light of a need and their ability to meet that need, "it seemed good to the apostles and the elders, with the whole church, to choose men from among them and send them to Antioch" (Acts 15:22, ESV). This category of calling involves far more logical deduction, and yet it was good enough grounds for the church leaders in Jerusalem to move forward.

These three categories are helpful as we seek to bring clarity to the confusion. I have met students who have had a dramatic experience of being called by God in a way that would certainly classify as a *mysterious call*, but it is important to note that these mysterious calls are most likely the exception rather than the rule. Often the result is a dramatic and almost instantaneous life change. The *commissioned call* confirms that it is a very biblical concept for the elders in a church to speak specific direction into an individual's life as they watch and discern the ministry and gifting of members.[19] Church leaders should not be timid to

---

[18] Taylor and Hoke, 67.

[19] Bob Sjogren and Bill and Amy Stearns, *Run with the Vision: A Remarkable Plan for the 21st Century Church* (Minneapolis, MN: Bethany House, 1995), 126.

allow God to use them in this way, and believers should heed this type of counsel very seriously. Unfortunately, this type of leadership is not the norm today. Finally, this generation has grown up with the news reports of the wars, seen images on the Internet depicting the needs of the world, and have had exposure to the poverty that exists worldwide both physically and spiritually. How logical it may be for many of these students to conclude that the best use of their time, energy, and talents is to serve God cross-culturally. It should just seem good to them!

It is evident that no two Christians are alike in their spiritual walk, be it in their conversion experience or in the way God daily communicates with them. Therefore, it should be no wonder that we see a variation in God's leading here too. The problem comes when we isolate one narrow way in which God guides today (the mysterious call) and define it as normative.

HEARING GOD'S VOICE

I have seen several ways in which God navigates students' lives to bring them to a realization of His will for them in regards to missions.[20] God uses human agents. He brings into our lives brothers, sisters, friends, and spiritual mentors who shape, challenge, and direct us in His heart for the world. Many young adults have made their way to the field because of the vision for missions they gleaned from a

---

[20] These five are adopted from George Peters, *A Biblical Theology of Missions* (Chicago, IL: Moody Press, 1972), 279-284.

peer. Also, God issues His call through the reading of His Word. From Genesis to Revelation God invites the reader to lay down his or her life for His greater purpose. It is difficult to be consistent in God's Word and deny outreach. Next, God extends His call through missions studies. As a student begins to read biographies of missionaries, articles about the state of the world, and as they gain exposure to facts, figures, maps of the world, pictures, and reports of the field—all of these act as mighty forces that God uses to extend His call. Lastly, God uses prayer. Remember Matthew 9:38 (ESV), "Pray earnestly to the Lord of the harvest to send out laborers into his harvest." Many have been led by God personally as they were obeying this passage and asking God to send out workers to the field. It is in the context of prayer that sensitivity is cultivated, and they recognize by the prompting of the Holy Spirit that they indeed may be the answer to their own prayer!

As we have seen, the excuse—I have no special call—is one that mobilizers have encountered for years. It may be one that students will continue to struggle with as long as we are talking about missions. The Student Volunteer Movement handled it with some pretty strong appeals for needs abroad and the logic of simply volunteering to meet those needs. At times, they issued a very harsh rebuke. And it worked! Students responded under the Spirit's influence by laying down their lives and volunteering even without a mysterious call. Today's generation requires a petition that covers a wider spectrum of personal experience. God does audibly call some, but He also uses the body of Christ and the common sense of believers as motivation to go. The argument against the necessity of a call should be based in Scripture with honest, yet careful presentation of the needs overseas to avoid the appearance of manipulation. The Spirit will bring clarity to our confusion and mobilize many in this generation to go!

CHAPTER 20
MONEY, MATERIALISM, AND DEBT

I will never forget an interview my dad and I saw. One of the wealthiest men in the world was interviewed and it was televised nationally. Toward the end, the interviewer asked a very bold question: "With all the wealth you already have at your fingertips, why do you still work sixty hours a week? How much money do you want?" His answer shocked both my dad and me. He replied, "I just want a little bit more."

Jesus said it simply, "The love of money is the root of all kinds of evil." John Mott said it like this: "Materialism is among the strongest influences to be overcome if young men are to be led to devote their lives to the service of the church either abroad or at home. The eagerness for wealth and the ability to acquire it rapidly combine powerfully to attract young men in the direction of money-making pursuits."[1] Greed is no respecter of persons. Nor does its seduction subside with the accumulation of possessions. This timeless temptation affects every level of society and it takes on many forms. Those devoted to Christ are not insusceptible and, as we shall see, neither are those committed to a life of serving

---

[1] John R. Mott, *The Pastor and Modern Missions* (New York: SVM, 1904), 160.

others overseas for the sake of the gospel. Money and materialism have been a snare for students in every step of the journey.

Greed is no respecter of persons.

For the student of the S.V.M.'s generation who had undertaken the investment of college, the craving of money and materialism was felt very strongly. For some, this took the form of a blatant desire for the finer things in life. For others, materialism manifested as an innocent pursuit to live comfortably and avoid the stress of financial burden. College students of this generation were already considered the indulged upper class; going to a foreign land meant great material sacrifice.

The S.V.M. equated the increased interest in legal and medical vocations with the desire for material possessions and wealth. By comparison, those pursuing careers in full-time ministry were waning. During the years of 1870-1906 the number of divinity students increased by 137 percent, the number of medical students increased 302 percent, and law students increased by 848 percent.[2] John Mott wrote:

> **Material success is the charmed word of our present-day vocabulary... Even in Christian homes the topic of most absorbing interest in conversation is money and the things that money can buy. Young men come to feel that success means the accumulation of property or the gaining of great worldly**

---

[2] John R. Mott, *The Future Leadership of the Church* (New York: SVM, 1908), 61.

power and prominence rather than self-denying service for God and man.[3]

On the self-proclaimed Christian students who sat in their audience with hearts full of greed, selfishness, and personal ambition, the S.V.M. unashamedly brought the lordship of Christ to bear. Robert Speer, at the 1891 student convention in Cleveland, Ohio, spoke these words:

> Do you know that if we added up all the money we have given for the evangelization of the world since the beginning of this century, it would not amount to more than $75,000,000— less, by far, than the drink bill of this nation for thirty days. And, the church of God in this land had money enough buried in rings, jewelry, and useless ornaments, in gold and luxuries that we might easily dispense with, to thrust forth missionaries sufficing to cover every field in this world more completely than even the most sanguine missionary has ever dared to pray for.[4]

Armored with an understanding of the brevity of wealth, the students were challenged to chart a course of self-denial in order to further the kingdom of God to all nations, exhorted by passages like Philippians 3:7-9, "But whatever was to my profit I now consider loss for the sake of Christ. What is more, I consider everything a loss compared to the surpassing greatness of knowing Christ Jesus my Lord, for whose sake I have lost all things. I consider them rubbish,

---

[3] Mott, *The Future Leadership of the Church*, 58.
[4] John R. Mott, *Student Mission Power: Report of the First International Convention of the Student Volunteer Movement for Foreign Missions* (Pasadena, CA: William Carey Library, 1891), 78.

that I may gain Christ and be found in him."

If a student safely navigated the difficult and tempting waters of materialism and decided to volunteer for the mission field, he was not completely free from money issues. It inevitably reared its head in another, equally crucial way—raising funds. Historically, it rested upon the denominational mission boards to provide financially for their missionaries. However, if the mission boards did not have sufficient funds to send them, the student was encouraged to allow God to provide funding in other ways.[5]

When a student fell into this category, the S.V.M. presented three means of obtaining the necessary funds so they could sail. First, students were encouraged to challenge the peers involved in their own campus ministry to give. A second option was to enlist churches to send them out. Beginning in 1888, Robert Wilder started encouraging students to use this approach more and more to alleviate the burden of financial provision from mission boards. Third, students could solicit funds from individuals in the churches for support. The volunteer assumed that if the person in the pew could not go, then they should send. The S.V.M. felt that as large numbers of volunteers utilized these three approaches, at some point down the road, this method of personal support raising would become the new norm.

While support raising is definitely an issue today, it seems to have been a different type of struggle for the S.V.M. era in light of the expectation for mission boards to fund one's expenses. The majority of missionaries today

---

[5] Robert P. Wilder, "The Rejected Volunteer," *The Student Volunteer Movement Bulletin*, Jan. 1925, 23.

sign on knowing that they will be responsible to raise support; it is just the way things are done! But in the S.V.M.'s generation, the shift in perspective from sending as the church's responsibility to solicitation of his or her own salary as the individual's responsibility was only just beginning to take place. And, for some volunteers, the unmet expectation of having funds provided was discouraging.

> Students in one of the leading theological seminaries said to me: "It will do no good for us to apply for foreign service. Two of our best men applied, and were rejected for lack of funds. They were far superior to us." To such I answer, "Do the Boards say, 'Go ye into all the world and preach the gospel to the whole creation'? If so, then the Boards' dictum should settle matters. But it is Christ who commands this world-wide campaign. A Christ-sent man no empty Board treasury can stop."[6]

The S.V.M. was correct in saying that utilizing the above three approaches would eventually redefine "normal" as personal support raising, but that shift was a long time in coming. Because this redefines the issue somewhat, we will deal with our current perspectives of support raising in a later chapter.

KNEE DEEP IN DEBT

I can remember two sisters coming up to me after I spoke at their campus. They were both so excited to go overseas as missionaries after they graduated; they were

---

[6] Mott, *Student Mission Power*, 164.

just worried about their debt. I asked them how much they had. They said $60,000. I asked, "Oh, $30,000 each?" They replied, "No, $60,000 each!"

Today, one of the greatest financial strongholds keeping students back from following God's lead overseas is their debt. For every $1 an American makes, they spend $1.10.[7] With credit card booths set up in the Student Center, as incoming freshmen wander the halls, and with the price of tuition on the rise, debt is an ever-lurking evil for the college student. Nearly two-thirds of college graduates have student-loan debt after completing their studies. The average debt is now as high as $19,000.[8] Some wish their debt was as low as $19,000! When asked, "What are you most fearful of at this time?" only 13.4 percent of students said a terrorist attack, while 32.4 percent answered "college debt."[9]

How the Christian student deals with the subject of missions will be affected by their debt situation. Some will use their debt as an automatic excuse to never go overseas; some will procrastinate their involvement until they get it taken care of. It is important to know how missions agencies are responding to the growing amount of tuition-incurred debt. Most of them are allowing candidates to apply with some school debt.[10] They do this because they require applicants to have a college degree and therefore, they feel partly responsible for the acquired debt. In light of the rising

[7] Mark Nolan, "Get Out of Debt." Available from morejoyinlife.com.

[8] Mike Woodruff, "The Ivy Jungle Network," *Campus Ministry Update*, June 2006.

[9] Greg Toppo, "Graduates Fear Debt More Than Terrorism," *U.S.A. Today*, May 18, 2005.

[10] The agencies consulted were Pioneers, Overseas Missionary Fellowship, WEC International, New Tribes Missions, Café 10-40, United World Mission, Avant Ministries, Chosen Peoples, Operation Mobilization, and Middle East Christian Outreach. New Tribes Missions and WEC International were the only agencies that will not accept students for long-term service with debt unless someone commits to full responsibility for paying it.

cost of college and their desire to recruit students to join as soon as they graduate, agencies understand that debt comes with the territory. The amount of debt allowed varies; the agencies surveyed range between $20,000-$25,000, though some do not put a precise number on what is permissible. When creating a budget to go long-term to the mission field, school debt is added to the suggested salary just like housing, car, food, and insurance. If it is too much to raise in financial support, agencies suggest that an applicant work for a few years before going overseas. However, it seems more beneficial to allow a missionary to build school debt into their monthly support budget than it is to ask them to pay it off over a period of time prior to joining the agency. Many by that time will have been sidelined by other issues. This tale of two students provides the perfect example.

Jennifer graduated from the University of Arkansas with a school loan payment of $400 a month, but felt strongly that she should go to the Middle East to reach Muslims. Her debt was a potential roadblock. She talked to various mission agencies and, after choosing one, was given permission to budget her debt into her overall support plan. As Jennifer raised her funds, she did not allow debt to sideline her, and her supporters didn't mind that their money was going to this end.

James, on the other hand, decided that instead of raising money for his college debt he would wait to go until he paid it off. His total monthly payment was $110. James's problem was that it never happened. Though his intentions were good, life's expenses caught up to him. After graduation he got a job to pay off the debt, only to incur more debt.

Car repairs, rent, food, and, of course, fun. James looked up at age thirty only to find himself deeper in debt. Jennifer was reaching the Middle East, James was reaching for help!

Don't get me wrong, this is not a way to justify the debt of irresponsible spending on the new up-to-date surround sound; rather, it is a viable way for people who sincerely desire to serve overseas to be freed from the bondage of school debt. The distinction between school debt and the debt incurred from careless spending is an important one. If someone is locked into excessive credit-card payments, they will find it very difficult to raise support from friends, family, and churches due to their lack of integrity and poor management of funds. Missions agencies handle this type of debt differently. Often they require that a candidate take care of all credit-card debts prior to applying.

This leads us to an issue to consider: should someone who is already in debt go on a short-term mission trip for the summer? Should those who are in debt spend even more money to go on a six-week trip, or should they focus on getting out of debt? All agencies I consulted have no problem with how much a student is in debt in order to participate in short-term trips.[11] The reasoning is that colleges usually allow students to defer loan payments for some time, which enables a student to experience a short-term mission. Also, many agencies agree that a short-term trip serves as an incredible motivator for students to get debt-free and live a simpler lifestyle upon returning to the States. Overseas exposure stimulates the desire to proactively eliminate debt on two fronts. The first is the stark reality that most of the world lives on far

---

[11] Though each agency has a different definition of short-term, the average represent between one week and three years. Anything over three years is considered long-term.

less than the average American. The shocking image of true poverty helps a student to readily surrender the standard of living that they previously held. The second is that taste of being used by God to affect a physically and spiritually impoverished world. Students are often inspired to remove all obstacles that stand in the way of their return, including debt. Simply put, debt is a real issue, but it is not a valid excuse.

Money, materialism, and debt have presented a roadblock for students for generations. Financial issues go straight to the heart of our trust in God, our obsession with status, and our addiction to comfort and independence. In the past it was confronted by the strong words of the S.V.M., who challenged students to leave behind the selfish notions of wealth and prestige. Missions agencies today are adapting to the almost universal presence of college debt by allowing it to be covered in the missionary's budget. They are also recognizing the incredible power of short-term trips to combat the lure of materialism at home.

C. T. Studd lived in the late 1800s and as a student at Cambridge was captain of its cricket team. He came from a wealthy background and when his father passed away, inherited an enormous sum of money. On top of that, everyone knew he would go on and make his own fortunes in professional athletics. For all practical purposes, he had the world at his fingertips. Studd could not have wanted for more money, and he could have had any of the luxuries a materialistic heart would covet. And then Studd heard a visiting speaker from America, D. L. Moody, and Studd's life caught fire with passion to serve God. He was convicted that he should give his life to the spiritual needs of China. So what did he do? He gave his entire fortune away to other ministries and then raised

Financial issues go straight to the heart of our trust in God.

support.[12] Studd possessed what today would make him a millionaire. But he was driven by passages like "Do not store up for yourselves treasures on earth" (Matthew 6:19); "Selling their possessions and goods, they gave to anyone as he had need" (Acts 2:45); and "You still lack one thing. Sell everything you have and give to the poor, and you will have treasure in heaven. Then come, follow me" (Luke 18:22). Studd was decisive that these verses were as "equally binding on himself as a present-day disciple of the Lord Jesus Christ, as on those to whom they were spoken. Therefore, in light of God's Word, he decided to give his fortune to Christ, and to take the golden opportunity offered him of doing what the rich young man had failed to do."

C. T. Studd denied himself any opportunity to trust money more than God and any temptation to love money more than God. Let us follow in C. T. Studd's example and remove any financial hindrance which so easily entangles us from doing that which He has given His followers to do.

---

[12] On January 13, 1887, C. T. gave away his fortune so he could live by faith as a missionary. He gave £5,000 to D. L. Moody, which he used to start Moody Bible Institute. C. T. Studd gave £5,000 to George Muller. He gave £5,000 to George Holland and London's poor as well as £5,000 to Booth-Tucker to start the Salvation Army in India. He gave another £6,000 to other ministries reaching the poor in England. He gave £3,400 to the Salvation Army of England and a few thousand pounds to the China Inland Mission which Hudson Taylor founded. Klaus Fiedler, *The Story of Faith Missions from Hudson Taylor to Present Day Africa* (Oxford: Regnum Books International, 1994), 160.

CHAPTER 21
THE NEEDS AT HOME

I couldn't have gotten two more opposite phone calls in one day—if they had been separated by a week maybe, but one day? The first was a friend of mine who called to inform me that a mission trip his agency was planning had just been canceled. They could not find a team of five to go to North Africa on a short-term mission trip. Zero applicants. Two hours later my pastor friend called me. He sounded really stressed, so I asked him what was going on. He said he had put out an ad to hire a youth pastor and had received over sixty applicants in two weeks. He could not even look through them all. He was drowning in responses.

One thing is sure about needs—they are everywhere and they are here to stay. I can't imagine a world without them! Needs, authentic needs, are found on campus, in government, in the inner city, at church, in our neighborhoods, families, and even our individual lives. And meeting these needs is a very real issue.

Looking back, a very common obstacle in the minds and hearts of the students was a misconception of the needs at home. Students knew that people were lost everywhere, and they rea-soned, "Why sail across the ocean when on campus, in this town, next door, there are those who need to hear

"Am I to stay or am I to go?"

the gospel?" Though it has an initial appearance of sincere piety and concern for reaching the lost, the S.V.M. heard it so commonly that they began to recognize it, more often than not, as the students' favorite guise for self-justification. They countered this protest on three fronts.

First, they challenged the heart of the question being asked. The S.V.M. was not opposed to meeting the needs at home, *if* one was called to stay. They were opposed, how-ever, to a student using the needs at home as a mask to cover an underlying distrust in the Lord or a wavering com-mitment to Him. Was the student asking the question be-cause he simply did not want to go overseas, or because he truly felt God calling him to stay? A. T. Pierson tried to guide students through the difference:

> All I want of you gentlemen is that you, each of you, should go and simply lay yourself at the feet of your Lord Jesus with hearty self-surrender, and be willing to go anywhere and do anything that God gives you to do. There is an argument for the foreign field which I beg you to notice as I close. Paul says: "I strived to preach the Gospel, not where Christ was named, lest I should build upon another man's foundation."

> You cannot go to any place in Christian lands without building on another man's foundation… My brethren make up your minds that you will do whatever God calls you to do, or go where He calls you to go. Say with simplicity: "Dear Lord, here I am. Send me."[1]

The emphasis of this message was not that overseas work was the only work ordained or blessed by God. Indeed, He *has* consecrated some to stay in their homeland and minister—but they need a call to stay! It is God who directs both the one who goes and the one who stays. The S.V.M. was satisfied only upon hearing a student's testimony of receiving a homeward call. S. C. Mitchell, a student at Georgetown College, was committed to the foreign field. Before he graduated and set sail for the mission field he told his fellow students:

> It is a privilege, not a duty, to labor for Christ wherever He places you. There are two alternatives, one on each side. Shall we labor where we prefer to go? Or shall we lay ourselves upon the altar and ask to be sent anywhere? Every man here before me is a Christian. He says he is willing to work for Christ wherever He sends him. Ah, my friend; can you hear a voice that calls more loudly than the voice that calls you to the work of foreign missions? It seems to me if we would only turn ourselves loose upon the world, we could just turn it upside down for Christ.[2]

---

[1] T. J. Shanks, *A College of Colleges: Led by D. L. Moody* (New York: Fleming H. Revell, 1887), 273.
[2] Shanks, *A College of Colleges,* 193.

The second way they answered the argument was by explaining that though the needs here were real and important, by comparison the non-Christian nations were entitled to receive a greater priority because their incredible need is met by insufficient workers and resources. They proved their point by compiling the numbers of Protestant workers in the States and those abroad and contrasting those figures to the number of non-Christians in the States and those in other countries. Scott Macfie of Cambridge University stated, "Take these statistics and work it out this way. Suppose there are four hundred men here. You will find that three hundred at least of you ought to go out to the heathen... Ask yourself: 'Am I to stay at home? Or am I to go abroad?' The most of us ought to go abroad."[3]

At the 1891 convention, in front of 680 participants, Robert Speer explained a conversation he had had with a doctor on a recent train ride. The doctor asked, "How are you able to give so much attention to the work abroad? How is it that the church wastes so much energy on the work abroad... when there is so much to be done in this land of ours?" Speer recounted:

> I asked him what he would consider a fair proportion of workers to keep in this land and a fair proportion to send abroad. He said, "I suppose two-thirds here and one-third abroad would be treating ourselves fairly." If we sent one-third of our workers abroad and kept the other two-thirds at home, we would more than ten-fold multiply the ordained missionaries

---

[3] Shanks, *A College of Colleges,* 191-192.

in the heathen fields from all the Christian nations in the world, and would send 400,000 lay workers out into the foreign world.[4]

Some in the church actually feared that if a mass departure of Christians to the mission field occurred, it would result in too few believers to meet the home-side *needs*. Robert Wilder argued that this fear was unwarranted.

Some talk as if they feared a general exodus of Christians out of this country. There is no immediate danger of that... We have in the United States an average of one Christian worker to every forty-eight of our population... Home work will not suffer by reason of foreign missionary activity... If the building is on fire and eight men are upstairs perishing while one is in the cellar—and if six are already helping the one in the cellar where do I need to go to offer my assistance?[5]

In short, the major emphasis of the S.V.M. was not to go to meet needs, but instead to meet the *greatest need*.

The third way they responded to the excuse of meeting the needs at home was to explain that a church actually maintains its own health by following in obedience the command of the Lord.

I say to you the hope of the church of God is missions. It is not simply how we shall save the world, but how we shall

---

[4] John R. Mott, *Student Mission Power: Report of the First International Convention of the Student Volunteer Movement for Foreign Missions* (Pasadena, CA: William Carey Library, 1891), 77.

[5] T. J. Shanks, *College Students at Northfield* (New York: Fleming H. Revell, 1888), 259-262.

save ourselves. The church that forgets the world will speedily be forsaken of the Holy Spirit; and the church that embraces the world in her love and in her labor is the church that, in losing herself for her Master's sake, shall gain herself, her Master, and the world.[6]

The congregation that raised protective walls around America and refused to export men and women to the field in a measure of self-protection and self-promotion was actually defeating itself. The reason the S.V.M. argued there was a Church at all was to meet the needs of the world. J. Ross Stevenson, a regular speaker at the conventions, elaborated on this point: "Napoleon once said, 'It is a maxim in the military art that the army which remains in its entrenchment is beaten.'" The non-missionary Church sins against its own best interest and is inviting defeat. A stay-at-home Christianity is not real Christianity at all."[7]

Involvement in missions blessed the home-side church by displaying the true Christian life. Sacrificially following the Lord in reaching the nations produces a mighty in-pouring of souls into the Church as they are convinced by genuine obedience. Missions never steals energy from the Church; on the contrary it provides the energy. Robert Wilder said, "I believe that for every God-sent man who leaves this country for foreign fields, four will fill his place at home. Dr. Judson Smith said: 'If young men should rise in large numbers and go to the foreign field, there would be such a revival at home that men would flock into the ministry.'"[8]

This stance on the place of home missions is the one

---

[6] Mott, 88.

[7] The Report of the Toronto Convention 1902: Missionary Campaign Library No. 1, Toronto, Feb. 26-March 2, 1902 (Chicago: Student Missionary Campaign Library, 1902), 34.

[8] Shanks, *College Students at Northfield*, 265.

that characterized the S.V.M. as long as its founding fathers were in command. After the 1920 convention, various denominations' home mission councils implored the S.V.M. to give home missions a greater platform in their venues. Robert Speer firmly demonstrated that recruitment for home missions was not the role of the S.V.M. He reasoned that if the two were allowed to have the same priority, the line between home and foreign service would be blurred.[9] At the 1924 convention the leading missions historian of the day, Kenneth Scott Latourette, challenged the students regarding the unreasonableness of meeting the home-side needs first as he traced the expansion of Christianity:

> In the first place, may I suggest to you that we have no right to keep Christ to ourselves. Suppose that the Christians of the fourth and fifth centuries had said, "We will wait until the Roman Empire is Christian before we carry the gospel to these barbarians of Northern Europe..." Had the Graeco-Romans waited until the Roman Empire was really Christian, you and I would still be pagan.[10]

The S.V.M. never denied that there were legitimate needs at home. They only implored students to ask the question, Where is the greatest need? With statistics to prove that the vast majority of Christians would remain at home, the S.V.M. presented to every student audience their brazen challenge to go into overseas missions.

---

[9] Michael Parker, *The Kingdom of Character: The Student Volunteer Movement for Foreign Missions 1886-1926*, 2nd ed. (Pasadena, CA: William Carey Library, 2008), 200.
[10] Milton T. Stauffer, *Christian Students and World Problems: Report of the Ninth International Convention of the Student Volunteer Movement for Foreign Missions, Indianapolis, Indiana, December 28, 1923 - January 1, 1924* (New York: Student Volunteer Movement for Foreign Missions, 1924), 402-403.

TYRANNY OF THE IMMEDIATE

Imagine that there are five cruise ships that are simultaneously sinking off the coast.[11] They are spaced at five-mile increments and the ship closest to the shore is five miles out. This means you have sinking cruise ships that are five, ten, fifteen, twenty, and twenty-five miles away from the coast. Rescuers are dispatched as hundreds aboard each cruise ship await help. The rescuers must make a choice. Which cruise ship do they go to first? The one five miles out seems the most logical since valuable time and energy would seemingly be wasted in going to the ship twenty-five miles out. Perishing lives would necessarily be passed over in reaching that farthest ship. Even after the first decision of who to reach, every subsequent rescue mission would involve a difficult choice of who to help next. These would be tough choices *if* no definition had been given as to the end goal. If the desired end was to save as many people as possible—simply a numeric issue—then it makes sense to focus solely on the closest cruise ship. But if the definition were *not* simply numeric in nature, the rescue strategy would have to conform to this desired end. This is the situation in which we find ourselves with the needs of the world. John Piper clarifies this idea for us:

> God may have in mind that the aim of the rescue operation should be to gather saved sinners from every people in the world, even if some of the successful rescuers must leave a

---

[11] This illustration is adopted from John Piper, *Let the Nations Be Glad: The Supremacy of God in Missions* (Grand Rapids, MI: Baker Books, 1993), 168-169.

fruitful *reached people*, in order to labor in a (possibly less fruitful) *unreached* people. The task of missions may not be merely to win as many individuals as possible from the most responsive people groups of the world, but rather to win individuals from *all* the people groups of the world.[12]

Piper is operating from a definition of missions that is dictated by Revelation 5:9, "And they sang a new song: 'You are worthy to take the scroll and to open its seals, because you were slain, and with your blood you purchased men for God *from every tribe and language and people and nation*.'" His goal is to have a representative from every tribe, tongue, and nation; and, therefore, we participate in the completion of this goal by engaging in missions. All of our efforts, energy, money, and time need to be poured into seeing this become a reality. We need to make sure that our definition of missions aligns correctly with God's. Given that His desire is to save some from every people, rescuers necessarily have to go to every cruise ship, not just the ones that yield the most fruit.

It is imperative that our definition of and participation in missions are not dictated by culture or by human reason. You see this in the ministry of the apostle Paul. He says in Romans, "So from Jerusalem all the way around to Illyricum, I have fully proclaimed the gospel of Christ. It has always been my ambition to preach the gospel where Christ was not known, so that I would not be building on someone else's

---

[12] Piper, 168-169.

foundation… But now that there is no more place for me to work in these regions… I plan to do so when I go to Spain" (Romans 15:19-24). This is a pretty incredible statement! From Jerusalem all the way around to Illyricum he cannot find a place to minister! That covers 1,400 miles, the equivalent distance from Dallas, Texas, to Los Angeles, California! How can he not find needs in those areas to meet? Paul was operating from a different paradigm, one defined by a desire to "preach the gospel where Christ was not known." He knew that it is not simply a matter of asking *where are the needs*, but of asking the question *where are the greatest needs*?

Jesus encouraged His disciples to look up to the harvest field. It takes intentional effort to see the harvest for what it truly is. This is as true today as ever,

We need to make sure that our definition of missions aligns correctly with God's.

It is not simply a matter of asking… where are the needs, but of asking the question where are the greatest needs?

especially since 95 percent of believers in the United States stay where they are. If the needs in the U.S. are the only needs to which 95 percent of American Christians are exposed—if we never leave the first cruise ship—the harvest field may start to look a little skewed since the sweeping majority of the world's needs exist outside the borders of America. We, like the disciples and the volunteers of old, need constant encouragement to look up and see the harvest.

There is certainly nothing wrong (and a lot of things right) with meeting domestic needs. It is an entirely viable ministry. Crossing an ocean never made anyone more spiritual. However, needs are perpetual. We will never meet them all, and we must make sure that the immediate needs are not blinding us from the needs overseas.

Steve Hawthorne challenges us to not let the home-side needs obscure our vision of the world. He calls it the "tyranny of the immediate":

> Here's how it works: Close-up needs such as those in our family or home church press in so demandingly that immediate needs begin molding life-shaping priorities. Certainly, the immediate needs are real and working to meet them is entirely legitimate. But too often, the close-up hurts and needs eclipse even greater ones an ocean away.[13]

Let's look at it from another perspective, because we all make strategic decisions like this on a daily basis. When

---

[13] Steve Hawthorne, "Tyranny of the Immediate: Another View of Acts 1:8." Available from thetravelingteam.org.

I am checking out at a grocery store, I'm not looking to be in the long line. In fact, finding the shortest line has really become an art for me. I am always calculating the fastest means to the end. I am meticulously checking not only the length of the lines, but how much is in the shopping carts. As I approach a stoplight, I look at which lane has the fewest cars. I have even made a second phone call with another phone if I was put on hold from the first call. Be honest— you were just thinking about how you do the same thing! I have come to find that most people do. Our commitment to the shortest line is second nature. Isn't it interesting that we naturally align our lives with that principle until it comes to the needs of the world? When I think about the hardest places in the world, the places with no access to the gospel—the places with the shortest line of people willing to go—all of a sudden I gravitate to a longer line. I wish my theology of the shortest line would just naturally overflow to the nations. I really want my first question to be, "Lord, where is the shortest line to the neediest place?" And I want to respond in obedience; I want to go and stand in it.

David Bryant says, "God cannot lead you on the basis of facts that you do not know." I believe that many Christians make the best decision they can on the basis of the needs they have had exposure to. If more believers were consistently informed about the world's needs, going to meet those needs would be seen as far more normal. Don't get me wrong, it is not purely an education issue, but the intake of more regular information would deal a significant blow to our current situation.

Let me reiterate, staying and ministering in the United States is not second-class; it is perfectly legitimate. In fact, for lots of people, it is even the very best, most strategic way to live. But God has a plan, and it includes every nation! Our lives as Christians must be lived and filtered through that ultimate reality. The desire to meet needs at home becomes misguided only when it proceeds out of a heart that is holding something back from God. In all we do, may the underlying purpose be the total fulfillment of God's mission in the world and in our personal lives.

CHAPTER 22
INDIFFERENCE

I remember challenging a group of college students in Michigan with the biblical basis of missions and the need of the millions of Muslims, Buddhists, and Hindus to hear the gospel. I noticed while I was speaking that one student jotted a note and passed it to another student. After the meeting and after the students had cleared the room, I saw the note on the floor so I picked it up to throw it away. Honestly, I was just trying to serve. On the way to the trash my curiosity got the best of me. I peeked. It read, "This is a complete waste of time." After picking up my shattered ego, I truly felt sorry for this student; he was caught in the timeless trap of indifference.

Though in terms of missions mobilization the Student Volunteer Movement's era was the most successful in all of history, it is obvious that apathy was a great hindrance to the work. Out of a crowd of thousands of college students who had just heard the missionary message, some would respond with a yawn; many would walk away in indifference. Students not only turned a cold shoulder on God's mandate in Scripture, but they went on unmoved by the blatant appeals for help that came from the missionaries themselves.

Face to face with unprecedented opportunities to advance, the missionary says to himself, "Surely the Christians at home will eagerly respond as soon as they know the need and the opportunity here." Letters are written and appeals are sent far and wide. The courageous missionary holds on until at last it dawns upon him that the church at home has little interest in his work, and in fact would not be really concerned were he compelled to retreat or even should he fall at his post.[1]

At the 1902 convention a church's annual report was read to illustrate the point of apathy:

Number added to the church last year by baptism, *none*; number added by letter, *none*; number dismissed by letter, *five*; number of members who had died, *three*... Amount raised for state missions, *nothing*; amount raised for home missions, *nothing*; amount raised for foreign missions, *nothing*." And then the letter closes each year, "Pray for us, brethren, that we may continue faithful to the end."[2]

The Student Volunteer Movement took the matter very seriously, as indifference meant another generation lost. Instead of lowering the bar and softening the challenge or padding the harsh realities, they presented the needs with even greater forthrightness. They went as far as to say that the person who doesn't believe in taking the message of Jesus Christ to the nations, in the end, does not believe in Jesus Christ. "No interest in missions means no interest

---

[1] James L. Barton, *The Unfinished Task* (New York: Student Volunteer Movement, 1908), 98.
[2] The Report of the Toronto Convention 1902: Missionary Campaign Library No. 1, Toronto, Feb. 26-March 2, 1902 (Chicago: Student Missionary Campaign Library, 1902), 124.

for that particular thing for which Jesus was content to be born and to live and to die."[3] Their definition of apathy spoke less of one's motivation or enthusiasm and more about one's personal walk with God and ability to care for the things He cares for.

The S.V.M. shared with students about the sale of kerosene lamps and sewing machines in the far corners of the earth. The point was to convict Christians that they cared more

"No interest in missions means no interest for that particular thing for which Jesus was content to be born and to live and to die."

about exporting these products and making a profit than they did about getting the gospel to those nations. Pleading with his audience to not be halfhearted, A. T. Pierson stated, "It seems to me that the Church of God is trifling with the whole subject of missions… lying in sluggish idleness in her hammock of ease, one end fastened to mammon and the other end nominally to the cross."[4]

The task of missions was presented as arduous and exceptionally demanding. They shared the inevitable hardships followed by an invitation to students to step up. This challenge proved fruitful in the transformation of many

---

[3] The Student Missionary Appeal: Addresses at the Third International Convention of the Student Volunteer Movement for Foreign Missions, Cleveland, Ohio, Feb. 23-27, 1898 (New York: Student Volunteer Movement for Foreign Missions, 1898), 149.

[4] John R. Mott, *Student Mission Power: Report of the First International Convention of the Student Volunteer Movement for Foreign Missions* (Pasadena, CA: William Carey Library, 1891), 84-85.

hearts from indifferent to involved. The S.V.M. kept a detailed list of students who had died on the field and read the names at different gatherings. John Mott's reasoning for this was that he believed Jesus "never hid His scars to win a disciple."[5] When the students realized the worthy and significant purpose before them and the opportunity they had to participate by giving up their lives, lack of interest was not a viable or even possible response. J. Campbell White challenged the students at the 1906 convention to move out of unresponsiveness and toward a life purpose:

> I ask myself, as I ask you tonight, whether there is anything so divine that we can do with this life of ours as to bind it in perpetual voluntary slavery to Jesus Christ for lost humanity's sake, and to say to Him: "If God will show me anything that I can do for the redemption of this world that I have not yet attempted, by His grace I will undertake it at once; for I cannot, I dare not go up to judgment until I have done the utmost that God expects me to do to diffuse His glory throughout the whole world." My fellow students, I expect to be satisfied with that life purpose a hundred years from tonight. Are you perfectly sure that you will be satisfied with yours?[6]

One reason given for students' indifference was the inherent desire to live for self. Death to self was, in the S.V.M.'s mind, the fulcrum point on which a fervent heart rested. A. T. Pierson echoed Christ's call to self-surrender when he spoke to students:

---

[5] John R. Mott, *Modern World Movement: God's Challenge to the Church* (London: Student Christian Movement, 1908), 29.

[6] The Students and the Modern Missionary Crusade, Addresses Delivered before the Fifth International Convention of the Student Volunteer Movement for Foreign Missions, Nashville, Tennessee, Feb. 28-March 4, 1906, 36.

When our Lord hung upon the cross His enemies tauntingly said; "He saved others; Himself he cannot save." No sneer ever hid a truth so sublime. In the Christian life, saving self and saving others are utterly incompatible; and the one great difficulty with the whole body of professed disciples is that most of them are trying to save themselves and yet be saved. And so it comes to pass that, while thousands go to church, come to the Lord's Table, say their prayers, and bear the name of Christ, they live life essentially worldly, are engaged in no soul saving work, and have no relish for it.[7]

A second reason given for students' indifference was the lack of vision for missions in the leadership of many local churches. It was believed that if pastors were regularly presenting the needs and challenging their congregations to move out of indifference, the job of the S.V.M. on campus would be much easier. Mott believed the role of a pastor should include building world vision into the life of every member. He shares, "Thousands of well qualified young men and young women are not even thinking of the missionary enterprise, simply because it has never been brought before them in such a way as to suggest that they could engage in it if they so desired."[8]

THE BIRTH OF A BURDEN

I once heard a pastor open his sermon with the question, "What is the greatest need in the world today?" Some

---

[7] Arthur T. Pierson, *The Divine Enterprise of Missions, 2nd ed.* (London: Hodder and Stoughton, 1891), 47-48.

[8] John R. Mott, *The Pastor and Modern Missions* (New York: SVM, 1904), 162.

people in the congregation responded with various news reports of natural disasters here and there; war tragedies of that particular time were mentioned; I think world hunger was even cited. The pastor acknowledged the truth and severity of each need, but continued on to gently challenge the people that, if they were honest, they would have to admit that the greatest needs in the world were their own felt needs. His point was this—no matter how great someone else's spiritual or physical plight, if that person lived in Mongolia, my own sore finger or sick grandmother would always take priority in my prayer life. This is the root of indifference. Needs that are not experienced by us go unacknowledged by us. Churches in the 1800s felt the "need" for floral decorations to adorn the sanctuary and it trumped the needs of the lost overseas. Today, the average Christian spends more money on dog food than on missions. Why? Because we experience the immediate "need" to feed our pets more readily than we enter into the needs of those without the gospel in Central Asia.

While, in many ways, we are responding to apathy much like the Student Volunteer Movement did at the turn of the 20th century, I can see two very distinct approaches that mobilizers and missions agencies utilize today. We have identified some consistent underlying causes for indifference: the lack of personal attachment and the obvious difficulty that the task of reaching the world presents. As a result, our counterargument addresses these two issues.

First of all, I can completely understand the difficulty in truly feeling a burden for a people from whom I am totally detached. I know the statistics, I know what the Bible says about it, I have missions-minded friends, and I still struggle to intercede for Laos in a heartfelt way. Why? Even though it is largely unreached and desperately in need of Christ's rescue from Buddhism, I still have no personal attachment to the people of Laos. The S.V.M. would respond to me by rebuking my self-absorption and challenging me to step up despite my feelings. This approach has its place, but I think something else is needed in today's generation. That is, it is important for students to recognize that they don't necessarily need to identify with or even care deeply for the people of Laos; they simply need to recognize that Laotians are extremely dear to the heart of God. He loves them infinitely and desires a relationship with them in the same way that He loves and desires us! Students need to hear that if they love God, it is imperative that they embrace His love for the lost of the world—not that they feel a love for them, but that they love the God who loves them.

I illustrate the point in this way: When my wife and I began dating, one obvious chasm stood between us—my deep devotion to coffee and her total lack of it. If you love coffee, you know how devastating this was to me. I begged her, "Jess, please try to come toward me in this!" At first she'd order hot chocolate. But gradually she advanced to mochas and lattes with tons of sugar stirred in. Then that thrilling day came when Jess ordered straight coffee! Jess didn't start out loving coffee; she started by loving me. Because she desired to move toward me in my passions she developed a love for coffee. One key to answering students' apathy is to redirect their love to God. He loves the nations and we love Him. That is enough.

He loves the nations and we love Him. That is enough.

Second, when apathy is caused by the difficulty of the task, missions agencies are confronting it by customizing their appeal to students and their specialties. It is not hard to find short-term trips overseas that are centered on hiking the Himalayas, surfing the Mediterranean, choreographing dances to indigenous music, or even creating worship music that is culturally contextual! Every personality and gifting can find a very specific expression overseas. The S.V.M. responded with a "pull up your boots straps and do the hard thing" mentality. They emphasized the difficulty and sacrifice of going even more. It is still true that reaching the world will be difficult and will require sacrifice, but a healthy dose of meeting students where they are is needed to maximize our recruitment of this generation.

Because we are human, indifference has always and will continue to be a primary response to the needs of the nations. With God's help we can overcome our own heart as we love Him and move toward His heart.

CHAPTER 23
ISSUES UNIQUE TO WOMEN

B y the time I met my wife, Jessica, she had just spent a summer in Papua New Guinea, enrolled in a missionary training school, and spent most of her time with the lost or in her Bible—I could barely get her to slow down to go on our first date! She knew well the struggles of a missional life and had wrestled with them personally—I just had to convince her that I wasn't one of them. I knew the life ahead of us would involve rigorous traveling, living in the Middle East, and all kinds of sacrifice. What was so attractive about her was that, as a single woman, I had already seen her incredible capacity to make the sacrifice.

It is no secret that the emotional, mental, and spiritual makeup of women differs significantly from that of men. And this fact is what helps family life, social life, and spiritual life run more smoothly. God, in His wisdom, allowed for relational balance by creating men and women to work in a complementary fashion. Just as men tend to struggle in areas that come naturally for women, so women have their own unique battles to fight.

The first female missions agency was established in the 1860s, and by the birth of the Student Volunteer Movement there were approximately twenty in existence.[1] Also by this time in history, mission boards had done away with the rule that required a woman to be married to go to the field. The S.V.M. came along at the perfect time in history to capitalize on the shift of missionary thinking regarding women. By the beginning of the 1900s there were over 600 institutions of higher learning that women could attend, and the enrollment of women in colleges and universities had reached over 110,000.[2] The Student Volunteer Movement went after the female recruits with the same tenacity that they went after the male ones, and this is attested to in the numbers of those who sailed. Michael Parker, in his book *The Kingdom of Character,* reminds us that "By 1905 women became the majority of the S.V.M.'s members who annually sailed as missionaries, and by 1908 the majority of its new members. Men continued to dominate the leadership of the Movement, but women became its mainstay."[3] Of the missionaries who sailed between the years of 1886 and 1920, over half were women.[4]

In light of this, it is no wonder that there were issues in recruitment that were unique to women. The biggest issue addressed was marriage. Women at the turn of the century were getting married at a young age, and yet the S.V.M. challenged them to heed the command of the Lord and go as missionaries to the field. A "yes" to this challenge meant almost certain lifelong, yet voluntary, singleness.

---

[1] Michael Parker, *The Kingdom of Character: The Student Volunteer Movement for Foreign Missions 1886-1926, 2nd edition* (Pasadena, CA: William Carey Library, 2008), 74.
[2] Bertha Conde, "The Women Students of the United States," *The Intercollegian,* Fourth Series, XXIII. No. 7 (April 1901): 149.
[3] Parker, 55.
[4] Parker, 56.

Bertha Conde, a single missionary in Latin America, at the 1920 S.V.M. convention in Des Moines tried to comfort the girls regarding their fear of singleness if they went to the field:

Of the missionaries who sailed between the years of 1886 and 1920, over half were women.

There is one question that I think most girls face, and that is, if I should go out into the foreign field, would that cut off all opportunity for marriage in my life? In the first place, the Mission Board probably will not want you for the foreign field before you are twenty-five years old. There will be ample opportunity for many social contacts before you reach that age... In the second place, if you form a purpose to go into foreign missionary work and live a life that is just as wide as God's horizon and as big as the world, you won't be likely to engage yourself to a man whose horizon in life is just about as wide as an inch and a half.[5]

If still unmarried when the time came for her departure, this wasn't to hold her back. In this situation the woman was challenged to find strength in the fact that God was her first love over all, deserving of her absolute faithfulness to Him and her total obedience to His call. Ruth Rouse, a pioneer in the movement and Traveling Secretary, declared:

---

[5] North American Students and World Advance, Addresses Delivered at the Eighth International Convention of the Student Volunteer Movement for Foreign Missions, Des Moines, Iowa, Dec. 31, 1919 – Jan. 4, 1920, 288.

If you are a Christian woman, you have absolutely no right to hold that life as your own. It is not yours any more than the dress that belongs to a friend is yours; and if you are holding it as your own possession, you are holding it not by right but by robbery... Oh, I ask every woman in the room today to fill out that other sentence, "I so love that I give"—what? A little time, a little strength, a little money, or my life? Your gift will be the measure of your love.[6]

The second issue involving the recruitment of women was family requirements at home. Women were expected to be the ones who cared for the family's needs; not financial needs, but hands-on service like managing the household, caring for ailing parents, and even helping with extended family. Those were commonly the responsibilities that women took on, even those who had graduated from the university. This made it even more difficult for the female of the family to decide to move

Ruth Rouse

[6] The Students and the Modern Missionary Crusade, Addresses Delivered before the Fifth International Convention of the Student Volunteer Movement for Foreign Missions, Nashville, Tennessee, Feb. 28-March 4, 1906, 262-263.

abroad; in essence, she was abandoning her responsibility to meet these needs at home. Again, Ruth Rouse states, "You are balancing home work against work in the foreign field. Remember that home claims have on their side all the vividness of sight... Of the nature of foreign missionary work, on the other hand you can have but a vague notion— no words of appeal, written or spoken, have the force of need personally seen."[7] The fact that her family opposed her being a missionary was not accepted as a viable excuse. "I do not suppose there is a woman in the foreign field today, unless she may be a missionary's daughter, who has not had to face at one time or another some kind of opposition from those that love her best; and just because they loved her best did they at first oppose this thing."[8] While the women may have felt torn between the pressures of meeting the needs at home and the pressure to meet the great needs overseas, the emphasis was placed on their hearts. Above all, women should *desire* to be used of God overseas. Bertha Conde speaks to the fact that God is not looking for those who need to be shoved to the field, but those who go voluntarily:

I have learned that God never takes advantage of anybody, never. Don't forget that, girls. He never takes advantage of anybody, and He never is going to take you by the shoulders and push you out to China, or push you out to Africa, or India, or any place in this world. We only want volunteers, people who want to go. This is not a draft proposition, and not one

---

[7] Ruth Rouse, "An Appeal to Women Students for Missionary Decision," *The Intercollegian*, Fourth Series, XXIII. no. 7 (April 1901): 151.

[8] The Students and the Modern Missionary Crusade, Addresses Delivered before the Fifth International Convention of the Student Volunteer Movement for Foreign Missions, Nashville, Tennessee, Feb. 28-March 4, 1906, 268.

of us in this room is fit to go if God has to take her by the shoulders and push her. She would not be much use to Him in any land.[9]

The first two issues women dealt with were family and marriage, both rooted in cultural expectations and pressures. This third issue, while connected to the cultural norms of the day, resided more in the minds of women. They felt at their core they were not qualified like the men were. Not only were women denied the privilege to be ordained at this time, but they could not even attend seminary. And as I mentioned before, only recently had women even been allowed to go without a husband. These factors left an immense feeling of ill-preparedness that affected recruitment. Grace Wilder in her short pamphlet *Shall I Go?* tries to come against this mind-set and encourages the women:

> 1 Corinthians 1:18-31 mentions five things which God uses: the weak, foolish, base, and despised things, and things that are not. Why? That no one may glory in his own strength, wisdom, or power… Our only fear need be that we are not offering to God the very *best we* have… One who has been a missionary a quarter of a century sends us girls this message: "If you have given yourselves a living sacrifice unto God, fear not the foreign field."[10]

Nettie Dunn pleaded with the women in the audience at the 1891 convention to look not at their qualifications, but

---

[9] North American Students and World Advance, Addresses Delivered at the Eighth International Convention of the Student Volunteer Movement for Foreign Missions, Des Moines, Iowa, Dec. 31, 1919 – Jan. 4, 1920, 287.

[10] Grace Wilder, *Shall I Go? Thoughts for Girls,* 5th ed. (SVM: New York, 1888), 10-11.

to focus on the incredible scarcity of females going out. As a challenge she added:

> There are a hundred thousand young women in our American colleges today; fifty thousand of them are Christian women, and only one or two thousand are volunteers for the foreign field. There are between four and five million Christian young women in this country, and only this handful going out to this great and needy field.[11]

As the S.V.M. wisely dealt with these issues and sought to show the female students why they were so critical to the overall success of the missionary movement, there were two primary ideas that were emphasized.

Only women can reach women: Men cannot get behind the veil of Islam. Though men were going out, half of the world's population were women and this fact mandated a proportionate amount of female recruits. Una Saunders exhorted women all over the United States regarding the missionary possibilities of women:

> The great mass of the women in the non-Christian countries can only be reached by the women of the Christian countries. Men preachers, men doctors, men teachers, cannot get access to the greater number of those women... It is only the human voice, and it is only the voice of a woman that can reach the closed homes and the closed hearts of the women of those countries.[12]

---

[11] John R. Mott, *Student Mission Power: Report of the First International Convention of the Student Volunteer Movement for Foreign Missions* (Pasadena, CA: William Carey Library, 1891), 184.

[12] The Students and the Modern Missionary Crusade, 77-78.

Liberation: The S.V.M. specifically rallied women to go by speaking to their unique ability to address the physical needs and help stop the degradation of women in non-Christian lands. As women in the States were fighting for their rights, they could identify with the longing of women in the world for liberation. This was a great motivation as Western women viewed themselves as liberators of oppressed women around the world. Helen Montgomery wrote the first history of American women in missions in a book titled, *Western Women in Eastern Lands*. A keynote speaker at the 1920 convention, she challenged women in the audience with the theme of social justice: "What are you going to do for these other sisters of ours who need schools and hospitals and friends? Who needs to give the training to them that they can take up the great work in their own land for the Son of God?"[13]

Women in the S.V.M.'s day brought unique challenges to the question of student recruitment. But they also brought unique gifts and blessings to the missionary cause. The Volunteers carefully crafted their efforts for their female audience, and as a result, over half of the volunteers raised up during the peak years of the movement were women.

SETTLING FOR MR. WRONG

Today, we don't deal with mission boards who only accept married couples. We are also not burdened by an ex-

---

[13] North American Students and World Advance, Addresses Delivered at the Eighth International Convention of the Student Volunteer Movement for Foreign Missions, Des Moines, Iowa, Dec. 31, 1919 – Jan. 4, 1920, 175.

pectation for a woman to be married off by her 21st birthday. Women today can avail themselves to seminary education, missionary training, and every field of ministry imaginable. Yet even with the changes that have occurred in the last one hundred years, some things remain the same in the hearts of women. Singleness is just as big an issue today as it was in the past. I have sat down with a countless number of students who, in the back of their mind, equate going to the field with taking a vow of singleness. For women, whose basic composition is relational, this is especially overwhelming. The temptation to position herself in the most strategic situation for meeting potential prospects is very great. Often it seems that a five-year commitment to Indonesia flies in the face of this relational strategy.

Ironically, I have seen the complete opposite! I have a surprising amount of friends who met their mate while they were serving the Lord overseas. It does make sense. Where could you go to find the guys or girls who are the most like-minded about missions and ministry? How about overseas! Don't get me wrong, just going overseas in no way guarantees you will meet your spouse, but it doesn't guarantee indefinite singleness either. I can still remember when I was in college and I heard Steve Shadrach, longtime veteran in student ministry, explaining to a crowd of eager students how to find one's mate. He said college students need to understand the appropriate order of life pursuits: The first priority is to know the Master. Second, students should pursue His mission for them, and only when those two are more established is it finally time to start thinking about a mate. If these get out of order, there is great potential for a mate not to share one's perspective of the Master or His mission. Of course, the other option a woman today has is to settle. Here is an e-mail I received.

> I just wanted to let you know I came across your website today. At 18, I spent a summer in student missions and knew at the end of that summer that God wanted me in missions work—but then I met "a guy" and basically sold God out just to get married. I am now 41 and have regretted that decision in so many ways. Please keep telling young people that the day to minister for Christ is today—not tomorrow or next semester or next year. And tell them to never, ever, ever let any person or anything deter you from the mission that God has placed in your heart. I am speaking from experience. –Amy

While the proverbial grass may look greener on the marriage side, if compromise has to be made to get there, a woman may soon find that singleness was greener after all. Truly nothing is more fulfilling than doing what God has designed a person to do—not even marriage. It must be remembered that God is a good, faithful Provider who has our absolute best in mind. When you follow Him without reservation, I guarantee you will never miss out on what He intends for you.

Another issue that I feel is alive and well from the past is the feeling of inadequacy that resides in the hearts of some women. When we consider the task at hand, we have to admit that, in our strength, we are all inadequate! "Such confidence we have through Christ toward God. Not that we are adequate in ourselves to consider anything as coming from ourselves, but our adequacy is from God" (2 Corinthians 3:4-5, NASB). Only when we focus on God's ability is He able to achieve His plans through us. Did you know that single women account for about two-thirds of the missionary force today? This statistic has held true for decades! Some of the greatest missionaries in history have been women, such as Amy Carmichael, Helen Roseveare, Gladys Aylward, Grace Wilder, Darlene Diebler-Rose, Catherine Booth, Ann Judson, Nettie Dunn, and Lottie Moon—women who trusted in God rather than in their own adequacy. Undeniably, women have left their mark on the world, and you can too!

When you follow Him without reservation, I guarantee you will never miss out on what He intends for you.

The era of the Student Volunteer Movement was ripe for the recruitment of women, not because it was easy or because students weren't dealing with any issues. No, it was ripe because despite the presence of cultural, spiritual, and personal challenges they never shied away from having honest conversations with students. They kept the commitment high, the education quality and the encouragement steady. In light of this, the Student Volunteer Movement received the fruit of their labor as hundreds of women signed up to become cross-cultural missionaries. The potential for women to be used incredibly by God to impact the nations still remains as potent as ever! No single woman should ever have to choose between God's leading and marriage prospects. I know it is a temptation and a fear, but it is only that. Allow God to use you no matter your relational status. When we decide that our fulfillment and our adequacy come from God alone I believe we will see an even greater uprising of women who say "Yes!" to what God is asking of them.

CHAPTER 24
SUPPORT RAISING

I graduated from college and was so excited to hit the workforce, become a real man, and get a job! I accepted a position as a campus minister, and finally I would get to do what I loved—reach college students! I sat down with my mentor, he laid out my salary structure, and I was pumped because it seemed like a lot! Then he said, "You have the summer, go raise it!" Emotions flooded my mind. I was nervous, scared, and knew my parents might freak. But I did it, and I'm so glad! The support-raising process affirmed that ministry was exactly what God had directed me to do. I had to convincingly cast the vision over and over to potential donors. I had to trust God. It developed me in areas I would not have gained naturally. Had I lived in the late 1800s, I most likely would not have had the opportunity to raise support, but today, approximately 70 percent of Christian workers raise their own financial support in this way.

In the following two chapters we will look at two issues that exist today without a historical counterpart in light of the theological shifts that have occurred over the last one hundred years. They are support raising and the destiny of the lost.

When the Student Volunteer Movement was recruiting for missions, it was still the norm for churches to cover all the missionary's expenses. Primarily, sending was their responsibility. We saw, however, how this era was just beginning to transfer that duty to the few and newly founded missions agencies.[1] Today, the parachurch has definitely come into its own as hundreds upon hundreds exist. As a result, support raising is now the primary means for students to go overseas in this generation. Not many college students have $3,000 tucked away in their savings waiting to be spent at a moment's notice on a short-term mission trip. Similarly, missionaries aren't always able to get a salary-paying job to sustain them on the field. Though culturally difficult, support raising is biblical, and understanding the biblical basis of support raising provides a foundation.

JESUS, PAUL, AND ME

There are several passages that speak of support raising as a means God uses to provide for those who are working for His kingdom.

When Jesus sent out the twelve disciples for ministry in Matthew 10, He gave them specific instructions on where to go, what to do, and what to take. "Do not take along any gold or silver or copper in your belts; take no bag for the journey, or extra tunic, or sandals or a staff; for the worker

---

[1] Andrew Walls, *The Missionary Movement in Christian History* (Maryknoll, New York: Orbis Press, 1996), 252.

is worth his keep" (Matthew 10:9-10). Jesus, with abundant resources at His disposal, instructed His disciples that, because of the nature of their work, they were worthy to receive compensation; others were to provide for their physical needs so they could focus solely on the spiritual needs of the people. Not only did He exhort the disciples in this approach, Jesus Himself modeled it. The gospel of Luke tells us that His needs were met by various women in the community. "Joanna the wife of Cuza, the manager of Herod's household; Susanna; and many others. These women were helping to support them out of their own means" (Luke 8:3). William Dillon writes:

> Jesus, who so easily could have turned stones into bread and who multiplied loaves and fishes, lived off the gifts of His friends during His public ministry. Then He pulled the economy rug out from under the feet of those He called into His service. He insisted that the fishermen should leave their fishing, the tax collector his tax collecting, and the tent maker his tent making... They were to accept the hospitality of those who would open their homes, "eating and drinking such things as they give: for the laborer is worthy of his hire" (Luke 10:7, KJV).[2]

It's no surprise that the apostle Paul echoed this concept in his writings. Paul is clear that he has full privileges to receive financial gifts from others; however, he did not exercise this right because of the Corinthians' immaturity.[3]

---

[2] William P. Dillon, *People Raising: A Practical Guide to Raising Support* (Chicago, IL: Moody Press, 1993), 24.

[3] Scott Morton, *Funding Your Ministry: An In-Depth, Biblical Guide for Successfully Raising Personal Support* (Colorado Springs, CO: NavPress, 2007), 42.

> Don't you know that those who work in the temple get their food from the temple, and those who serve at the altar share in what is offered on the altar? In the same way, the Lord has commanded that those who preach the gospel should receive their living from the gospel. But I have not used any of these rights (1 Corinthians 9:13-15).

Parachurch organizations have different convictions as to how support is raised. Some groups have no problem with their staff meeting face-to-face with potential donors and asking them for a monthly financial commitment. Other groups allow their staff to meet with individuals or groups, make their needs known, yet discourage them from asking for a specified amount.[4] No matter what the organization's policy, funds need to be raised before the next stage of ministry can begin. If it is God who has led us to ministry, it is God who will guide our efforts. Betty Barnett exhorts us, "Our long-term success in support raising is dependent upon Him being our source of wisdom and ideas: His strength when we're weak; His encouragement when we're discouraged; and His spiritual tactics for battle against our enemy."[5]

I'M SO NERVOUS

Again, raising support is not unbiblical as much as it is un-American. We are a very self-sufficient society, so

---

[4] This policy is a result of the "Faith Mission Movement" influenced by Hudson Taylor, who in 1865 founded the first faith mission organization, called China Inland Mission. He was heavily influenced by George Mueller, who believed that needs should be made known only to God. For more information about the faith mission movement, see the comprehensive work Klaus Fiedler, *The Story of Faith Missions: From Hudson Taylor to Present Day Africa* (Regnum/Lynx, Oxford, 1994).

[5] Betty Barnett, *Friendraising: Building a Support Team That Lasts* (Seattle, WA: YWAM Publishing, 1991), 58.

some inherent fears are attached to the process.[6]

Failure: It is a big step to join a parachurch ministry that requires support raising. What will happen if deadlines are not met and money is not raised? Since no salary is guaranteed, the possibility of being viewed as a failure is very real.

Raising support is not unbiblical as much as it is un-American.

Rejection: What will the people I love most think of me when I ask for money? It can be quite uncomfortable to have a close friend decide he/she will not give financially. Will the awkwardness change the relationship in the future? Fear of offending people and the risk of losing friends is enough to keep some people from raising support. I can remember making my list of potential donors, and there was one particular couple I was so intimidated to ask. I just felt a weird vibe, for some reason. I knew it was going to be uncomfortable. I decided that if I never asked I would be at the same place as if I had asked and been rejected. So, I decided to go for it. They not only came on our support team, they are our biggest givers and have not missed a month!

Weakness: Phrases like "begging for money," "get a real job," "how long is this phase?" often surround the subject of support raising. The new graduate can feel dis couraged that support raising is a sign that he can't really

---

[6] These fears were adopted from Steve Shadrach, "The Top Five Fears in Support Raising," Support Raising Solutions, July 2009. Available from thebodybuilders.net.

make it on his own. Fears are genuine, but our identity is in Christ, and at the end of the day all people, no matter what their profession may be, rely on God to provide financially.

Ministry does not begin after support has been raised; rather, support raising is its own ministry.

Support raising should not be viewed as a necessary evil, but as its own type of ministry.[7] I have a friend, Dean, who went on a support appointment, and the couple was so challenged by the needs of the world they decided to downsize, not only their possessions, but their cars and house! Dean called me and said, "Todd, I think this couple just put their home on the market so they could give more to missions!" Ministry does not begin after support has been raised; rather, support raising is its own ministry.[7] Casting vision to others and exposing them to the world is an incredible opportunity that support raisers repeatedly have with people who might otherwise never be exposed. Think of how many people in all seasons of life will be met during the process—potentially hundreds! And each one represents another opportunity to encourage a believer in his or her role in missions.

No doubt the best recruiter for missions is the missionary

---

[7] Morton, 21.
[8] Dillon, 4.

himself. Support raising calls for the missionary to interface with other believers who make up the Body of Christ. When they meet face-to-face, the missionary communicates his vision, his call. His enthusiasm and dedication stimulate interest and involvement in missions.[8]

The body of Christ, by its very nature, is interdependent. The gifts and roles that God has given each individual are meant to be mutually beneficial and reciprocal. Support raising is one of the most obvious opportunities that we have to act out these qualities. Some are privileged to fill the role of missionary. Some are privileged to stay behind and financially send out those missionaries. This give-and-take relationship truly is a blessing to all who submit themselves to it and participate according to God's leading. May we not allow cultural and personal discomforts to keep us from this biblical provision that God has designed to bless us and further His kingdom!

CHAPTER 25
DESTINY OF THE LOST

Leonard Ravenhill once said, "Jehovah's Witnesses don't believe in hell and neither do most Christians." Few topics are as sensitive as the destiny of the lost. When those questions go unanswered, students will often fill that knowledge gap with a mix of theological fallacies. I received an e-mail that echoes what I have heard multiple times from students:

> What happens to people who never hear the Gospel? It is a paradox. From what I know/understand, they never ascend to Heaven. Yet it is seemingly unreasonable to condemn them to Hell. — Gabe, University of Illinois

Unbiblical reasoning about the lost must be addressed, because it undermines the urgency and necessity of reaching them.

The students in the late 1800s and early 1900s, for the most part, did not question the destiny of the lost. Christians were exclusivists whose categories were clear-cut and straightforward. It was understood that salvation came through Christ alone and this foundation meant that there were only two evident ways to spend eternity: in heaven or in hell. Today, because so many other alternative solutions have been introduced, students are treading in some pretty murky waters. What students truly believe about the afterlife is an incredible motivator (or de-motivator) behind how they live their life. Removing the straightforward categories of absolute truth has created a domino effect of unanswered questions. Some of these questions may include: What happens when the nonbeliever dies? Will they be reincarnated? Do they simply cease to exist? Will they enter a state of innocent bliss? Will they suffer forever for their sin? But, inevitably, at least one of the questions is why does missions even matter? In 1997, 56 percent of Americans claimed to believe in hell. That number spiked to more than 74 percent after the terrorist attacks on September 11, 2001. However, recent polling indicates the number has once again dropped significantly.[1] It is one thing to believe in a hell that is escaped by engaging in good works. It is quite another to believe that the sacrifice of Jesus Christ is the one and only hope for bypassing eternal damnation. The former paradigm motivates a person to act and respond in kindness; the latter challenges a person to step out with the gospel and proclaim it to the nations.

LOVE AND JUSTICE

For many, the doctrine of eternal punishment is difficult to fathom, much less accept. It is more difficult when applied to those who have never heard the gospel. Thankfully,

---

[1] Charles Honey, "Belief in Hell Dips, but Some Say They've Already Been There," Pew Forum on Religion and Public Life (August 14, 2008). Available from pewforum.org.

Scripture is far from silent regarding the destiny of man and eternal punishment. All men are declared sinners, children of wrath, and held under condemnation (Romans 3:23; 5:12; Ephesians 2:3). This means there are two destinies for mankind, one of everlasting joy in the presence of God and one of everlasting torment apart from God (Matthew 25:41; Luke 15:10; Revelation 22:3-5). J. Herbert Kane states,

> The word *Gehenna* (hell) occurs twelve times in the New Testament; eleven times it came from the lips of Christ. It was not John the Baptist or the apostle Paul, or Martin Luther, or John Knox who first coined those awful words we would prefer to drop from our present day preaching: "the unquenchable fire," "the worm that dieth not," "outer darkness," "weeping and gnashing of teeth"... These are not the wild, irresponsible words of some flaming evangelist who goes up and down the country preaching hell, fire, and brimstone in an attempt to scare people into the kingdom. These words, terrible though they are, fell from the lips of the meekest Man who ever lived, the Friend of publicans and sinners, the Man who gave His life and shed His blood that men might be forgiven; and they were spoken, we may be sure, with a tear in the eye and a quiver in the voice.[2]

There is nothing in the New Testament that gives the reader hope that there exists after death the possibility of a second chance. Actually, the opposite is true. Scripture states, "It is appointed for men to die once, and after this

---

[2] J. Herbert Kane, *Understanding Christian Missions* (Grand Rapids, MI: Baker Book House, 1982), 131.

comes judgment" (Hebrews 9:27, NASB; also see Luke 16:19-31).[3] Serious philosophical and theological problems exist for those who reject that hell is the destiny of the lost.[4] First, it robs the death of Christ of its atonement. If mankind could be saved apart from the cross then God erred horrifically in allowing His Son to suffer and die. Secondly, why would Jesus have made preaching the gospel the primary mission of the Church? His final command to His followers was to preach this message of repentance to all the nations (Matthew 28:18-20; Mark 16:15; Luke 24:46-49; and John 20:21). This mission would be incredibly undercut if all are eventually to be saved. Third, as mentioned previously, Christ clearly taught about hell and a division after death between the righteous and the unrighteous. So to deny this truth is to open the door for discrimination between truth and error in the Bible. Robertson McQuilkin states,

> The ones who call on *the name* are the ones who will be saved. But what of those who have not heard so they cannot call? Paul does not assure us that those who have not heard may simply believe on whatever they have heard (Romans 10:17). But suppose no one goes? Will God send some angel or some other special revelation? Even if God did have such an alternative plan, were He to reveal that to us, we who have proved so irresponsible and disobedient would no doubt cease altogether obedience to the Great Commission.[5]

---

[3] For a more in-depth study on the topic of hell, see R. A. Torrey, *Heaven or Hell* (Springdale, PA: Whitaker House, 1985). Also see W. G. T. Shedd, *The Doctrine of Endless Punishment*, reprinted (Carlisle, PA: Banner of Truth Trust, 1986); as well as J. M. Humphrey, *The Lost Soul's First Day in Eternity* and *A Soul's First Day in Heaven* (Shoals, IN: Old Paths Tract Society, 1912).

[4] The three problems listed are adapted from Robertston McQuilkin, *The Great Omission* (Grand Rapids, MI: Baker Book House, 1984), 41-43.

[5] McQuilkin, 45, 49.

HOW LONG IS FOREVER

In an attempt to offer a softened approach to Christ's teachings on hell, some have propagated a perspective called annihilationism. This view states that the nature of hell is total destruction rather than the endless torture of those who have died without Christ.[6] The fire of hell is totally consuming rather than eternally tormenting. This position employs Matthew 7:13; 10:28; Romans 9:22; and Hebrews 10:26-27 for support, though it is extremely difficult to reconcile these passages completely with their claims.[7] The major focus on the debate regarding annihilationism is on the Greek word *aion,* which is translated "ever" and "eternal." *Aion* is used sixty-four times in the New Testament and refers to "the divine and blessed realities of the other world." Ajith Fernando shares significant insight into the debate regarding annihilationism and the use of *aion*:

> Sometimes this idea is expressed with even more stress by repeating the word "ever." Revelation 4:10 and 10:6 say that God lives "forever and ever." Revelation 11:15 says, "He will reign forever and ever." It would be unnatural to take "ever and ever" in these statements as meaning anything other than "everlasting." The phrase "ever and ever" is used in Revelation for eternal punishment too... Here too the words must mean everlasting.[8]

---

[6] Evangelical Alliance Commission on Unity and Truth Among Evangelicals, *The Nature of Hell* (London: Acute Publishing, 2000), 4-5.

[7] Michael J. Murray, *Reasons for the Hope Within* (Grand Rapids, MI: Eerdmans Publishing, 1998), 315.

[8] Ajith Fernando, *Crucial Questions about Hell* (Wheaton, IL: Crossway Books, 1991), 46.

John Walvoord states correctly, "one is faced with the fact that the only place one can prove absolutely that God is a God of love and grace is from Scripture. If one accepts the doctrine of God's love and grace as revealed in the Bible, how can that person question, then, that the same Bible teaches eternal punishment?"[9]

Annihilationism diminishes the urgency of evangelism. However, a correct view of hell, the destiny of the lost, and their impending judgment provides tremendous motivation to move today's believer out of spiritual lethargy and into active evangelism, especially as the Church becomes complacent.

If one accepts the doctrine of God's love and grace as revealed in the Bible, how can that person question, then, that the same Bible teaches eternal punishment?

Yet the church today seems to be content to ignore the plight of the lost. Its people have become complacent in the enjoyment of the church's nice building and their own middle-class incomes... Perhaps this urgency has been lost because the church no longer teaches or preaches about hell, even though the idea still might be found in our doctrinal statement.[10]

[9] William Crockett, ed., *Four Views on Hell* (Grand Rapids, MI: Zondervan, 1996), 27.
[10] W. Edward Glenny and William H. Smallman, eds., *Missions in a New Millennium* (Grand Rapids, M: Kregel Publications, 2000), 152.

Paul Borthwick suggests three areas of our lives that will change when we take seriously the biblical doctrine of hell: an increased urgency in evangelism, a deeper level of compassion, and a greater desire to target those with no opportunity to hear the gospel.[11] He states, "In spite of the wonderful advances of the Christian church around the world, experts still estimate that between two and three billion people have no opportunity to hear the gospel and respond. The doctrine of hell ought to burden us deeply to mobilize the church to get the good news to these people."[12]

The doctrine of hell ought to burden us deeply to mobilize the church to get the good news to these people.

The tossing out of the difficult doctrine of hell is, I believe, motivated by compassion and love for humanity—qualities initiated by God Himself! In the end just the opposite is achieved. People are left with little motivation to share the great news of salvation, and Christ's words on the topic are completely ignored. In complacency, we sit by while lost people and nations go on in their folly. Jeremiah says that nations will come before the throne of God and confess, "Our fathers possessed nothing but false gods, worthless idols that did them no good" (Jeremiah 16:19). Let us boldly embrace that

---

[11] Paul Borthwick, *Six Dangerous Questions to Transform Your View of the World* (Downers Grove, IL: InterVarsity Press, 1996), 81-83.

[12] Borthwick, 83.

which the Bible affirms: that hell is real and that God has made an incredibly gracious provision for lost humanity in His Son, Jesus Christ. Let it be a challenge to us to move out in compassionate, missions-minded action toward all people and nations with no current access to this truth.

MOVING
FORWARD

"If I have seen further than others, it is by standing on the shoulders of giants."

— Isaac Newton

CHAPTER 26
CONNECTING THE PAST TO THE PRESENT

"Would you tell me, please, which way I ought to go from here?"

"That depends a good deal on where you want to get to," said the Cat.

"I don't much care where…" said Alice.

"Then it doesn't matter which way you go," said the Cat.

—Lewis Carroll, *Alice in Wonderland*

Where do we go from here? We have journeyed back to look at mobilization in the past, but if we've done it only for the sake of studying history, then it does not matter where we go from here. If we care, however, about the nations and about students finding their place, then we move forward to learn from what we have studied. The first step is to see where our road merges with the Student Volunteer Movement's and where the two separate. I want to draw out some general and specific connections between the ways the S.V.M. recruited and the ways in which we do today, so that we can improve our efforts.

Methods: The S.V.M. embraced specific methods that contributed greatly to the longevity of the movement and to the number of students who sailed to the field. They followed up new recruits with the Mission Study Courses, used the printed page, brought students together collectively with their quadrennial conventions, deployed Traveling Secretaries, and prayed. Though we are separated by over one hundred years, similar methods are in use today. The Mission Study Courses of old have a modern-day component: the Perspectives course. The conventions of the past are much like the Urbana, Passion, and other conferences today. Though air travel and the personal vehicle have replaced the train, the spirit of Traveling Secretaries can still be seen in The Traveling Team. There are two methods, however, used today that were simply not available to the S.V.M.: the Internet and short-term mission trips. One wonders how that powerful movement would have utilized these if they'd had them.

Issues: Though our methods are similar, we see a great deal of discrepancy when we compare issues. Students have always dealt with the dilemmas of family and calling, but there are issues unique to this generation. One hundred years ago students did not go to college unless they could pay for it. Today the paradigm is quite different. Students are now graduating with debt beyond what they feel they can control. Debt is compounded by the fact that students are at times apprehensive about and even resistant to the idea of support raising. One of the more difficult heart issues is that, more than ever, students doubt the destiny of the lost. It's clear that today's mobilizers have tough challenges to face.

Theological: Our theology has shifted from history's theology. Students today have a different outlook on church in light of the many parachurch groups that they have exposure to. The fact that the nations are now at our door (and in the dorm) offers an incredible opportunity, but it also brings the Christian student face-to-face with his or her understanding of salvation and casts doubt as to whether or not Christ *is* the only way. In addition, we see today a significant downplaying of truth. Absolute truth has been kicked to the curb in favor of relative truth (even among Christians). There have been some progressive shifts too in the last century. The study of missions has developed greatly during these years, and the conceptual move from nations to people groups was a huge breakthrough for mobilizers.

Organizational: The Student Volunteer Movement was an incredibly tight, structured, and well-connected organization. One man, John Mott, led the movement for thirty-two years. The Young Men's Christian Association, which was the campus ministry of the day, viewed this movement as their primary missions arm. The result of this union was unprecedented inroads to students and quick, dramatic impact on the collegiate Christian culture in response to the S.V.M.'s challenge. Another result of the unique atmosphere of the day was that the watchword "the evangelization of the world in this generation" could be the rallying cry that was embraced by all. Today, there are dozens of campus ministries who each have their own watchword to drive them. Movements now are more diverse and multifaceted, and momentum is building within each one.

Technological: More has happened in the last one hundred years than probably in the last one thousand! Not only can students fly overseas in less than half a day, but they can, with the click of a button, be in a live video chat with students who have never stepped foot on this continent. The Internet can be utilized to pursue any desired information and the news is a constant source of global images. The world has become smaller as we have become interconnected. The downside is a calloused response to information overload. Crossing cultures is simply less intriguing.

Practical: Other paradigms have been effected

John Mott as an older man

The world has become smaller as we have become interconnected.

The motivation for missions truly has shifted from duty to delight.

today that make mobilization different. In the past when missions came up, the automatic definition was "going." Crossing cultures for the purpose of evangelism was the normal way to apply the Great Commission and be obedient as a Christ-follower. They did not have to interact with other cultures on a daily basis as we do in our day. Therefore, today's emphasis is not solely calling students to go long-term, but to live a lifestyle that exhibits World Christian priorities. That might mean boarding a plane and going anywhere from six weeks to ten years. It may also mean reaching out to internationals on campus, praying for the world, giving financially, or mobilizing; all our resources are geared toward this effort.

Motivational: The motivation for missions truly has shifted from duty to delight. The S.V.M.'s approach to mobilizing students kept the reality of the lost, the heathen, and hell always at the forefront of their messages—both written and spoken. Students' tolerance for the subject of hell is considerably lower today than it was one hundred years ago. Therefore, it is rarely talked about and has the reputation of being a guilt technique effective only in pushing an audience away instead of spurring them to action. This is not necessarily a negative, it is just different. Students are less man-centered in their motivation; focused on saving people from hell, and more God-centered; focused on God receiving the worship He deserves.[1]

As we attempt to look to the past to reach the present, let's summarize the most valuable finds from our short survey of mobilization and see how we can move forward.

---

[1] The theologian at the forefront of this concept is John Piper. For more insight into duty versus delight see, John Piper, *Desiring God: Meditations of a Christian Hedonist* (Sisters, OR: Multnomah Books, 1986). John Piper, *Let the Nations Be Glad: The Supremacy of God in Missions* (Grand Rapids, MI: Baker Books, 1993). John Piper, *Don't Waste Your Life* (Wheaton, IL: Crossway Books, 2003). John Piper, *When I Don't Desire God: How to Fight for Joy* (Wheaton, IL: Crossway Books, 2004).

CHAPTER 27
SEVEN COMMON PRINCIPLES

Try to picture for a minute that you are walking into your church's Sunday service for the annual missions conference. You're pretty pumped because it's a guest speaker and you've heard he has a powerful presentation. You work your way to the front of the sanctuary to get a great seat; you don't want to miss anything. Finally, the announcements and singing are done and it's time for the speaker to deliver his message. Ready for a great challenge, you get your journal and pen in position. Then the lights dim and some scratchy music starts playing. A minute later, a black-and-white video starts playing and you think you hear what sounds like a movie reel laboring in the back. You manage a peek, even though you're in the front, and sure enough, a cinema-sized reel is whirring back there! The scratchy music changes abruptly from smooth and comforting to very intense. You realize it's scratchy because someone is operating it from two record players—it's the guest speaker! He begins to narrate the eight-millimeter film strip of tribal people. You can tell he has some great things to say, but you can't take notes because you're too distracted by the contraption he's rigged around his entire head and neck. Turns out the head gear is actually a hands-free harmonica holder with a bulky corded mic attached to the front, the speakers for which are dangling awkwardly from this man's equipment-laden body. The guest continues this very "multimedia" presentation and you shut your journal to ponder what kind of time warp you've found yourself in.

Sounds hilarious, doesn't it? How long would this guy's speaker circuit be in the 21st century? Incredibly, this is an actual scenario of a real missions mobilizer who lived in the 1940s. Not only was his presentation considered high-tech and extremely cutting edge, but it was amazingly fruitful in raising up laborers for the world! What's the point? Today, we probably wouldn't duplicate any of this man's methods— they are time-bound. I mean, you could try the record player thing, but I did this two weeks ago and it was a flop! The principle, however, that drove this mobilizer is enduring. He used all the methods at his disposal to communicate with the widest audience possible—that's timeless! That's what we want to do now. Look back to the past, sift through the time-bound periphery, and emerge with some timeless principles.

God has never stopped interrupting lives for His purpose, but for those who wish to mobilize, we must know our times and our audience. Based on what we have learned from the S.V.M. and from our own historical context I will highlight seven of these common principles to show that, if appropriately applied, a person, group, or church can experience a significant increase in their vision for missions. These are not a blueprint to be followed; rather they are principles to be implemented.

PRINCIPLE ONE – PRAYER SHOULD BE SPECIFIC IN ORDER TO BE MOST EFFECTIVE

It would be impossible to study the Student Volunteer Movement without seeing the preeminent place they gave to prayer. Prayer for the nations was at the heart of Robert Wilder's home where the Princeton Foreign Missionary Society was established. It was the force behind the recruitment of the first one hundred students at the Mount Hermon summer project and therefore, prayer was the foundation for the Movement itself. The S.V.M. produced an ample amount of resources to help students engage in prayer. Their intercession for the student, the campus, the Movement, and the various parts of the world communicates to the mobilizer today that this must be a valued principle.

It is true that prayer should be the primary work of the ministry. The problem is that students do not know what to pray. They have the world at their fingertips through the Internet and globalization in general, but instead of taking advantage of this and responding through a more informed prayer life, they do just the opposite. They react to the over-stimulation by withdrawal. They are unable and untrained to process the enormous amount of information. The mobilizer today must help students learn how to wade through today's overwhelming global exposure.

I have been in prayer groups all over the country, and it is common to hear requests for family issues, relationships, grades, or futures. What is often absent from these prayer meetings is the very request that Jesus commanded: *"Pray earnestly to the Lord of the harvest to send out laborers into his harvest"* (Matthew 9:37-38, ESV). This command assumes we are aware there is a harvest field in need of workers and believers who need to be sent there. Obviously, we need to pray for one another and lift up our family and friends, but God also desires that we join together to intercede on behalf of the world. What would it take to truly see a prayer movement for the nations?

Today, we need students who echo the words of Luke 11:1, "Lord, teach us to pray." We also need mobilizers who can help with the answer by specifically training students in intercession for the nations. This is where today's world prayer resources play a significant role. Effective prayer mobilizers will take prayer resources and help students utilize them. Print off a people group profile from the Joshua Project database, learn about a missionary or a team that has gone out to the world, gather information about current events in the world and have some news at your fingertips, or just open up *Operation World*![1] Pray specifically for others and the excuses they are wrestling with about going overseas or fears they may have. Ask God to raise up specific students from the campus to the harvest field. I have a friend who purchased *Operation World* and started praying specifically for the first country— Afghanistan. It is no surprise he is currently working there. Specific prayer yields tremendous results.

PRINCIPLE TWO – KEEP THE BIBLE AS THE PRIMARY MEANS OF RECRUITMENT

The second principle evident from the Student Volunteer Movement is that they used the Bible as the primary motivator for missions. They emphasized the Great Commission texts and encouraged students to step out in obedience to the clear command of Christ.[2] In every opportunity to mobilize, they brought the Bible, its message and claims, to bear upon students' lives. They moved students on the grounds that the subject of missions is not found in one or two verses, but it is the very theme of Scripture and the core of the Christian life.[3]

For centuries the Bible has communicated in a relevant way to its readers; therefore, it is the only foundation on which to build a timeless message. From Genesis to Revelation the question is not *Where can we find missions?* but *Where is it not?* God's plan is made clear beginning in Genesis 12 with Abraham, through the Prophets and into the Gospels, from the book of Acts and even into Revelation—

---

[1] Joshuaproject.net.

[2] Elizabeth Goldsmith, *Roots and Wings: Five Generations and Their Influence* (Waynesboro, GA: Paternoster Publishing Publication, 1998), 50.

[3] Robert Speer, *Christianity and the Nations* (London: Fleming H. Revell Company, 1910), 17.

God's Word articulates His plan on every page. His desire to use people to reach the world is unquestionable. What role does this overarching biblical narrative play in mobilization? It is the *only* method that will bear lasting fruit in a student's life. He invites us to be a part of

> *It is a privilege to lose our life for the greatest story of all time.*

His story, but He mandates we give up our ambitions. God's plan must transcend our own, but when we catch a glimpse of His purpose, we genuinely desire to submit ours. No one is willing to lay down their life for a lesser story. It is a privilege to lose our life for the greatest story of all time.

Our own testimony and experiences are important, and those should be told; however, never as a replacement for God's Word. Tragically, many times when returning missionaries are given the opportunity to challenge an audience, they center their messages on personal stories. Again, these have their place and that place is in the support and context of the Bible's missions theme. Personal experiences are inspiring, but without God's Word which acts as the authority in a Christian's life, the missions vision we seek to pass on will only be event/experience-oriented. I don't know anyone who has maintained a steadfast vision for the long haul when it was based merely on a testimony, a statistic, a moving video, or a heart-wrenching story.

I have come to realize that one's commitment to missions mirrors one's view of missions in Scripture. If God's heart is recognized on the pages of Scripture, our lives will be missional. If a person thinks missions is found in only one or two random verses, he will never allow God's heart to have an influence on his or her life or decisions.

What's the best way to implement this principle today? The mobilizer must be able to simply and thoroughly share this biblical theme. Genesis is a great starting place to show that through Abraham, Isaac, and Jacob (Genesis 12:1-3; 26:4; and 28:14), God sought to establish Israel as a missionary nation. The theme continues on through the Old Testament—God consistently acted on behalf of His name being made known in all the earth (examples: the parting of the Red Sea, Joshua 2:9-10; the wisdom of Solomon, 1 Kings 4:34; and Daniel the prophet, Daniel 6:26). In the New Testament, the majority of Christ's miracles involved those who were non-Jewish. Every gospel account ends with a passage commissioning the disciples (Matthew 28:18-20; Mark 16:15; Luke 24:44-48; and John 20:21). The book of Acts opens with an exhortation to the disciples to see this message taken to the ends of the earth (Acts 1:8), and Paul the apostle made this purpose his life ambition (Romans 15:20). The conclusion is found in Revelation 7:9 where Scripture culminates with a representative from every people, language, and culture around the throne.

The Word of God convicts, challenges, and guides

every person in every culture and every generation. Further-more, it consistently reveals God's unchanging purpose to redeem every nation. Therefore, it must be the forerunner for today's missions mobilizer.

PRINCIPLE THREE –
EXCUSES SHOULD BE LOGICALLY AND BIBLICALLY DISARMED

When students encountered obstacles, the mobilizer helped navigate them. For some, excuses represented a smoke screen behind which to hide their true, uncommitted heart. Others genuinely desired to go, but had immense pressure either from family or fiancée, the allure of affluence, or the fear of singleness. The S.V.M. thought that every person, both student and staff, needed to be equipped to counter these excuses. Print materials were published to address them, as seen in the *Shall I Go?* pamphlet by Grace Wilder. Missions speakers prepared talks with excuses in mind, and they challenged the students, without hesitation, to press through. The Traveling Secretaries also allowed time following their talks for students to ask about these excuses in a question–and-answer format.

Today, mobilizers will be confronted with excuses that were both familiar and unfamiliar to the S.V.M. It is important that we model their boldness to tackle these issues head-on with the truth. Mobilizers need to balance rebuke, exhortation, and humility. This is not just an argument to be won. Mobilizers need to handle excuses honestly and authentically, sharing about their own struggles and how they faced the same challenges themselves.

We should constantly encourage students that God is more interested in their availability than in their ability. God's abiding presence has always been the missionary's source of encouragement. The premise of Matthew 28:18-20 is that Jesus possesses all authority and that His presence is always with us: "All authority in heaven and on earth has been given to me. Therefore go and make disciples of all nations, baptizing them in the name of the Father and of the Son and of the Holy Spirit, teaching them to obey everything I have commanded you. And surely, I am with you always, to the very end of the age."

An excuse represents a stopping point in the student's Christian life, an area where Jesus has yet to be confessed as Lord. One must deal with the underlying issue of lordship; otherwise it will resurface in the form of another excuse. For example, if a student says his refusal to go is based on a struggle to raise support, part of the mobilizer's job is to help the student discern the true heart issue. Is it pride? Is it that they would rather provide for themselves by working for it? Is it a trust issue? Helping a student fully surrender his heart must be the primary motive of a mobilizer rather than getting one more student to sign the dotted line of missions. This approach not only deals more effectively with the true issue, it communicates a selfless desire for the student's spiritual health.

PRINCIPLE FOUR – DIVERSIFY YOUR METHODS IN ORDER TO REACH THE WIDEST POSSIBLE AUDIENCE

There are many motivations that God uses to guide us toward following Him. To name a few: love (John 4:21), obedience (Matthew 28:18-20), compassion (Matthew 9:36), and purpose (Matthew 16:26-27). As has been the case in every era, people are diversely motivated; each one is challenged in a different way to engage God's Word and God's world. In response to this, mobilizers need to expand their methods in order to be understood by as many students as possible.

The mobilizer at the beginning of this chapter tapped into various methods to reach the widest possible audience. So did the Student Volunteer Movement. Not only did volunteers present the Word of God, its claim upon students' lives, and its clear theme of God's heart for all nations, but they also held up maps of the world and showed charts and graphs to illustrate the desperate needs of the lost. They used print resources, large-group meetings facilitated by the Traveling Secretaries, prayer, and conferences to stir missions vision.

Today, we must take the same diversified approach.

Remember that while the ultimate goal is to win the hearts of the unreached to Christ, the immediate goal is to win the hearts of students to the nations. We should appeal to students on several levels to see this established in them. It is important not only that the methods be assorted, but that missions be advocated both by an outside voice (those with whom they are not connected day in and day out) as well as those who are regularly in their lives.

Students need to be exposed to practical resources such as books, websites, magazines, and videos. Books have the incredible power to sear a reader's mind with significant insight into missions. Biographies allow students to look to the men and women of the past and find mentorship in the narrative.[4] The world is up close and personal through the Internet. Students should be given well-established websites where, through videos, links, and statistics, students can essentially educate themselves in some areas of missions. They definitely need experience in initiating conversation with international students both for the incredible ways in which a student's vision will be expanded and for the benefit of the international who may hear the gospel for the first time. Students need constant reminders of the opportunity and challenge that lies in developing these friendships. Every mobilization effort should include an opportunity for a short-term trip for firsthand exposure.

Missions must be seen as something normal. Let's not marginalize it to a once-a-year announcement. When we

---

[4] A few biographies to start with are Norman Grubb, *C. T. Studd: Famous Athlete and Pioneer* (Grand Rapids, MI: Zondervan, 1933); Elisabeth Elliot, *A Chance to Die: The Life and Legacy of Amy Carmichael* (Grand Rapids, MI: Revell, 1987); Courtney Anderson, *To the Golden Shores: The Life of Adoniram Judson* (Valley Forge, PA: Judson Press, 1987); Ruth Tucker, *From Jerusalem to Irian Jaya* (Grand Rapids, MI: Zondervan Publishing, 1983).

talk about it regularly, it becomes the DNA of a group, congregation, or ministry. Let's consistently employ all the above means of exposure and see if students don't respond by adapting missions as an everyday lifestyle.

Mobilizers should know where each student is and challenge them in a way they understand. There is an important rule for mobilizers found in Habakkuk 2:2: "Then the Lord replied: 'Write down the revelation and make it plain on tablets so that a herald may run with it.'" Habakkuk was to write down the vision God gave him and put it on a level that the people could understand. A modern-day application of *making it plain* would be that before you discuss how to plant churches in Nagaland, you teach students what a church plant is! Before they are given statistics of unreached people groups, they need to know what the phrase "unreached people" means. Mobilization is not just the transmission of data; it also includes confirmation that students understand what has been presented. How does a mobilizer put the resources on the "bottom shelf" to be easily accessed and understood? By first asking the question, where are students in the pipeline of growth and in what areas do they need further exposure? Like Habakkuk, enabling them to comprehend is the first step in enabling them to obey. It is critical that as mobilizers we vary our methods and also communicate on a level appropriate to the understanding of our audience.

PRINCIPLE FIVE –
BE EQUIPPED TO FOLLOW UP YOUR
EFFORTS WITH RESOURCES

Thousands of people each year contact missions agencies, yet very few move past the stage of initial interest. There are as many reasons for this as there are people, but one thing is for sure, anyone seeking to raise up World Christians must have follow-up as a top priority. Because excuses are real, often unforeseen, and usually unprepared for, it is insufficient to stop casting vision after only minimum exposure. It's a mobilizer's responsibility to continue interacting with students until they have successfully navigated the entire process. Giving a student vision where there is none is difficult, but it pales in comparison to helping a student sustain and grow that vision. However, once initial interest has begun, it will take an incredible amount of energy and follow-through to keep the vision alive and active. There are plenty of case studies of students who have motivation and information, yet still do nothing. Why? There is no shortage of recruiters; everything is pulling for their passion, time, and resources. Christian students desperately need personal attention if they are going to thrive as World Christians.

Follow-up is another thing that the Student Volunteer Movement did remarkably well. They understood that the student's signature on the Volunteer Declaration was merely the first step in a long journey. After this first level of involvement, students were encouraged to begin reading a collection of eight books and pamphlets packaged together called *Choice Missionary Literature*.[5] These were considered the foundation that would supply confidence for the student. The S.V.M. had an entire department dedicated to follow-up, called the "Mission Study Department." Its primary function was to encourage students through the Mission Study Courses. Every student was challenged to plug into these courses because they offered accountability for students dealing with life issues. Hundreds of books and pamphlets were also printed that covered everything from the call of God to the neediest countries.[6]

Today, mobilization must take place in the context of relationship. There is no substitute for the kind of mentoring that will both encourage and confront. Praying for students, addressing their specific needs, and casting vision for their potential are essential components in the process. Training students in mobilization and exposing them to opportunities for growth are imperative to the journey towards a World Christian lifestyle. It is insufficient for resources to simply be made available. Follow-through is life-on-life coaching and is the necessary part if believers are to be established as authentic World Christians. Make no mistake, students will be

---

[5] The eight books and pamphlets are 1) *History of the Student Volunteer Movement for Foreign Missions*, by John R. Mott; 2) *Shall I Go? Thoughts for Girls*, by Grace E. Wilder; 3) *Prayer and Missions*, by Robert E. Speer; 4) *The Volunteer Band*, by J. Campbell White; 5) *The Self-Perpetuation of the Volunteer Band*, by J. Campbell White; 6) *Ten Lessons on the Bible and Missions*, by J. Campbell White; 7) *The Volunteer Band Meetings*, by J. Campbell White; 8) *The Bible and Missions,* by Robert P. Wilder. For a detailed description, see Robert Wilder, *The Great Commission: The Missionary Response of the Student Volunteer Movement in North America and Europe; Some Personal Reminiscences* (London, England: Oliphants Publishers, 1936), 45.

[6] Robert Speer, *What Constitutes a Missionary Call* (New York: Student Volunteer Movement, 1901); and Samuel Zwemer, *The Unoccupied Mission Fields of Africa and Asia* (New York: Laymen's Missionary Movement, 1911).

bombarded with obstacles that challenge their confidence and tempt them to lose focus; the mobilizer will be the primary means by which a student will navigate the inevitable storms.

PRINCIPLE SIX – MOBILIZERS MUST GIVE A LONG-TERM CHALLENGE

The Student Volunteer Movement did not have the luxury of recruiting students to short-term trips. In their day, it took months to cross the ocean to reach their desired destination, and once they had sailed the only reasons for return were sickness or death. People signed on with their life, knowing that it already belonged to Christ. The S.V.M. set a high bar. Students responded. Thousands of students went to reach the world. They graduated and gave up their careers on the home front and the assurance of a comfortable lifestyle in exchange for a life lived cut off from their own culture for the purpose of reaching another.

One thing noticeably missing from today's missions mobilization is the challenge to go long-term. Today, it is extremely rare for a student to be given the opportunity to commit more than a spring break or summer to missions. Only 5 percent of the time is a long-term challenge given by a missions speaker. On average, the missions focus is once a semester, so that means that a long-term challenge happens once every ten years.[7] Why is a long-term challenge not present in today's mobilization? Is it because we do not feel like the audience is ready for this kind of commitment? Is it because we feel students are not equipped to decide until they've gone? Is it neglected out of fear that the audience may be offended by this kind of challenge? None of these suffice when compared to the incredible fruit that we will see when students are asked to rise to a higher standard. We must bring back the challenge to go long-term!

Without a doubt there are low expectations for this generation. It is not odd for the main challenge of a missions conference to be for students to skip a meal and remember the hungry, or to give $20. Students are asking the question, "What can I give my life for?" To answer, they look to their parents for advice, watch where their friends are going, listen to what their own heart is feeling, consider what they enjoy, and then they decide. Rarely does a Christian student pray, "God, in light of Your Word and Your world, where is the most strategic place for me?" This is not what they are encouraged by our culture to do. Mobilizers need to challenge them to ask this question and encourage them at a minimum to consider going long-term.

The Student Volunteer Movement challenged big and so must we. Many key components of church-planting will never be achieved through short-term missions, not the least of which is Bible translation. Without this challenge students can and will consider their short-term trip as something to be checked off the list of spiritual achievements. The mobilizer needs to cast vision that they are going to do

---

[7] This statistic is provided by Paul Van Der Werf with GoCorps, who has spent a good portion of his life traveling the United States, gaining a pulse on mid-term and long-term missions commitment.

something for the next five to ten years of their life; why not consider going overseas!

Jesus was never afraid of difficult statements nor did He sidestep the hard issues. Early on in His ministry He looked at the people and said:

Truly, truly, I say to you, unless you eat the flesh of the Son of Man and drink his blood, you have no life in you. Whoever feeds on my flesh and drinks my blood has eternal life, and I will raise him up on the last day... When many of his disciples heard it, they said, "This is a hard saying; who can listen to it?"... After this many of his disciples turned back and no longer walked with him (John 6:52-66, ESV).

Jesus was unapologetic for raising the bar, and we can confidently follow His example knowing that big challenges lead to big commitments.

Students who sense that God wants to use them in missions begin to feel a greater urgency about the condition of their life and heart. Vision helps encourage a student toward holiness. An example may be students who after several years of being believers are still weak in Bible study, content with their sinful habits, and in a relationship they know they need to break off. They are unmotivated because no one has challenged them with a big vision; they have never considered that they might make an eternal impact. The usual response to this kind of vision is that students begin to live with a greater drive.

Unfortunately, many times those who hold the greatest influence in students' lives desire to keep them on the home front. It may be a pastor who has an internship available, a former boss who has a job lined up for them, or a fiancée who would rather remain in her hometown. Oftentimes the counsel will be to stay. Very few people, if any, will challenge students to take their degree and utilize it overseas long-term. I can remember being at Washington State University, and I asked the campus staff worker why she decided to go into full-time ministry. She said, "The lady discipling me said, 'The world will shamelessly recruit you to itself every day. For the next fifteen minutes I want to shamelessly recruit you to full-time ministry.'" We can't underestimate the power of casting vision for students.

There are four very practical ways this can be done today. First, give a vocal challenge toward long-term service (either as a large-group speaker or in a one-to-one meeting). Students need to hear it presented as a compelling option. Second, encourage students to pray and seek God for His leading. Third, expose students to missionaries who have spent significant years on the field and let missionaries share their life experience. Finally, be upfront when communicating about missionary realities.

Casting long-term vision is a lost art in this generation's mobilization, yet to effectively carry out the last command of Christ to go and make disciples of all nations it is a necessity!

PRINCIPLE SEVEN –
ENCOURAGE ALL CHRISTIANS TO HAVE
A ROLE IN MOBILIZATION

A mobilizer is a normal, everyday Christian who walks with God, yet has a global perspective and stays on the home front to rouse others to action. Anyone who has a vision for the world has at one time been mobilized. Someone may have asked them to go on a short-term trip, invited them to a missions conference, taken them to a Bible study on the topic, or introduced them to a missionary; somehow that interest was ignited. Now they, in turn, seek to be the spark that sets others ablaze with a passion for missions. A mobilizer is a recruiter looking to enlist others in God's agenda. Their focus is on Christians who are unaware of God's global plan, and they consistently seek to raise an awareness of missions in creative ways, no matter the setting—small group, large group, one-on-one, formal and informal conversation.

Think about the awesome potential that would be generated if every World Christian saw themselves as a mobilizer! Every Christian would be orchestrating their life around God's heart for the world and fulfilling the Great Commission while at the same time passing that vision on to the next generation. The mobilizer is a key player in the process of raising up laborers. Mobilization has happened in every World Christian's life, and every World Christian can and should be involved in passing it on.

The leaders of the Student Volunteer Movement realized that each student played a significant role in mobilization. Every student involved in this historical movement was expected to pass the vision on to their peers on campus. One way they did this was by having students invite other students to sign the Volunteer Declaration. Each student was also challenged to lead Mission Study Courses and to introduce others to the Watchword. Students recruiting students proved to be a mighty force.

Today, when many of us think of being involved, we immediately think of going overseas. As a result, the student paradigm about missions is still very closely linked with a call to go. Consequently, among those who are passionate about missions there still exists this attitude of belonging to a specific, if not elite, class of Christians. They often cling to one another, go to conferences together, socialize with each other; all the while it never crosses their minds that perhaps those around them might, if given the chance, catch the vision as well.

The jump from "called to missions" to mobilizing others is not a natural one. I have met many students who are excited to graduate and pursue a one- to two-year overseas commitment with an organization yet had no idea their college experience could have been spent mobilizing others. In talking with these students about their future plans I ask,

"How many others have you passed your vision on to while in college?" Fifteen seconds of awkward silence is usually what follows. They have not naturally arrived at the concept of looking beyond their personal convictions about life after college to engage others around them for the purpose of mobilizing them. Having made what feels like the biggest lordship decision in the Christian life, they often think they arrived at a place of full surrender. No further thought is given to passing it on.

What if those fresh young students who have captured the grand purpose of being used by God to reach nations were challenged to utilize the college years to spread that vision to their peers? The World Christian student is served greatly because it removes the frustration of feeling forced to wait to do something until the summer or graduation. There is no "holding pattern" of inactivity in World Christianity; no waiting until the real ministry begins when one crosses an ocean. What better way to make an impact than by raising up others to be World Christians around you! They are also served, because if they are actively engaged in mobilization, the accountability is there for when they encounter dry spells or obstacles. They will hunger to take their vision and knowledge deeper so they can lead others.

Students who are untrained in mobilization yet possess raw passion for the nations have great potential and their impact should not be underestimated! Their approach—"come with me"—can be a powerful force to influence their peers. In the same way that every Christian is to actively share their faith, read the Word, pray, and give, mobilization is the DNA of the Christian life.

Every Christian... a World Christian; every World Christian a mobilizer.

Mobilization doesn't have any prerequisites of being a rock-solid World Christian who knows all the latest statistics and is an excellent public speaker. Rest at ease, great mobilizers are made from those for whom the World Christian vision is very new. Pure excitement is contagious, and others are sure to catch it! Start where you are. Teach what you know, and soon you will see how doable it is for every Christian to be a World Christian, every World Christian a mobilizer.[8]

---

[8] The phrase "Every Christian a World Christian, every World Christian a mobilizer" was brilliantly and succinctly coined by Claude Hickman.

CHAPTER 28
THE GOAL AND GETTING THERE

I think it was just bad timing. My wife and I were driving down the highway obeying the speed limit at 70 mph when all of a sudden there were brake lights as far as the eye could see. This is the last thing you want on a five hour trip. As we slowly made our way up to the cause of the congestion, it became obvious that there had been a huge accident. There was glass on the road, a bumper in the median, and a few cars in the ditch. But what really shocked me was the body bag I saw on the side of the road. As we made our way through the pile-up I noticed something interesting. I was not going 70 mph. I was not even going 65 mph. I had consciously dropped all the way down to 60 mph. It was my immediate response to what I'd seen! But do you know what happened? The farther away I got from the wreck, the faster I went until I was back at my regular speed of 70 mph, enjoying my Coke and fries as if nothing had happened.

This is a perfect illustration of what we *don't* want in mobilization—recruitment to an event. Take short-term trips for example. Countless students have gone on an overseas trip, been broken by the reality of the poor, experienced true joy in sharing Jesus with someone, and seen the Lord work in new ways. When they got home, there was a short season when they re-evaluated their dating life, the movies they watched, how they spent their money, and how they used their time—they drove 60 mph. But as the highway of life carried them farther and farther away from the event, they drifted back into their old routines. Before they knew it, the trip was a distant memory and they were driving 70 mph again.

There are two crucial questions we must ask in order to know our goal and how to get there.

"What do we want to mobilize this generation to do?" We are mobilizing individuals to fulfill their role in world evangelization. This may mean a student never goes on any short-term trip, never leaves his country, but loves the Lord and has a ministry with the Cambodians in his community, works a full-time job, and seeks to further the Kingdom by giving and living sacrificially. He feels this is exactly what God wants him to do. The student is not only mobilized, but mobilized to his role in God's overall purpose. No two journeys are the same. Each plays a part in God's global plan. Every individual Christian will experience changes in circumstances and surroundings throughout life, but World Christianity is not defined by these. We mobilize to a journey; a journey of walking with a missionary God through the good works He has set out for His followers to do. We are not

mobilizing to a time commitment or task, but to a lifestyle of being engaged with God and engaging the nations.

"How do you know when someone has been mobilized?" For the Student Volunteer Movement, a mobilized person was defined as someone who had been relocated in another culture for the purpose of ministry. The only exceptions were those who could prove that greater impact was being made in the nations by their staying. Inspired by the amount of missionaries God raised up in the 1800s, the S.V.M.'s *only* paradigm for mobilization was recruiting more people to go. Today, in light of our cultural context, the mobilized individual takes on an entirely new description. We are no longer living in the 1880s, so what does a mobilized person look like today? What characterizes him or her?

It goes without saying that no one, no matter where they are in the process, can claim to have arrived. The apostle Paul said, "Not that I have already obtained this or am already perfect, but I press on to make it my own, because Christ Jesus has made me His own" (Philippians 3:12, ESV). We never stop growing in our knowledge and understanding of who God is, what He has for us, and what the world looks like. That being said, we greatly undercut our efforts to raise up laborers for His kingdom if we fail to make our end goal identifiable. We need a scoreboard of some kind to help guide us.

Some automatic parameters are set for us in the definition of the term World Christian. The World Christian is a believer who has discovered the truth about God's unfulfilled global purpose and the need to reach all peoples. They know that with this knowledge they are now responsible to act, pray, think, and believe according to this truth.[1] World Christians have come to the conclusion that God's Word is a missions book, and they understand

We are not mobilizing to a time commitment or task, but to a lifestyle.

that this theme runs throughout His Word. They are also aware of the needs of the world and build on this basic understanding by continually growing in their knowledge of the major people blocs of the world. They understand where the gospel has not been. Also, the mobilized are those who are living out the World Christian life by regularly reaching out to the internationals among them, praying for the world, giving sacrificially, raising awareness around them, and sometimes going overseas either short-term or long-term. The World Christian goal embraces a lifetime commitment to God's purpose. We must do whatever it takes, going or staying. And we must be ready at any time or season in life; not just to pursue an event, but to strive for lifelong labor for the sake of His name among the nations. Therefore, the mobilized are not categorized as such based on their location, nor are they dubbed this title because of an overseas experience they had one summer or any other single, specific role in which they are participating. The mobilized are on the journey.

---

[1] David Bryant, *In the Gap* (Ventura, CA: Regal Books, 1979), 73.

FULL CIRCLE

The Student Volunteer Movement was faithful. Faithful to know their generation. Faithful to use the methods they had access to. Faithful to confront the issues. Because of their faithfulness, students were faced with the question— how can my whole life be leveraged for the nations? I think it is possible that a lot of students in that generation were able to look back on their lives without regret. John Mott stated, "Radical decisions and choices are the founding fathers of my life. Can I now waver?" The S.V.M. mobilized with total abandon. And based on their commitment to the evangelization of the world in their generation, students responded to Christ unreservedly. They gave their lives to see Him proclaimed among the nations.

In the same way, we stand at the door of opportunity. We have a generation before us; methods at our disposal; issues to hurdle. As we move out in faithfulness to live for Christ without reservation and as we call students to do the same, may we bring the efforts of the Student Volunteer Movement full circle—may we strive for the evangelization of the world in this generation. Will students today allow God to interrupt their lives? Will we be faithful to confront them with that question? Will we walk through the door of opportunity open before us? Or will we look back with regret? We only have today—we only have our generation, for this generation of believers is responsible for this generation of souls.

One day there will cease to be Watchwords and declarations, there will be no more training, no more overseas trips. Conferences and print material will be no more and prayers will have been answered. The season for mobilization will have passed. We look forward to the day when the great promises of God are an achieved reality. Until then may this generation echo the words of Luther Wishard, "What others have begun is ours to complete."

"Radical decisions and choices are the founding fathers of my life. Can I now waver?"

To this great end we strive, we hope, we pray. This goal is worthy of our study and our passionate devotion because the raising up of more laborers committed to living as World Christians gets us that much closer to the multicultural worship of God around His throne.

After this I looked, and behold,
a great multitude that no one could number, from
every nation, from all tribes and peoples and
languages, standing before the throne
and before the Lamb.
(Revelation 7:9, ESV).

EPILOGUE

EPILOGUE

What happened to this great Movement? How is it that so few believers are aware of what God did with the Student Volunteers? Where is their home office so I can visit and take a tour? Today there is no home office, no staff because there is no more Student Volunteer Movement. What happened?

The Student Volunteer Movement's peak period was from 1886-1920. Though it lived well beyond 1920 as a movement, it suffered to the point of extinction. If sheer numbers were telling the story, 1920 was the high water mark. In that year they had the largest Convention with 6,890 attendees and a whopping 1,171 missionaries were sent out. However, numbers are not always an accurate measurement; the downward spiral had begun.

World War I impacted that generation by producing what is called a post-war era mindset. Consequently missions recruitment was deeply affected. Students who attended the conventions charged the S.V.M. with imperialism because in their post-war minds the S.V.M. was sending people in Christ's name to conquer weaker cultures. To them it was a wolf in sheep's clothing tactic. Students also accused the S.V.M. of ignoring the needs at home. This led many to believe that the "day of the foreign missionary is rapidly drawing to a close."[1] The 1924 Convention was the last one to display the Watchword, *"The evangelization of the world in this generation"* on the platform.

A second reason for the downturn was a continual lack of biblical understanding in basic Christian concepts. Truth became less absolute and was based more on someone's personal experience. Therefore, students on the college campus became harder to recruit overseas to save souls. Wilder commented on the new type of college student that was emerging on campus, "Jesus is accepted by them not as *the* way, but as *one* of the ways to God"[2] He became an option on the multiple-choice question. Near the end of his life John R. Mott stated that the "mission force had become the mission field." Typically, the S.V.M. stood before students and gave them a straightforward challenge to go to the nations. Slowly the message transitioned to an attempt to convince them that Jesus was the only way. More energy was spent on getting Christians to embrace the uniqueness of Christ than it was on getting them to the world.

A third devastating blow to the S.V.M. was the Great Depression of the 1930s. People were focused on survival; trying to feed their families and keep their heads above water in this unforgiving economic crisis. It is no wonder that sending volunteers got relegated to the end of the list of needs, and by then the money had long since been depleted.

A fourth contributing factor was Walter Rauschenbusch's book titled, *Christianity and the Social Crisis*, which introduced ideas that became the Social Gospel Movement.

---

[1] Michael Parker, *The Kingdom of Character: The Student Volunteer Movement for Foreign Missions 1886-1926* (2nd edition) (Pasadena, California: William Carey Library, 2008), 281.

[2] Parker, 281.

Basically, he propagated that Christ's death was not an act of substitutionary atonement, but that Christ was merely demonstrating an individual's responsibility to be socially benevolent; making contributions to society.[3] This idea picked up steam especially in light of the previous war. The Student Volunteer Movement took a pulse of students at each convention and found that they were increasingly following in the steps of the Social Gospel. The pervading thought became, "if Christianity is a superior religion, how could it have produced a civilization that would subject two-thirds of the world's people to total war?"[4]

Another factor that influenced the downfall was the transition of leadership. One man led this movement for thirty-two years, John R. Mott. He was there at the beginning at Mount Hermon in 1886, and spent his life raising millions of dollars for the Movement and raised up many leaders. He was a difficult person to replace and with the external problems on the rise; little room was allowed for internal re-organization.

The last thirty years of the S.V.M.'s existence can be described in one word: mergers.[5] Several organizations came together until eventually the S.V.M. was only a memory. It eventually voted itself out of existence in 1969.[6] This marked the end of a fruitful organization that God used to glorify Himself as North American Christian students, following Him in obedience, attempted to evangelize the world in their generation.

---

[3] Walter Rauschenbusch, *Christianity and the Social Crisis* (Association Press: New York, 1912).

[4] Parker, 180.

[5] Parker, 239.

[6] Nathan D. Showalter's, *The End of a Crusade: The Student Volunteer Movement for Foreign Missions and the Great War* (Lanham: The Scarecrow Press, 1998).

BIBLIOGRAPHY

ABC News. "Idol Gives Back Over $64 Million to Charities." Nov. 12, 2008. Available from abcnews.go.com. 2009.

Anderson, Courtney. *To the Golden Shores: The Life of Adoniram Judson.* Valley Forge, PA: Judson Press, 1987.

Baker, David W., ed. *Biblical Faith and Other Religions: An Evangelical Assessment.* Grand Rapids, MI: Kregel, 2004.

Barna Group, "Despite Benefits, Few Americans Have Experienced Short-Term Mission Trips." Oct. 6, 2008. Available from barna.org. 2009.

Barna Group, "Most American Christians Do Not Believe That Satan or the Holy Spirit Exist." April 10, 2009. Available from barna.org. 2009.

Barnett, Betty. *Friendraising: Building a Support Team That Lasts.* Seattle, WA: YWAM Publishing, 1991.

Barrett, David B., Todd M. Johnson, and Peter F. Crossing. "Missio metrics 2006: Goals, Resources, Doctrines of the 350 Christian World Communions." In *Speaking About What We Have Seen and Heard: Evangelism in Global Perspective*, edited by Jon Bonk, Dwight P. Baker, Daniel J. Nicholas, and Craig A. Noll. New Haven, CT: OMSC Publications, 2007.

Barton, James L. *Educational Missions.* New York: Student Volunteer Movement, 1913.

Barton, James L. *The Unfinished Task.* New York: Student Volunteer Movement, 1908.

Beach, Harlan P. "Sketch of the Student Volunteer Movement for Foreign Missions." *The Intercollegian* 24, no. 3, Fourth Series (December 1901).

Blincoe, Robert. "The Strange Structure of Mission Agencies, Part 1: Still Two Structures After All These Years?" *International Journal of Frontier Missions* 19:1 (Spring 2002).

Borthwick, Paul. *How to Be a World Class Christian (Abridged Ed.).* Wheaton, IL: Victor Books, 1991.

Borthwick, Paul. "Lessons Learned about Mobilizing the Next Generation." *Pulse*, Feb. 2004.

Borthwick, Paul. *A Mind for Missions.* Colorado Springs, CO: NavPress, 1987.

Borthwick, Paul. *Missions: God's Heart for the World.* Downers Grove, IL: InterVarsity Press, 2000.

Borthwick, Paul. "My Five Concerns about the Emerging Generation." *Pulse*, April 2004.

Borthwick, Paul. *Six Dangerous Questions to Transform Your View of the World*. Downers Grove, IL: InterVarsity Press, 1996.

Borthwick, Paul. *Youth and Missions: Expanding Your Student's World View*, 2nd ed. Waynesboro, GA: Operation Mobilization Literature, 1998.

Bosch, David J. *Transforming Mission: Paradigm Shifts in Theology of Mission*. MaryKnoll, NY: Orbis Books, 2005.

Bowen, William G. "The Quest for Equity: 'Class' (Socio-Economic Status) in American Higher Education." The Thomas Jefferson Foundation Distinguished Lecture Series, University of Virginia, April 7, 2004.

Braisted, Ruth Wilder. *In This Generation: The Story of Robert P. Wilder*. New York: Friendship Press, 1941.

Bromley, Dana, ed. *Mission Maker Magazine*. Minneapolis, MN: STEM Press, 2009.

Broomhall, Benjamin. *The Evangelization of the World - A Missionary Band*. London: Morgan and Scott, 1887.

Brumbaugh, T. T. "Convention Mistakes" in "The Open Forum." *S.V.M. Bulletin* 5 (Feb. 1924): 122-124.

Bryant, David. *In the Gap*. Ventura, CA: Regal Books, 1979.

Buckley, William. *God and Man at Yale*. Washington, DC: Regency Publishing, 1951.

Burgin, Patricia. *The Powerful Percent: Students at the Heart of the Great Commission*. Orlando, FL: WSN Press, 1991.

Bush, Luis. "A Brief Historical Overview of the AD2000 & Beyond Movement and Joshua Project 2000." Paper presented in Seoul, May 27-30, 1996.

Campus Crusade for Christ. "About Us." Available from uscm.org. 2009.

Campus Crusade for Christ Midsouth Region. *When God Says "Go" and Parents Say "No."* Orlando, FL: CCC, 2002.

Carey, William. *An Enquiry into the Obligations of Christians to Use Means for the Conversion of the Heathen*. England: Ann Ireland, 1792, reprint edition Dallas, TX: Criswell Publications, 1988.

Carson, D. A. *The Gagging of God: Christianity Confronts Pluralism*. Grand Rapids, MI: Zondervan, 1996.

Carson, D. A., ed. *Telling the Truth: Evangelizing Postmoderns*. Grand Rapids, MI: Zondervan, 2000.

Christian Century. "Church Attendance on the Decline." Sept. 11, 1996. Available from findarticles.com. 2009.

CNN News. "Koinange: Oprah School Opens Hearts, Minds in S. Africa." August 25, 2006. Available from cnn.com. 2009.

Conde, Bertha. "The Women Students of the United States." *The Intercollegian* 23, no. 7, Fourth Series (April 1901).

Crockett , William, ed. *Four Views on Hell*. Grand Rapids, MI: Zondervan, 1996.

Daniels, Roger. *Coming to America: A History of Immigration and Ethnicity in American Life*, 2nd ed. New York: Harper Perennial, 2002.

Dharmanand, Premraj. *Your Questions Our Answers,* vol. 1. Uttaranchai, India: Premraj Dharmanand, 2003.

Dillon, William P. *People Raising: A Practical Guide to Raising Support*. Chicago: Moody Press, 1993.

Douglas, J. D. *Let the Earth Hear His Voice: International Congress on World Evangelization Lausanne, Switzerland*. Minnesota: World Wide Publications, 1975.

Elliot, Elisabeth. *A Chance to Die: The Life and Legacy of Amy Carmichael*. Grand Rapids, MI: Revell, 1987.

Elmer, Duane. *Cross-Cultural Servanthood: Serving the World in Christlike Humility*. Downers Grove, IL: InterVarsity Press, 2006.

Erickson, Millard J. *Postmodernizing the Faith: Evangelical Responses to the Challenge of Postmodernism*. Grand Rapids, MI: Baker Books, 1998.

Evangelical Alliance Commission on Unity and Truth among Evangelicals. *The Nature of Hell*. London: Acute Publishing, 2000.

Every Ethne. *XPlore: God's Heart for the Nations*. Fayetteville, AR: U.S. Center for World Missions, 2007.

Fernando, Ajith. *Crucial Questions about Hell*. Wheaton, IL: Crossway Books, 1991.

Fiedler, Klaus. *The Story of Faith Missions from Hudson Taylor to Present Day Africa.* Oxford: Regnum Books International, 1994.

Fraser, Donald. *Make Jesus King: The Report of the International Students Missionary Conference.* London: The Student Volunteer Missionary Union, 1896.

Gairdner, W. H. T. *Echoes from Edinburgh, 1910.* New York: Fleming Revell Company, 1910.

Giglio, Louie. *I Am Not But I Know I Am.* Sisters, OR: Multnomah Publishers, 2005.

Glenny, Edward W. and William H. Smallman, eds. *Missions in a New Millennium.* Grand Rapids, MI: Kregel Publications, 2000.

Goldsmith, Elizabeth. *Roots and Wings: Five Generations and Their Influence.* Waynesboro, GA: Paternoster Publishing Publication, 1998.

Gordon, A. J. *The Holy Spirit in Missions.* New York: Fleming H. Revell Company, 1893.

Green, Keith. *Why You Should Go to the Mission Field.* Wise Tracts from Last Days Ministries. Lindale, TX: Pretty Good Printing, 1982.

Greene, H. Leon. *A Guide to Short-Term Missions: A Comprehensive Manual for Planning an Effective Mission Trip.* Waynesboro, GA: Gabriel Publishing, 2003.

Grenz, Stanley J. *A Primer on Postmodernism.* Grand Rapids, MI: Eerdmans, 1996.

Groothuis, Douglas. *Truth Decay: Defending Christianity against the Challenges of Postmodernism.* Downers Grove, IL: InterVarsity Press, 2000.

Grubb, Norman. *C.T. Studd: Famous Athlete and Pioneer.* Grand Rapids, MI: Zondervan, 1933.

Guder, Darrell L., ed. *Missional Church: A Vision for the Sending of the Church in North America.* Grand Rapids, MI: Eerdmans Publishing, 1998.

Gundry, Stanley. *Four Views on Salvation in a Pluralistic World.* Grand Rapids, MI: Zondervan, 1995.

Hall, Gordon and Samuel Newell. *"The Conversion of the World: Or the Claims of Six Hundred Millions, and the Ability and Duty of Churches Respecting Them."* 1818.

Hansen, Collin. "Passion Takes It Higher." *Christianity Today*, March 3, 2007. Available from ctlibrary.com. 2009.

Harder, Ben. "The Student Volunteer Movement for Foreign Missions and Its Contribution to 20th Century Missions." *Missiology*, April 8, 1980.

Hawthorne, Steve. "Tyranny of the Immediate: Another View of Acts 1:8." Available from thetravelingteam.org. 2010.

Hawthorne, Steve. "Perspectives." *Mission Frontiers*, U.S. Center for World Mission, May-August 2009, 28.

Hefley, James and Marti. *Uncle Cam.* Huntington Beach, CA: Wycliffe Bible Translators, 1984.

Henry, Carl F. H. *God, Revelation, and Authority* , vol. 1. Waco, TX: Word, 1976.

Hick, John. *God Has Many Names.* Philadelphia, PA: The Westminster Press, 1980.

Hick, John. *The Metaphor of God Incarnate: Christology in a Pluralistic Age,* 2nd ed. Louisville, KY: Westminster John Knox Press, 2005.

Hickman, Claude. *Live Life on Purpose.* Enumclaw, WA: WinePress Publishing, 2003.

Hickman, Rebecca. "When God Says Go and Family Says No." Available from thetask.org. 2009.

Honey, Charles. "Belief in Hell Dips, but Some Say They've Already Been There." Pew Forum on Religion and Public Life, August 14, 2008. Available from pewforum.org. 2009.

Hopkins, C. Howard. *20th Century Ecumenical Statesman John R. Mott: 1865-1955.* New York: Eerdmans Publishing Company, 1979.

Hopkins, C. Howard. *History of the YMCA in North America.* New York: Association Press, 1951.

Hopkins, Charles Howard. "The Legacy of John R. Mott." *International Bulletin of Missionary Research*, April 5, 1981.

Howard, David. *Student Power in World Evangelism.* Downers Grove, IL: InterVarsity Press, 1970.

Humphrey, J. M. *The Lost Soul's First Day in Eternity* and *A Soul's First Day in Heaven.* Shoals, IN: Old Paths Tract Society, 1912.

Hutchison, William R., ed. *Between the Times: The Travail of the Protestant Establishment in America, 1900-1960.* Cambridge: Cambridge University Press, 1990.

The Intercollegian. *The Student World*. Fourth Series (November 1900). Vol. XXIII No. 2.

The Intercollegian. *The Student World*. Fourth Series (December 1900). Vol. XXIII No. 3.

The Intercollegian. *The Student World*. Fourth Series (January 1901). Vol. XXIII No. 4.

Irvin, Dale T. "John R. Mott and World-Centered Mission." *Missiology*, April 12, 1984.

Johnson, Alan. "The Frontier Mission Movement's Understanding of the Modern Mission Era." *International Journal of Frontier Missions* 18, no. 2 (Spring 2001).

Johnson, Todd. *Countdown to 1900: World Evangelism at the End of the 19th Century*. New Hope Publishing, 1989.

Johnstone, Patrick. *The Church Is Bigger Than You Think*. Great Britain: Christian Focus Publications, 1998.

Johnstone, Patrick and Jason Mandryk. *Operation World,* 6th ed. Waynesboro, GA: Authentic Media, 2006.

Joshua Project. "What Is Joshua Project?" Available from joshuaproject.net. 2009.

Kane, J. Herbert. *Understanding Christian Missions*. Grand Rapids, MI: Baker Book House, 1982.

Kim, Sandra and Todd Johnson. "Describing the Worldwide Christian Phenomenon." *International Bulletin of Missionary Research* 29, no. 2 (April 2005): 80-84.

Knitter, Paul. *No Other Name? A Critical Survey of Christian Attitudes Toward the World Religions*. Maryknoll, NY: Orbis Books, 2005.

Kraemer, Hendrick. *The Christian Message in a Non-Christian World*. New York: International Missionary Council, 1938.

Kyle, John. *Should I Not Be Concerned? A Mission Reader*. Downers Grove, IL: InterVarsity Press, 1987.

LaVallee, Andrew. "Facebook to Nonprofits: More Pages, Fewer Apps." *Wall Street Journal*, August 28, 2009.

Lewis, Jeff. *God's Heart for the Nations*. Riverside, CA: The Global Center California Baptist University, 2000.

Livermore, David A. *Serving with Eyes Wide Open: Doing Short-Term Missions with Cultural Intelligence*. Grand Rapids, MI: Baker Book House, 2006.

Lo, Jim. "Concerns Regarding Short-Term Missions." Available from drurywriting.com. 2009.

Lotz, Denton. "The Watchword for World Evangelization." *International Review of Mission* 68 (April 1979).

Maclure, David. "Wholly Available? Missionary Motivation Where Consumer Choice Reigns." *Evangel* 20, no. 3 (Autumn 2002): 3.

Marsden, George M. *The Soul of the American University*. New York: Oxford University Press, 1994.

Mathews, Basil. *John R. Mott: World Citizen*. New York: Harper and Brothers Publishers, 1934.

McDermott, Gerald. *Can Evangelicals Learn from World Religions? Jesus, Revelation, and Religious Traditions*. Downers Grove, IL: InterVarsity Press, 2000.

McGavran, Donald. *Bridges of God*. London: World Dominion Press, 1957.

McQuilkin, Robertson. *The Great Omission*. Grand Rapids, MI: Baker House, 1984.

Montgomery, Helen Barrett. *Western Women in Eastern Lands*. New York: The Macmillan Company, 1910.

Moody, D. L. "Study of the Bible at the Mt. Hermon School." *Springfield Magazine*, August 2, 1886.

Morton, Scott. *Funding Your Ministry: An In-Depth, Biblical Guide for Successfully Raising Personal Support*. Colorado Springs, CO: NavPress, 2007.

Mott, John R. *Addresses and Papers of John R. Mott Volume 1: The Student Volunteer Movement for Foreign Missions*. New York: Association Press, 1946.

Mott, John R. *Addresses and Papers of John R. Mott Volume 2: The World's Student Christian Federation*. New York: Association Press, 1947.

Mott, John R. *Addresses and Papers of John R. Mott Volume 3: The Young Men's Christian Association – Parts I, II, and III*. New York: Association Press, 1947.

Mott, John R. *Addresses and Papers of John R. Mott Volume 4: The Young Men's Christian Association – Parts IV, V, and VI*. New York: Association Press, 1947.

Mott, John R. *Addresses and Papers of John R. Mott Volume 5: The International Missionary Council.* New York: Association Press, 1947.

Mott, John R. *Addresses and Papers of John R. Mott Volume 6: Selected Papers and Addresses.* New York: Association Press, 1947.

Mott, John R. *Confronting Young Men with the Living Christ.* New York: Association Press, 1923.

Mott, John R. *The Decisive Hour of Christian Missions.* Canada: Missionary Educational Movement, 1911.

Mott, John R. *The Evangelization of the World in This Generation.* New York: S.V.M., 1901.

Mott, John R. *Five Decades and a Forward View.* New York: Harper and Brothers, 1939.

Mott, John R. *The Future Leadership of the Church.* New York: S.V.M., 1908.

Mott, John R. *The Larger Evangelism.* New York and Nashville: Abingdon-Cokesbury Press, 1944.

Mott, John R. *Liberating the Lay Forces of Christianity.* New York: Macmillan Co., 1932.

Mott, John R. *Modern World Movement: God's Challenge to the Church.* London: Student Christian Movement, 1908.

Mott, John R. *The Pastor and Modern Missions.* New York: S.V.M., 1904.

Mott, John R. *The Present World Situation.* New York: S.V.M., 1915.

Mott, John R. *The Present-Day Summons to the World Mission of Christianity.* Nashville, TN.: Cokesbury Press, 1931.

Mott, John R. *The Place of Prayer in the Volunteer Movement, Vol. III, No. 1.* New York: Student Volunteer Movement, October 1894.

Mott, John R. *Student Mission Power: Report of the First International Convention of the Student Volunteer Movement for Foreign Missions.* Pasadena, CA: William Carey Library, 1891.

Murray, Michael J. *Reasons for the Hope Within.* Grand Rapids, MI: Eerdmans Publishing, 1998.

Myers, John Brown. *William Carey: The Shoemaker*. Scotland: John Ritchie Publishers, 1887.

Nash, Ronald H. *Is Jesus the Only Savior?* Grand Rapids, MI: Zondervan Publishing, 1994.

Netland, Harold A. *Dissonant Voices: Religious Pluralism and the Question of Truth*. Vancouver: Regent Publishing, 1991.

Nicole, Roger. "The Biblical Concept of Truth." In *Scripture and Truth*, edited by D. A. Carson and John D. Woodbridge. Grand Rapids, MI: Zondervan, 1983.

Nolan, Mark. "Get Out of Debt." March 15, 2010. Available from morejoyinlife.com. 2010.

"North American Students and World Advance," Addresses Delivered at the Eighth International Convention of the Student Volunteer Movement for Foreign Missions, Des Moines, Iowa, Dec. 31, 1919 – Jan. 4, 1920.

Norton, Fred L. *A College of Colleges: Led by D. L. Moody*. New York: Fleming H. Revell, 1889.

Ober, C. K. *Exploring a Continent*. New York: Association Press, 1929.

Olson, Gordon C. *What in the World Is God Doing?* 3rd ed. Cedar Knolls, NJ: Global Gospel Publishers, 1988.

Parker, Michael. *The Kingdom of Character: The Student Volunteer Movement for Foreign Missions 1886-1926,* 2nd ed. Pasadena, CA: William Carey Library, 2008.

Passion Conferences. "About the Movement." Available from 268generation.com. 2009.

Patterson, James. "The Legacy of Robert P. Wilder." *International Bulletin of Missionary Research*, January 14, 1991.

Perspectives on the World Christian Movement. "What Campus Ministries Are Saying." Available from perspectives.org. 2009.

Peters, George. *A Biblical Theology of Missions*. Chicago, IL: Moody Press, 1972.

Peterson, Roger, Gordon Aeschliman, and R. Wayne Sneed. *Maximum Impact Short-Term Mission*. Minneapolis, MN: STEMPress, 2003.

The Pew Forum on Religion and Public Life. "Many Americans Say Other Faiths Can Lead to Eternal Life." Dec. 18, 2008. Available from pewforum.org. 2009.

Pierson, Arthur T. *The Acts of the Holy Spirit*. New York: Fleming H. Revell, 1895.

Pierson, Arthur T. *Crisis of Missions*. New York: Baker and Taylor Co., 1886.

Pierson, Arthur T. *The Divine Enterprise of Missions*, 2nd ed. London: Hodder and Stoughton, 1893.

Pierson, Arthur T. *Evangelistic Work in Principle and Practice*, rev. ed. London: Passmore and Alabaster, 1892.

Pierson, Arthur T. *The Greatest Work in the World: The Evangelization of All Peoples in the Present Century*. New York: Fleming H. Revell, 1891.

Pierson, Arthur T. *The Miracles of Missions* (4 volumes). New York: Funk and Wagnalls, 1891-1901.

Pierson, Arthur T. *The Modern Mission Century Viewed as a Cycle of Divine Working*. New York: Baker and Taylor, 1901.

Pierson, Arthur T. *The New Acts of the Apostles*. New York: Baker and Taylor, 1894.

Pierson, Arthur T. *The Problem of Missions and Its Solution: A Paper Presented to the Presbytery of Philadelphia*. 1885.

Pierson, Delavan Leonard. *Arthur T. Pierson: A Biography*. London: James Nisbet and Co, 1912.

Pinnock, Clark. *A Wideness in God's Mercy*. Grand Rapids, MI: Zondervan Publishing, 1992.

Piper, John. *Desiring God: Meditations of a Christian Hedonist*. Sisters, OR: Multnomah Books, 1986.

Piper, John. *Don't Waste Your Life*. Wheaton, IL: Crossway Books, 2003.

Piper, John. *Let the Nations Be Glad: The Supremacy of God in Missions*. Grand Rapids, MI: Baker House, 1993.

Piper, John. "Personal Tribute to the Late Ralph Winter." Desiring God Ministries. Available from desiringgod.org. 2009.

Piper, John. *When I Don't Desire God: How to Fight for Joy*. Wheaton, IL: Crossway Books, 2004.

Pocock, Michael, Gailyn Van Rheenen, and Douglas McConnell. *The Changing Face of World Missions*. Grand Rapids, MI: Baker Academic, 2005.

Priest, Robert and Kurt Ver Beek. "Are Short-Term Missions Good Stewardship?" *Christianity Today*, July 2005. Available from christianitytoday.com. 2009.

Rauschenbusch, Walter. *Christianity and the Social Crisis*. Association Press: New York, 1912.

The Report of the Toronto Convention 1902, Missionary Campaign Library No. 1, Toronto, Feb. 26-March 2, 1902. Chicago: Student Missionary Campaign Library, 1902.

Reuben, Julie A. *The Making of the Modern University*. Chicago: The University of Chicago Press, 1996.

Richards, Thomas C. *Samuel J. Mills: Missionary, Pathfinder, Pioneer and Promoter*. Boston: The Pilgrim Press, 1906.

Robert, Dana. *Occupy Until I Come: A. T. Pierson and the Evangelization of the World*. Grand Rapids, MI: Eerdmans Publishing, 2003.

Robert, Dana. "The Legacy of Arthur Tappan Pierson." *International Bulletin of Missionary Research*, July 8, 1984.

Robert, Dana. "The Origin of the Student Volunteer Watchword: 'The Evangelization of the World in This Generation.'" *International Bulletin of Missionary Research*, Nov. 4, 1986.

Rouse, Ruth. "An Appeal to Women Students for Missionary Decision." *The Intercollegian* 23, no. 7, Fourth Series (April 1901).

Rouse, Ruth. *The World's Student Christian Federation*. London: S.C.M. Press LTD., 1948.

Sailer, T. H. P. "Suggestions as to Policy in Mission Study." *The Intercollegian* 28, no. 6, Fourth Series (March 1906).

Schwartz, Glenn. "Two Awesome Problems: How Short-Term Missions Can Go Wrong." *International Journal of Frontier Missions* 20:4 (Winter 2003).

Seventy-Fifth Anniversary: Western India Mission of the Presbyterian Church in the United States of America. Presbyterian Church, U.S.A., 1929.

Shadrach, Steve. "The Top Five Fears in Support Raising." Support Raising Solutions, July 2009. Available from thebodybuilders.net. 2009.

Shanks, T. J. *A College of Colleges: Led by D. L. Moody*. New York: Fleming H. Revell, 1887.

Shanks, T. J. *College Students at Northfield*. New York: Fleming H. Revell, 1888.

Shaw, Ryan. *Waking the Giant: The Resurging Student Mission Movement*. Pasadena, CA: William Carey Library, 2006.

Shedd, Clarence P. *History of the World's Alliance of Young Men's Christian Association*. London: SPCK Publishing, 1955.

Shedd, Clarence P. *Two Centuries of Student Christian Movements: Their Origin and Intercollegiate Life*. New York: Association Press, 1934.

Shedd, W. G. T. *The Doctrine of Endless Punishment*. Reprinted. Carlisle, PA: Banner of Truth Trust, 1986.

Shehori, Steven. "37% of Americans Unable to Locate America on a Map." December 15, 2008. Available from huffingtonpost.com.

Showalter, Nathan. *The End of a Crusade: The Student Volunteer Movement for Foreign Mission and the Great War*. Lanham, MD: Scarecrow Press, 1998.

Sjogren, Bob, Bill Stearns, and Amy Stearns. *Run with the Vision: A Remarkable Plan for the 21st Century Church*. Minneapolis, MN: Bethany House, 1995.

Smith, James P. *The New Americans: Economic, Demographic, and Fiscal Effect of Immigration*. Washington, DC: National Academies Press, 1997.

Smith, Wilfred Cantwell. *Towards a World Theology*. Philadelphia: Westminster, 1981.

Speer, Robert. "Abiding Values of the Student Volunteer Movement." *The Student Volunteer Movement Bulletin*, Dec. 1926.

Speer, Robert. *Christianity and the Nations*. London: Fleming H. Revell Company, 1910.

Speer, Robert. *The Deity of Christ*. New York: Young Men's Christian Association Press, 1909.

Speer, Robert. *Missionary Principles and Practice: A Discussion of Christian Missions and of Some Criticisms upon Them*. London: Fleming H. Revell Company, 1902.

Speer, Robert. *Prayer and Missions*. New York: S.V.M., 1899.

Speer, Robert. *South American Problems*. New York: Student Volunteer Movement, 1912.

Speer, Robert. *What Constitutes a Missionary Call*. New York: Student Volunteer Movement, 1901.

Stackhouse, John G. Jr., ed. *No Other Gods Before Me? Evangelicals and the Challenge of World Religions*. Grand Rapids, MI: Baker Academic, 2001.

Stauffer, Milton T. *Christian Students and World Problems: Report of the Ninth International Convention of the Student Volunteer Movement for Foreign Missions, Indianapolis, Indiana, December 28, 1923 - January 1, 1924*. New York: Student Volunteer Movement for Foreign Missions, 1924.

Stearns, Bill and Amy. *2020 Vision: Amazing Stories of What God Is Doing Around the World*. Minneapolis, MN: Bethany House, 2005.

Stortz, Diane and Cheryl Savageau. *Parents of Missionaries: How to Thrive and Stay Connected When Your Children and Grandchildren Serve Cross-Culturally*. Colorado Springs, CO: Authentic Publishing, 2008.

The Student Missionary Appeal: Addresses at the Third International Convention of the Student Volunteer Movement for Foreign Missions, Cleveland, Ohio, Feb. 23-27, 1898. New York: Student Volunteer Movement for Foreign Missions, 1898.

The Students and the Modern Missionary Crusade, Addresses Delivered before the Fifth International Convention of the Student Volunteer Movement for Foreign Missions, Nashville, Tennessee, Feb. 28-March 4, 1906.

Tatlow, Tissington. *The Stoy of the Student Christian Movement of Great Britain and Ireland*. London: Student Christian Movement Press, 1933.

Taylor, Bill and Steve Hoke. *Global Mission Handbook: A Guide for Cross-Cultural Service*. Downers Grove, IL: InterVarsity Press, 2009.

Tennent, Timothy. *Christianity at the Religious Roundtable: Evangelicalism in Conversation with Hinduism, Buddhism, and Islam*. Grand Rapids, MI: Baker Academic, 2002.

Tiplady, Richard. *Post-Mission: World Mission by a Postmodern Generation*. Waynesboro, GA: Paternoster Publishing Publication, 2002.

Tiplady, Richard. *World of Difference: Global Mission at the Pic-n-Mix Counter*. Waynesboro, GA: Paternoster Press, 2003.

Toppo, Greg. "Graduates Fear Debt More Than Terrorism." *USA Today*, May 18, 2005.

Torrey, R. A. *Heaven or Hell*. Springdale, PA: Whitaker House, 1985.

Tucker, Ruth. *From Jerusalem to Irian Jaya*. Grand Rapids, MI: Zondervan Publishing, 1983.

Turner, Fennell. "Student Volunteer Series: The Call, Qualifications and Preparation of Candidates for Foreign Missionary Service." *Papers by Missionaries and Other Authorities* 4, no 4 (Oct. 1901).

Turner, Fennell. *Students and the World-Wide Expansion of Christianity: Addresses Delivered before the Seventh International Convention of the Student Volunteer Movement for Foreign Missions, Kansas City, Missouri*. New York: Student Volunteer Movement, 1914.

Van Engen, Charles. *God's Missionary People: Rethinking the Purpose of the Local Church*. Grand Rapids, MI: Baker Book House, 1991.

Vine, W. E., Merrill Unger, and William White, eds. *Vine's Complete Expository Dictionary of Old and New Testament Words*. Nashville, TN: Thomas Nelson Publishers, 1985.

Walls, Andrew. *The Missionary Movement in Christian History*. Maryknoll, NY: Orbis Press, 1996.

Wallstrom, Timothy C. *The Creation of a Student Movement to Evangelize the World*. Pasadena, CA: William Carey International University Press, 1980.

Wheeler, W. Reginald. *A Man Sent from God*. Westwood, NJ: Revell Publishing, 1956.

White, Stanley. *In Memoriam: Miss Grace E. Wilder*. New York: Board of Foreign Mission of the Presbyterian Church, 1911.

Widner, Wes. "Short-Term Mission Trips: Sanctified Vacations?" Available from reasontostand.org. 2009.

Wilder, Grace. *Shall I Go? Thoughts for Girls,* 5th ed. New York: S.V.M., 1888.

Wilder, Robert P. *Christ and the Student World*. London: InterVarsity Fellowship, 1935.

Wilder, Robert P. "Early Days in the Movement." *S.V.M. Bulletin* 7, no. 3 (Dec. 1926).

Wilder, Robert P. *The Great Commission: The Missionary Response of the Student Volunteer Movement in North America and Europe; Some Personal Reminiscences.* London: Oliphants Publishers, 1936.

Wilder, Robert P. "The Rejected Volunteer." *The Student Volunteer Movement Bulletin* (Jan. 1925).

Winter, Ralph. "Momentum Is Building! Many Voices Discuss Completing the Task by 2000 A.D." *International Journal of Frontier Missions* 3, no. 1-4 (1986).

Winter, Ralph and Steven Hawthorne. *Perspectives on the World Christian Movement*, 4th ed. Pasadena, CA: William Carey Library, 2009.

Wishard, Luther. *The Beginning of the Students' Era in Christian History.* New York: YMCA Library, 1917.

Wishard, Luther. *A New Programme of Missions: A Movement to Make the Colleges in All Lands Centers of Evangelization.* New York: F.H. Revell, 1895.

Wood, Rick. "The Third World Takes the Lead: The AD 2000 Movement." Jan-Feb. 1992. Available from missionfrontiers.com. 2008.

Woodruff, Mike. "The Ivy Jungle Network." *Campus Ministry Update*, June 2006.

Wright, Christopher J. H. *The Mission of God.* Downers Grove, IL: InterVarsity Press, 2006.

Wright, H. B. *Two Centuries of Christian Activity at Yale.* New York: The Knickerbocker Press, 1901.

Yep, Jeanette, ed. *Following Jesus Without Dishonoring Your Parents.* Downers Grove, IL: InterVarsity Press, 1998.

Zacharias, Ravi. *Can Man Live Without God?* Dallas, TX: Word Publishing, 1994.

Zumwalt, John. *Passion for the Heart of God.* Choctaw, OK: Heart of God Publishing, 2000.

Zwemer, Samuel. *The Unoccupied Mission Fields of Africa and Asia.* New York: Laymen's Missionary Movement, 1911.

To order more copies of this book,
please contact 800-366-7788.

To request the author to speak,
contact 501-329-7676
or todd@thetravelingteam.org.

www.thetravelingteam.org
www.inthisgeneration.org

Also by this Author

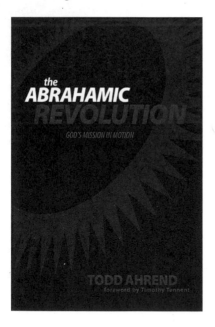

for a seminar by this author
visit www.missionrev.org